A GERMAN COURSE

A GERMAN COURSE

BY

R. H. HORSLEY, B.A.

Assistant Master at
Wellington College

CAMBRIDGE
AT THE UNIVERSITY PRESS
1933

CAMBRIDGE
UNIVERSITY PRESS

University Printing House, Cambridge CB2 8BS, United Kingdom

Cambridge University Press is part of the University of Cambridge.

It furthers the University's mission by disseminating knowledge in the pursuit of education, learning and research at the highest international levels of excellence.

www.cambridge.org
Information on this title: www.cambridge.org/9781316612651

First published 1933
First paperback edition 2016

A catalogue record for this publication is available from the British Library

ISBN 978-1-316-61265-1 Paperback

CONTENTS

PREFACE

This book is intended primarily to meet the need of a prose manual which may be used in form from the time a boy begins the translation of connected passages to the time he leaves school. The advantages of using one prose book throughout the school are obvious, the most important perhaps being the opportunities it gives for revision. In order to satisfy schools faced with competitive examinations, the proses which form the second half of the book have been divided into two parts, those in the first part reaching School Certificate standard, those in the second the standard of the Army Examination and of London Matriculation. The proses have been selected from a wide field in order to encourage the use of as large a vocabulary as possible; a few but not many have already been set in examinations. The first piece in each part has been treated in detail and takes the form of a model lesson. In the notes attached to the proses help is given with difficult phrases and idioms as well as numerous references to the grammatical sections which form the first half of the book. The matter in these sections covers roughly the same field as the proses. Since it is not the aim of this book to take the place of a Grammar, much that may be found in Grammars has been omitted (e.g. long lists of exceptions and tables showing the conjugation of verbs, etc.), and this has made possible inclusion of matter not always found in Grammars (e.g. the use of *ja, doch, einmal,* etc.). But since errors even in advanced work are often due to a failure to understand elementary principles, the most important points of elementary Grammar have been included at least in outline, so that reference may be made to them if necessary. An index to the Grammar is given at the end of the Grammar sections and a full vocabulary after the proses, and it is hoped that with these inclusions the book will be found complete in itself. This completeness as well as the fullness of the references will, I hope, appeal not only to schools but also to those who already have some knowledge of German and who wish to keep their knowledge fresh. For this purpose the occasional translation of short passages from English into German is as good a method as any, provided time need not be wasted in referring to Dictionaries and Grammars; it was to avoid this necessity that the index was added and the vocabulary made as complete as possible.

My grateful thanks are due to Mr Reginald Maxse, Lecturer of Brasenose College, Oxford, for constant help and advice.

Acknowledgment for permission to reproduce short copyright passages is due to *The Times Publishing Company, Ltd.* for part of a lecture by Sir James Jeans; to *Ernest Benn, Ltd.* for two extracts from *Quotable Anecdotes*, by D. B. Knox; to *Jonathan Cape, Ltd.* for an extract from the *Note Books* of Samuel Butler; to *Mr John Murray* for an extract from *The Creevey Papers*; to *Edward Arnold and Co.* for an anecdote from *German Composition from German Models*; to the *Insel-Verlag*, Leipzig for seven extracts from *Anekdoten von Friedrich dem Grossen*; to *Mr Lloyd Osbourne* for three Fables by R. L. Stevenson; to the *Oxford and Cambridge Schools Examination Board*; and to the *University of London* for examples taken from *Examination Papers*.

R. H. H.

WELLINGTON COLLEGE
July, 1933

I. VOCABULARY

The building up of a vocabulary which will be sufficiently large and varied not only to satisfy examiners but also to throw open the wide field of German Literature must be a gradual process. By extensive reading only can we gain an insight into those shades of meaning and subtleties of association which give colour and life to a language. But for the purpose we have before us, which is the correct translation of English into German, reading alone is not sufficient. Words whose meaning we understand well enough when reading German have an unhappy knack of escaping our memory when we wish to use them in a piece of prose. Memory is indeed fallible, and we cannot afford to neglect any means for strengthening it. Memory is a matter not only of the eye but of the ear: a word, then, should not only be seen but heard. Some people have a better memory for sound than for sight, and they would do well to cultivate the former talent provided that they do not neglect the latter. It is always advisable when learning a new word to write it down and if, when we do so, we take pains to write legibly we shall double our chance of remembering it. But words, besides appealing to the eye and ear, appeal also to the reason; a word will only become firmly fixed in its proper place when we know all about it, when we understand its habits and are acquainted with its relations. Any trouble we spend in organising our knowledge will be repaid; if, for example, when we learn for the first time the word *Schmerz* 'pain', we note that it is declined *der Schmerz, des Schmerzes, die Schmerzen*, and then take the trouble to discover that from it are formed *schmerzlich, schmerzen, Kopfschmerzen, Augenschmerzen, Weltschmerz*, etc., we shall have added depth and width to our knowledge with a minimum expenditure of energy.

The habit of forming groups of words will certainly be of value; German, above all other languages, is rich in the possibilities of word development. Let us take one example to show this.

From the word *ein* are formed: *der Verein* 'the club', *einig* 'agreed', *vereinigen* 'to join', *Einigkeit* 'unity', *einheitlich* 'uniform', *einsam* 'lonely', *Einsamkeit* 'loneliness', *einstimmig* 'unanimous', *übereinstimmen* 'to agree', *einst* 'once', *einäugig* 'one-eyed', *Einsiedler* 'a hermit', etc. These are but a few of the possible derivatives, but they serve to show the almost unlimited possibilities of word formation. Compound nouns in particular can be coined almost at will and even the largest dictionaries cannot contain all the possible combinations. For the sake of illustration a few examples are given:

Inseparable Prefix + Noun:
                das Mißverständnis, the misunderstanding.
Preposition + Noun: der Ausgang, the exit.
Adverb + Noun: das Heimweh, homesickness.
Verb + Noun: das Zündholz, the match.
                der Schreibtisch, the desk.
Adjective + Noun: die Großmut, the generosity.
Noun + Noun: der Schuhmacher, the shoemaker.
                die Hauptstraße, the main street.
                der Kirchhof, the cemetery.
                der Lieblingshund, the favourite dog.
                der Tagesanbruch, the daybreak.
                der Geburtstag, the birthday.
                die Freiheitsliebe, love of freedom.
                der Tannenbaum, the fir tree.
                der Riesenschritt, the giant stride.

This last class is by far the most numerous; no rule can be given as to whether the first compound should stand in the genitive or not; in the older formations the nominative was used (e.g. *der Schuhmacher*), but later formations almost always have the genitive (e.g. *der Tagesanbruch*) and use is now even made of a genitive in *-s* for feminine words (e.g. *der Geburtstag, die Freiheitsliebe*). If the first part of the compound is a feminine noun ending in *-e, -n* is generally added (e.g. *der Tannenbaum*). It should be clear from the above examples that the habit of forming words without proper knowledge is dangerous; learners should be content at first in noting compound words whenever they occur.

But phrases as well as words are a necessity for idiomatic translation. It would be beyond the scope of this book to give lists of idioms; let each rather make lists for himself and furthermore not be content with noting the infinitival form alone: if we learn that *grüßen lassen* means 'to send greetings', let us also learn how it is used:

Er läßt Sie alle vielmals grüßen.
He sends his kind regards to you all.
Meine Mutter hat Dich herzlich grüßen lassen.
My mother sends you her love.
Er vergaß mich grüßen zu lassen.
He forgot to send me his greetings.
Daß er mich nicht grüßen lassen wollte, glaube ich nicht.
I do not believe that he did not wish to be remembered to me.

The spelling of *grüßen* and *lassen* calls our attention to the difference between *ss* and *ß*. Double *s* in the middle of a word is written *ß* after a long and *ss* after a short vowel; thus in *grüßen, fließen, reißen*, etc. the vowels are long, but in *lassen, wissen, müssen*, etc. they are short. At the end of a word and before final *-t*, double *s* is always written *ß*; thus both *das Roß* and *der Fuß* are written with *ß* although the *o* in *Roß* is short and the *u* in *Fuß* long (a fact which may be seen from their genitives: *des Rosses* but *des Fußes*); thus we write *müssen* but *ich muß, du mußt, er muß*.

The only other point of spelling to which attention must be called is the usage with regard to foreign words. Most foreign words which have become part and parcel of the German language are spelt as if they were originally German. Thus: *Kalender, Katalog, Kompanie, Offizier, Justiz, Zigarre, Telefon, Büro, Schokolade*, etc.

II. ARTICLES AND PRONOUNS

§ 1. The Definite Article: The Indefinite Article:

	SINGULAR		PLURAL				
	M	F	N			M	F	N
Nom.	der	die	das	die	Nom.	ein	eine	ein
Acc.	den	die	das	die	Acc.	einen	eine	ein
Gen.	des	der	des	der	Gen.	eines	einer	eines
Dat.	dem	der	dem	den	Dat.	einem	einer	einem

Like *ein* are declined: *kein* 'no', 'not a', and the Possessive Adjectives *mein* 'my', *unser* 'ours', etc.

§ 2. The Demonstrative Pronoun:

	SINGULAR			PLURAL	So are declined:
	M	*F*	*N*		
Nom.	dieser	diese	dieses / dies	diese	*aller* 'all'
					jener 'that'
Acc.	diesen	diese	dieses / dies	diese	*jeder* 'each'
					mancher 'many a'
Gen.	dieses	dieser	dieses	dieser	*solcher* 'such a'
Dat.	diesem	dieser	diesem	diesen	*welcher* 'which'

§ 3. The Demonstrative Pronoun has an alternative form *der*, declined like the Relative *der* (see § 9) except that the Genitive Singular Feminine and the Genitive Plural is *derer* and not *deren*. This form:

(i) May replace *dieser* or *jener* in the Nominative or Accusative for the sake of emphasis (especially in conversation):

Diesen Mann \
or, **Den** } kenne ich nicht.

I don't know **this man**.

Geben Sie mir einen Bleistift.   Wollen Sie or, **den** diesen } haben?

Give me a pencil.   Will you have **this one**?

(ii) Replaces *jener* in the Nominative and Accusative Neuter Singular:

Dies ist mein Bleistift und **das** der seinige.
This is my pencil and **that** is his.

(iii) Is an alternative to *derjenige* (§ 14).

(iv) In the Genitive it replaces *seiner* and *ihrer* (see § 4) when they refer to inanimate objects:

Erbarme dich seiner, ihrer, etc.   Have pity on him, them, etc.

But:

Ich bin **dessen** sicher.   I am sure of it.

Er hat große Begabung, aber ist **derer** nicht würdig.
He has great talent but is not worthy of it.

Er versuchte mehrere Aufgaben zu lösen, aber er war **derer** nicht fähig.
He tried to solve several problems, but he was not capable of doing them.

§ 4. THE PERSONAL PRONOUNS:

1ST PERSON	SINGULAR		PLURAL	
Nom.	ich	I	wir	we
Acc.	mich	me	uns	us
Gen.	meiner	of me	unser	of us
Dat.	mir	(to) me	uns	(to) us

2ND PERSON				
Nom.	du	thou	ihr	ye
Acc.	dich	thee	euch	you
Gen.	deiner	of thee	euer	of you
Dat.	dir	(to) thee	euch	(to) you

SINGULAR AND PLURAL		
Nom.	Sie	you
Acc.	Sie	you
Gen.	Ihrer	of you
Dat.	Ihnen	(to) you

3RD PERSON	SINGULAR						PLURAL	
	M		F		N		All genders	
Nom.	er	he	sie	she	es	it	sie	they
Acc.	ihn	him	sie	her	es	it	sie	them
Gen.	seiner	of him	ihrer	of her	seiner	of it	ihrer	of them
Dat.	ihm	(to) him	ihr	(to) her	ihm	(to) it	ihnen	(to) them

§ 5. The formal mode of address **Sie** (borrowed from the 3rd person plural) is the same in the Singular and Plural; the intimate form **du** (Singular) and **ihr** (Plural) is used towards animals, children, parents and intimate friends. **Du** and **ihr** are also generally used in fables and fairy stories.

§ 6. THE POSSESSIVE ADJECTIVES are formed from the Genitive of the Pronoun, e.g. *seiner* 'of him', *sein* 'his':

ich	I	mein	my
du	thou	dein	thy
er	he	sein	his
sie	she	ihr	her
es	it	sein	its
wir	we	unser	our
ihr	ye	euer	your
Sie	you	Ihr	your
sie	they	ihr	their

They are declined like *ein*:

	SINGULAR			PLURAL
	M	*F*	*N*	
Nom.	unser	unsere	unser	unsere
Acc.	unseren	unsere	unser	unsere
Gen.	unseres	unserer	unseres	unserer
Dat.	unserem	unserer	unserem	unseren

The Plural of *unser* may be shortened to:

Nom.	unsre
Acc.	unsre
Gen.	unsrer
Dat.	unsren or unsern

§ 7. Distinguish between the Possessive Adjectives *mein, sein, unser*, etc. and the Possessive Pronouns *meiner, seiner, unserer*, etc.

The **Adjective** agrees with a noun which is expressed:

Mein, sein, unser Pferd, etc. My, his, our horse, etc.

The **Pronoun** replaces a noun which is omitted:

Wessen Pferd ist das? Meines, seines, unseres, etc.
Whose horse is that? Mine, his, ours, etc.

The Pronoun inflects according to the ordinary rule for the declension of adjectives (see § 22); it may have three forms: *meiner, meine, meines*, etc. (strong because nothing precedes it); *der meinige, die meinige, das meinige*, etc. (weak after *der*); and *der meine, die meine, das meine*, etc. (weak).

§ 8. When speaking of clothes or parts of the body, the Definite Article should be used instead of the Possessive Adjective, and if necessary the possessor indicated by the Dative of the Reflexive or Personal Pronoun (as in French):

Den Ranzen auf **dem** Rücken wandert er durchs Land.
With **his** knapsack on **his** back he wanders through the country.

Ich wasche **mir die** Hände.   I am washing **my** hands.
Ich schüttelte **ihm die** Hand.   I shook **his** hand.

Note the difference between:

> Der Soldat hat **sich** das Bein gebrochen.
> The soldier has broken his leg (i.e. his own).
> Der Soldat hat **ihm** das Bein gebrochen.
> The soldier has broken his leg (i.e. someone else's).

§ 9. THE RELATIVE:

(i) *Welcher*, declines like *dieser*.

(ii) *Der*:

	SINGULAR			PLURAL
	M	**F**	**N**	
Nom.	der	die	das	die
Acc.	den	die	das	die
Gen.	dessen	deren	dessen	deren
Dat.	dem	der	dem	denen

Der is generally used in preference to *welcher* except where variety is desirable.

§ 10.
The Relative agrees with its antecedent in Number and Gender, its case is governed by the construction of its own clause:

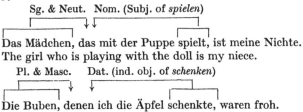

Sg. & Neut. Nom. (Subj. of *spielen*)

Das Mädchen, das mit der Puppe spielt, ist meine Nichte.
The girl who is playing with the doll is my niece.

Pl. & Masc. Dat. (ind. obj. of *schenken*)

Die Buben, denen ich die Äpfel schenkte, waren froh.
The boys to whom I gave the apples were glad.

§ 11.
The Genitive of the Relative often causes confusion. Note carefully the Genitive forms of *der* (*welcher* is rarely used in the Genitive) and distinguish particularly between the Genitive Singular Feminine *deren* and the Dative Plural *denen*:

Die Blume, deren Farbe im Frühling so schön war, ist jetzt verwelkt.
The flower, whose colour was so beautiful in Spring, is now withered.

Dies sind Leuten, denen man kaum trauen kann.
These are people whom one can hardly trust.

From the first of these examples it will be seen that the Article is omitted after the Relative in the Genitive Singular:

Das ist der Baum in dessen Äste Hans geklettert ist.
That is the tree into the branches of which Jack climbed.

§ 12. With Prepositions the form *wo* may be used when the antecedent is an inanimate object:

$$\text{Die Feder,} \begin{Bmatrix} \text{mit der} \\ \text{or, womit} \end{Bmatrix} \text{er schreibt, kratzt.}$$

The nib with which he is writing scratches.

But:

Der Junge, an den (not, woran) er schreibt, ist sein Bruder.
The boy to whom he is writing is his brother.

§ 13. In English the Relative Pronoun is often omitted, in German (as in French) never:

The letter you wrote has not arrived.
Der Brief, **den** Sie schrieben, ist nicht angekommen.

§ 14. Derjenige (declined like the Article *der* + the Adjective *jenig*) has a shortened form *der* (declined like the Demonstrative *der*, § 3). The short form is now generally preferred to the long, except where special emphasis is required or where *der* might be confused with the Definite Article. *Derjenige* or *der* is used, like the French *celui*,

(i) before a Relative,
(ii) before a Genitive.

Examples:

(i) Before a Relative, 'he who', 'the man who', 'the one which', etc.:

Ich kenne **den** nicht, der gestern bei Ihnen war.
I don't know the man who was at your house yesterday.

Erinnern Sie sich **derer**, von der ich spreche?
Do you remember the lady of whom I speak?

Trink nicht aus diesem Glas, trink aus **dem**, das auf dem Tisch steht.
Do not drink out of this glass, drink out of the one standing on the table.

Gedenke **derer**, die Ihnen geholfen haben.
Think of those who have helped you.

N.B. *Wer* ('whoever') is similarly used:

> **Wer** das glaubt, ist kein Freund von mir.
> He who believes that is no friend of mine.

> **Wen** der Krieg verschont hat, kann dankbar sein.
> Those whom the war spared can be thankful.

(ii) Before a Genitive, 'that of':

Er holte meinen Koffer und **den** meines Bruders.
He fetched my trunk and my brother's (i.e. that of my brother).

§ 15. Derselbe 'the same' declines similarly to *derjenige*:

> derselbe,   dieselbe,   dasselbe,
> denselben,   dieselbe,   dasselbe, etc.

Er hat dieselben Worte gesagt. He said the same words.

Derselbe may on occasion be used to translate 'it', referring to something already mentioned:

Er hat mir die Urkunde geschickt; eine Klausel **derselben** beweist daß....
He sent me the deed; one clause **of it** proves that....

§ 16. INTERROGATIVE PRONOUNS AND ADJECTIVES:

Pronouns: who?   what?   *Adjectives:* which (French *quel*)

Nom.	wer	was	welcher (declined like *dieser*)
Acc.	wen	was	what sort of?
Gen.	wessen		*Singular* was für ein
Dat.	wem		*Plural* was für

Examples:

Wer ist gekommen?	Who has come?
Wer von Ihnen hat es getan?	Which of you has done it?
Wen haben Sie gesehen?	Whom have you seen?
Wessen Hut ist das?	Whose hat is that?
Wem gehört der Hut?	To whom does the hat belong?
Was ist denn das?	What on earth is that?
Was haben Sie getan?	What have you done?
Mit welchem Zug kommen Sie?	By what train are you coming?
Was für ein Mann ist er?	What sort of a man is he?
Was für Männer sind sie?	What sort of men are they?

§ 17. Wer, 'who', is used in indirect as well as direct questions:

Wen haben Sie gesehen?   Whom have you seen?
Ich fragte ihn, wen er gesehen habe. I asked him whom he had seen.
Mit wem haben Sie gesprochen?   With whom have you spoken?

Ich weiß nicht, mit wem er gesprochen hat.
I do not know with whom he has spoken.

§ 18. Was? 'what?' (i) With Prepositions two forms are possible:

Wovon (or **von was**) sprechen Sie? Of what are you speaking?
Woran (or **an was**) leiden Sie?   From what are you suffering?

(ii) The German for 'what' in the sense of 'that which' is **das was** (French *ce que*). *Das* may, however, be omitted in the Nominative and Accusative:

> (Das) was Sie sagen ist Unsinn.
> What you say is nonsense.
>
> Er drückte (das), was ich nur dachte, aus.
> He expressed what I only thought.

But:

> Die Hälfte **dessen**, was Sie sagen ist Unsinn.
> Half of what you say is nonsense.
>
> Er erzählte mir von **dem**, was Sie sagten.
> He told me about what you were saying.

§ 19. Note that **was** and not the Relative **das** is used (i) when the antecedent is indefinite, (ii) when the whole and not a part of a sentence is the antecedent.

Examples:

(i) Alles **was** Sie sagen ist Unsinn. Everything you say is nonsense.
    (**Was** because *alles* is indefinite.)

Es war das Schönste, **was** ich je gesehen habe.
It was the most beautiful thing I have ever seen.
    (**Was** because *das Schönste* is indefinite.)

But:

Es war das schönste Bild, **das** ich je gesehen habe.
It was the most beautiful picture I have ever seen.
    (**Das** because *das schönste Bild* is definite.)

(ii) Leider konnte er nicht kommen, **was** zu bedauern war.
Unfortunately he could not come, which was to be regretted.

(*Was* because **the whole** of the previous sentence is the antecedent.)

§ 20. In **was für ein**, 'what sort of', the case of *ein* is decided by the construction of the sentence:

Was für **ein** Vogel ist es? What sort of a bird is it?

Was für **einen** Vogel hast du gesehen?
What sort of a bird did you see?

In the Plural *ein* is omitted:

Was für Vögel waren dies? What sort of birds were those?

N.B. *Für* should not be separated from *was*; *was ist das für ein Vogel?* though possible in conversation, should be avoided in prose.

§ 21. (i) Distinguish between **was für ein**, 'what sort of', and **welcher**, 'which of' (French *lequel*):

Wer ist da gewesen? Who was there?
Ein Herr. A gentleman.
Was für einer? What sort of one?

Einer der Herren aus Stuttgart.
One of the gentlemen from Stuttgart.

Welcher von ihnen? Which of them?
Herr Schmidt. Mr Smith.

(ii) **Welcher** is also the Interrogative Adjective (French *quel?*):

In welchem Haus wohnen Sie? In which house do you live?

Zu welchem Preis wollen Sie es verkaufen?
At what price will you sell it?

Like *quel*, *welcher* is also used in exclamations:

Welcher Erfolg! What a success!
Welch schöner Tag! What a beautiful day!

III. ADJECTIVES

§ 22. The Adjective may be declined either strong or weak:

	STRONG DECLENSION					WEAK DECLENSION			
CASE	SINGULAR			PLURAL *All genders*	CASE	SINGULAR			PLURAL *All genders*
	M	*F*	*N*			*M*	*F*	*N*	
Nom.	-er	-e	-es	-e	*Nom.*	-e	-e	-e	-en
Acc.	-en	-e	-es	-e	*Acc.*	-en	-e	-e	-en
Gen.	-es	-er	-es	-er	*Gen.*	-en	-en	-en	-en
Dat.	-em	-er	-em	-en	*Dat.*	-en	-en	-en	-en

Neither declension should be difficult, since the strong is like **dieser** and the weak has only two terminations, **e** in the Nominative Singular (all genders) and in the Accusative Feminine and Neuter, and **–en** for all other cases.

Rule. Either the word[1] preceding the Adjective or the Adjective itself must have a strong termination (since the strong termination alone shows gender and case clearly). If the word preceding the Adjective has a strong termination then the Adjective has a weak one; if not the Adjective must have the strong termination.

Examples:

I. *Nom.*   der gute Mann (*der* has the strong termination *-er*, therefore *gut* has the weak termination *-e*).

  Acc.   den guten Mann (*den* has strong termination *-en*, therefore *gut* has weak termination *-en*).

  Gen.   des guten Mannes (*-es* strong, therefore *-en* weak).

  Dat.   dem guten Mann (*-em* strong, therefore *-en* weak).

  Nom. Plur. die guten Männer (*-e* strong, therefore *-en* weak).

After words declined like *dieser* (see § 2) the Adjective has the weak termination in all cases.

---

[1] I.e. the Definite and Indefinite Articles and Pronouns such as *mein, kein, alle*, etc.

II. *Nom.* ein guter Mann (*ein* has not the strong termination *-er*, therefore *gut* must have it).

Acc. einen guten Mann (*einen* has the strong termination *-en*, therefore *gut* has the weak *-en*).

Gen. eines guten Mannes (*eines* strong, therefore *guten* weak).

Dat. einem guten Mann (*einem* strong, therefore *guten* weak).

After words declined like *ein* (see § 1) the Adjective has the strong termination in the Nominative, Masculine and Neuter, and in the Accusative Neuter, but the weak termination in all other cases.

III.

	SINGULAR	PLURAL	
Nom.	schlechter Wein	schlechte Weine	(no strong termination,
Acc.	schlechten Wein	schlechte Weine	therefore Adjective
Gen.	schlechten¹ Weines	schlechter Weine	strong)
Dat.	schlechtem Weine	schlechten Weinen	

Drei große Männer (no strong termination, therefore Adjective strong).

Hundert tapfere Soldaten (no strong termination, therefore Adjective strong).

§ 23. When two Adjectives follow each other the second has the same termination as the first:

Ein Glas guten roten Weines. A glass of good red wine.
Drei schöne süße Äpfel. Three beautiful sweet apples.

§ 24. *Einige* 'some', *manche* 'many', *mehrere* 'several', *viele* 'many', *wenige* 'few', are followed by the strong termination instead of the weak in the Nominative and Accusative Plural:

Einige gute Freunde. Some good friends.
Manche schöne Städte. Many beautiful towns.

§ 25. *Ander* 'other' is no exception to the ordinary rule; *ander* is an Adjective:

Andere gute Leute. Other good people.
Die anderen guten Leute. The other good people.

¹ The strong termination of the Adjective in the Genitive Singular Masculine and Neuter is altered from *-es* to *-en* for the sake of euphony:

Sei guten Herzens. Be of good cheer.
'Der Tisch' ist männlichen Geschlechts. 'The table' is of the male gender.

§ 26. *Aller* declines like *dieser* and is therefore followed by the weak termination:

> Alle reichen Männer. All rich men.
> Aller gute Wein. All good wine.

For further notes on *aller*, see § 58.

§ 27. Adjectives used as Substantives follow the above rules for the declension of the Adjective:

Nom. der Alte, the old man (**-er** strong, therefore *Alt*-**e** weak).
Acc. den Alten, „ „ (**-en** strong, therefore *Alt*-**en** weak).
Nom. ein Alter, an old man (*ein* not strong, therefore *Alt*-**er** strong).
Acc. einen Alten, „ „ (*ein*-**en** strong, therefore *Alt*-**en** weak).

Other examples are:

> Der Fremde, the stranger. Der Reisende, the traveller.
> Der Gefangene, the prisoner. Der Gelehrte, the scholar.
> Der Deutsche[1], the German.

§ 28. Note also Neuters of Adjectives:

Das Gute, das Wahre, das Schöne, the good, the true, the beautiful.
Gutes tun, to do good. Böses sprechen, to speak ill.
Etwas Gutes, something good. Nichts Schlimmes, nothing bad.
Von etwas Gutem (Dat.) sprechen, to speak of something good.

§ 29. A neuter termination may frequently translate the English word 'thing':

Er sagte **dasselbe**. He said the same thing.
Das erste was wir zu tun haben. The first thing we have to do.
Ich habe nur noch ein**s** zu sagen. I have only one thing more to say.

§ 30. Such words as *ein*, *kein*, etc. when standing alone also follow the Adjective Rule:

Ein**er** von uns. One of us.
Ich sah ein**en** von ihnen. I saw one of them.
Der eine ist jung, der andere alt. One is young, the other old.
Keiner von beiden. Neither of them.
Ich sprach mit kein**em** von beiden. I spoke with neither.

Ich habe das Glas Bier getrunken, geben Sie mir noch ein**s**.
I have drunk the glass of beer, give me another.

---

[1] *Der Deutsche* is the only Noun indicating nationality which is declined like an Adjective.

IV. COMPARISON

§ 31. The comparative of Adjectives is formed by adding *-er* to the positive, the superlative by adding *-st*:

klug, wise;	klüger, klügst;
bitter, bitter;	bitt(e)rer, bitterst.

These forms decline like Adjectives:

Ein klügeres Mädchen.	A wiser girl.
Der klügste Mann.	The wisest man.
Ein bittreres Getränk.	A bitterer drink.
Die bittersten Tränen.	The bitterest tears.

N.B. Most common monosyllabic Adjectives modify their vowel in comparison, e.g. *klug, klüger, klügst.* Exceptions are those with diphthong **au: blau, faul,** etc.

§ 32. The comparison of **Adverbs** is the same as that of Adjectives except that the superlative is formed with *am*:

klug, klüger, am klügsten.

Note that the adverbial form is used predicatively:

Er ist am klügsten.	He is the wisest.

§ 33. Distinguish between **als** 'than' (comparison of degree) and **wie** 'as' (comparison of quality):

Er ist größer **als** du.	He is larger than you.
Er ist ebenso groß **wie** du.	He is as big as you.
Hier ist es so warm **wie** im Ofen.	It's as hot as an oven here.

N.B. *Wie* may also be used as a Conjunction: *wie Sie wollen,* 'as you wish'; *wie Sie sagen,* 'as you say', etc.

§ 34. '**As ... as**' is usually to be translated by *ebenso ...wie*:

Er ist ebenso reich wie ich.	He is as rich as I am.

Note these two alternatives:

Er kam so schnell wie möglich. \
or, Er kam möglichst schnell. } He came as quickly as possible.

V. NOUNS

§ 35. The **Genders** of words would not cause so much difficulty if a serious attempt were made to master them from the very start; it is absolutely essential that whenever a new Noun is being learnt the Definite Article should be learnt with it. A few gender rules are of some help and should be known thoroughly.

§ 36. To the **Masculine Gender** belong:

(i) Names of Males:

Der Bube, the boy; der Lehrer, the teacher; der Wolf, the wolf; der Löwe, the lion.

Exception: die Wache, the guard.

(ii) Larger divisions of time (seasons, months, days) and the points of the compass:

Der Frühling, the Spring; der Januar, January; der Montag, Monday; der Morgen, the morning; der Norden, the north.

Exceptions: die Nacht, the night; die Woche, the week; das Jahr, the year.

§ 37. To the **Feminine Gender** belong:

(i) Names of Females:

Die Frau, the woman; die Nichte, the niece; die Königin, the queen; die Kuh, the cow; die Biene, the bee, etc.

Exceptions: das Weib, the woman; das Mädchen, the girl; das Fräulein, the young lady.

N.B. The feminine of male nouns is formed by adding -*in*; if the word is of one syllable, its vowel modifies:

Der Bauer, the peasant.	Die Bäuerin, the peasant woman.
Der Engländer, the Englishman.	Die Engländerin, the Englishwoman.
Der Wolf, the wolf.	Die Wölfin, the she-wolf, etc.

(ii) Nouns ending in -*ei*, -*heit*, -*keit*, -*schaft*, -*in* and -*ung*, and the foreign terminations -*ie*, -*ik*, -*ion*, -*tät*:

Die Sklaverei, the slavery; die Poesie, the poetry; die Kindheit, the childhood; die Musik, the music; die Schwierigkeit, the difficulty; die Nation, the nation; die Freundschaft, the friendship; die Universität, the university; die Warnung, the warning.

(iii) Most nouns of more than one syllable, ending in *-e*, which denote **inanimate** objects:

Die Eiche, the oak; die Gemeinde, the parish; die Sonne, the sun; die Straße, the street; die Stunde, the hour.

§ 38. To the **Neuter Gender** belong:

(i) Diminutives ending in *-chen* and *-lein*, e.g.

Das Mädchen, the girl; das Hündchen, the little dog; das Fräulein, the young lady; das Fischlein, the little fish.

N.B. These suffixes are often used to express the idea of endearment: *das Bübchen*, 'the dear little boy'; *das Stühlchen*, 'the nice little chair'; etc. *-lein* is used instead of *-chen* for the sake of euphony, e.g. *das Fischlein, das Büchlein*, etc.

(ii) Infinitives and all other parts of speech used as nouns, e.g.

Das Rauchen, smoking; das Leben, life; das Rot, red; das Ja und das Nein, the pros and cons.

(iii) Names of towns and countries, e.g.

Das freie England, free England; das große London, great London. Exceptions: die Schweiz, Switzerland; die Türkei, Turkey.

§ 39. The Gender of Compound Nouns is that of the last component, e.g.

Die Haustür, the front door (from *das Haus* and *die Tür*). Der Türriegel, the door-bolt (from *die Tür* and *der Riegel*).

§ 40. It would be outside the scope of this book to go into the declension of nouns. In the Vocabulary Genitive Singulars and Plurals are given where necessary.

The following practical rules may be found useful:

(i) The Genitive Singular of all Masculine and Neuter Nouns, except those which decline weak, ends in *-s* or *-es*. The Weak Declension (whose terminations are similar to the weak declension of the adjective, see § 22) comprises a number of words ending in *-e* denoting males; some like *der Mensch, der Herr*, etc.; and also foreign derivatives not ending in *-al, -an, -ar, -ast, -ier*: e.g. *der Soldat* 'the soldier', *der Polizist* 'the policeman', etc.).

(ii) The Dative Plural ends in *-n.*

(iii) Feminine nouns remain unchanged in the Singular. Feminine nouns of more than one syllable add *-n* in the Plural except **Mutter** and **Tochter** (Pl. **die Mütter** and **die Töchter**).

§ 41. (i) **Proper Names** have a Genitive in *-s.*

Alexanders Tod, Alexander's death; Goethes Werke, Goethe's works; Karls Fahrrad, Charles's bicycle.

(ii) Masculine **Christian Names** ending in sibilants (*s, ß, sch, x, z*) and feminines in *-e* or *-ie* take the Genitive in *-ens* or *-ns:*

Fritzens Rock, Fred's coat; Mariens Halskette, Mary's necklace.

With Foreign Names the Genitive must be shown by the Definite Article:

Die Tragödien **des** Sophokles. The tragedies of Sophocles.

§ 42. When modified by the Definite Article or by an Adjective the Genitive Singular of Proper Names remains uninflected:

Wilhelms Schuhe, but, Die Schuhe des kleinen Wilhelm.
Elisabeths Puppe, but, Die Puppe der kleinen Elisabeth.

§ 43. Note that there is a difference between the use of *von* and the use of the Genitive:

Eine Sonate von Beethoven = a sonata by Beethoven.
Beethovens Sonate = Beethoven's sonata (i.e. belonging to him).

§ 44. When a Proper Name is preceded by a Title either the Title or the Proper Name is inflected, but not both; if the Definite Article is present the Title is inflected, if not, the Proper Name:

Das Schloß des Königs Ludwig.⎱ The castle of King Louis.
or, König Ludwigs Schloß. ⎰

Der Bruder des Fräuleins Schmidt.⎱ Miss Smith's brother.
or, Fräulein Schmidts Bruder. ⎰

Der Sohn der Frau Schmidt.⎱ Mrs Smith's son.
or, Frau Schmidts Sohn. ⎰

N.B. The title *Herr* is an exception to this rule and always declines:

Herrn Schmidts Sohn. ⎱
Der Sohn Herrn Schmidts. ⎰ Mr Smith's son.
Der Sohn des Herrn Schmidt.⎰

§ 45. An appended title is declined as follows:

Nom.	Karl der Große.	Ludwig der Erste.
Acc.	Karl den Großen.	Ludwig den Ersten.
Gen.	Karls des Großen.	Ludwigs des Ersten.
Dat.	Karl dem Großen.	Ludwig dem Ersten.

§ 46. (i) Masculine and Neuter Nouns used as **measures** of weight, quantity, value, etc. are not inflected in the Plural:

Sechs Fuß hoch.	Six feet high.
Vier Glas Bier.	Four glasses of beer.
Zwei Paar Schuhe.	Two pairs of shoes.
Fünf Pfund Käse.	Five pounds of cheese.
Zwei Stück Kuchen.	Two pieces of cake, etc.

(ii) Feminine Nouns except *die Mark* are inflected in the Plural:

Zwei Flaschen Weißwein.	Two bottles of white wine.
Drei Tassen Tee.	Three cups of tea.

But:

Das kostet drei Mark.	That costs three marks.

§ 47. When any of the above nouns are not used as units of measure, they may of course have a Plural:

Der Mensch war sechs Fuß hoch. The man was six feet tall.

But:

Jeder Mensch hat zwei Füße. Every man has two feet.

§ 48. Note that words dependent on Nouns of Measure are not put into the Genitive:

Ein Glas Bier (not Biers).	Ein Pfund Käse (not Käses).
Eine Flasche Wein (not Weines).	

Similarly:

Eine Art Fisch.	A sort of fish.
Eine Menge Leute.	A crowd of people.
Eine Gruppe Kinder.	A group of children.

§ 49. Since the Dependent Noun is in apposition to the Noun of Measure, its case, which must be shown when an adjective

is present, should in strict Grammar be the same as that of the
Noun of Measure:

> Er kam mit einer Flasche starkem Wein.
> Er sprach mit einer Gruppe jungen Kindern.

The use, however, of the Genitive when an adjective is present
is common and should perhaps be preferred when the Dependent
Noun stands in the Plural:

> Eine Gruppe junger Studenten.
> Mit einer Menge alter Leute.

The Genitive of course must be used when the Dependent Noun
is preceded by some **determinative** adjective, or pronoun:

> Eine Flasche meines besten Weines.
> Ein Pfund dieses Käses (or, von diesem Käse).

VI. NUMERALS AND EXPRESSIONS OF TIME

§ 50. The simple Numerals are:

eins, zwei, drei, vier, fünf, sechs, sieben, acht, neun, zehn, elf,
zwölf, dreizehn, vierzehn, fünfzehn, sechzehn, siebzehn, achtzehn,
neunzehn, zwanzig, dreißig, vierzig, fünfzig, sechzig, siebzig, achtzig,
neunzig, hundert, etc.

Numerals are generally written as figures; if they are written
out in full, compound Numerals should be written as one word:
einundzwanzig, zweiunddreißig, hundertvierundfünfzig, etc.

The Ordinals (except *der erste* 'the first') are formed by adding
-t up to 20 and *-st* afterwards: *der vierte, fünfte, zwanzigste,
hundertste*, etc. [Note the spelling in *der dritte* and *der achte*.]

§ 51. The neuter form *eins* is used in counting, in Arithmetic,
and when standing alone in expressions of time:

> Eins und eins sind zwei.   One and one are two.
> Es hat eins geschlagen.   It has struck one.
> Er kam um eins.   He came at one.

§ 52. Distinguish the two nouns *das Hundert, das Tausend* from the cardinal numerals *hundert* and *tausend*:

Zweihundert Soldaten, two hundred soldiers; but, Hunderte von Soldaten, hundreds of soldiers.

Sechstausend Menschen, six thousand men; but, Tausende von Menschen, thousands of men (cf. *des milliers d'hommes*).

§ 53. There is the same difference in German between *halb* (adj.) and *die Hälfte* (noun) as between *demi* and *la moitié* in French:

Eine halbe Stunde, half an hour (*une demi-heure*).
Die Hälfte des Apfels, half the apple (*la moitié de la pomme*).

§ 54. Expressions of time occur so frequently in prose that it is worth while calling attention to a few common sources of error. Distinguish between the noun *der* **M**orgen 'the morning' and the adverb m*orgen* 'to-morrow', e.g. *heute* **M**orgen 'this morning' but m*orgen früh* 'to-morrow morning'.

Adverbs may be formed from *der Morgen, der Abend*, etc. by adding *-s*: *morgens* 'in the morning', *abends* 'in the evening', *nachmittags* 'in the afternoon', *vormittags* 'in the morning', *morgens früh* 'in the early morning'. In imitation of the above is formed *nachts* 'in the night', although *Nacht* is feminine.

§ 55. Adjectives are formed from *die Stunde, der Tag, die Woche, der Monat, das Jahr*, etc.; *stündig, tägig, wöchig, monatig, jährig*:

Eine zweistündige Fahrt.	A journey of two hours.
Ein sechsjähriges Kind.	A six-year-old child.

Distinguish the above adjectives from *stündlich, täglich, wöchentlich, monatlich, jährlich*, meaning 'hourly', 'daily', 'weekly', etc.:

Ein täglicher Besuch.	A daily visit.
Dreimonatlicher Urlaub.	Leave every three months.

§ 56. In expressions of time the English 'for' should not be rendered by *für*. There are three alternatives:

(i) **Auf**, which indicates **intention**:

Ich gehe auf einige Tage nach London.
I am going to London for a few days.
Ich wollte auf einige Tage gehen.
I wanted to go for a few days.

(ii) **Seit,** which is used of past time and indicates that the action continues up to the moment of speaking:

Ich bin seit drei Tagen in London.
I have been in London three days (and am still there).

Ich war seit drei Tagen dort.
I had been there three days (and was still there at the time of speaking).

(iii) In ordinary past time either omit the Preposition or use the Adverb *lang*:

Ich blieb drei Tage (or, drei Tage lang).
I stayed for three days.

§ 57. Distinguish between *das Mal* (French *la fois*) and *die Zeit* (French *le temps*):

Es ist die höchste Zeit, daß du schlafen gehst.
It is high time that you go to bed.

Ein jegliches hat seine Zeit.   To everything there is a season.
Zur Zeit Ludwigs des Vierzehnten.   In the time of Louis XIV.

But:

Das erste Mal, zum ersten Mal, zehnmal, jedesmal, etc.
The first time, for the first time, ten times, each time, etc.

VII. SOME PRONOUNS AND INDEFINITE NUMERALS

§ 58. ALL:

(i) *Aller* is declined like *dieser*:

Aller Wein ist nicht gut.   All wine is not good.
Alle Arbeit ist gesund.   All work is healthy.
Alle Menschen sind sterblich.   All men are mortal.

When followed by the Definite Article or a Possessive Pronoun *all* is not declined in the Singular:

All der Wein im Keller ist sauer.   All the wine in the cellar is sour.
All mein Geld ist ausgegeben.   All my money is spent.

In the Plural it may be declined:

Alle⎫ die Schüler in seiner or, All⎭ Klasse arbeiten.	All the boys in his class work.
Alle⎫ meine Freunde wohnen or, All⎭ im Ausland.	All my friends live abroad.

N.B. In translating the English 'all the' in the Plural the Definite Article is omitted in German except when particularising:

> Alle Blumen im Garten blühen.
> All the flowers in the garden are flowering.

But:

> Alle **die** Blumen, **die** ich gepflanzt habe, blühen.
> All the flowers which I planted are flowering.

(ii) 'All' must frequently be translated not by *aller*, but by *ganz*:

Die ganze Welt.	All the world.
Die ganze Stadt.	All the town.
Den ganzen Tag.	All the day.
Ganz Europa, London, etc.	All Europe, London, etc.

Ganz, which corresponds more to the English 'whole of', expresses the completeness or indivisibility of a thing, whereas *aller* indicates the individual parts of which the whole is composed:

> Alle Bäume in jenem Walde sind Eichen.
> All the trees in that wood are oaks.

But:

> Der ganze Wald besteht aus Eichen.
> The whole wood consists of oaks.

Thus *Ich habe alle Tage gearbeitet* = 'I have worked every day', but *Ich habe die ganzen Tage gearbeitet* = 'I have worked the whole of every day'.

(iii) The expressions 'all of us', 'all of this', etc. are rendered by 'we all', 'this all', etc., 'all' standing in agreement with the Pronoun:

Wir gingen alle ins Theater.	We all of us went to the theatre.
Das Geschenk ist von uns allen.	The present is from all of us.
Das alles ist Unsinn.	That is all nonsense.

§ 59. ANOTHER:

Distinguish between 'another' in the sense of 'one more' and 'another' in the sense of 'a different one':

> Geben Sie mir noch eine Ansichtskarte, eine andere.
> Give me another postcard, a different one.

§ 60. BOTH:

Beide directly precedes its Noun and must not be separated from it by the Definite Article:

> Die beiden Kinder. ⎱ Both the children.
> or, Beide Kinder. ⎰
> Meine beiden Hände. Both my hands.

The expressions 'both of us', 'both of them', etc. are rendered similarly to 'all of us':

> Wir beide gingen nach Hause. Both of us went home.
> Er sprach von Ihnen beiden. He spoke of both of you.

§ 61. IT:

(i) In German 'it' must agree in Gender with its antecedent:

> Ich leihe Ihnen diesen Bleistift, bringen Sie **ihn** wieder.
> I will lend you this pencil, bring **it** back.

> Wo ist die Gabel? **Sie** liegt unter dem Stuhl.
> Where is the fork? **It** is under the chair.

> Wer ist das Mädchen? ich kenne **es** nicht.
> Who is the girl? I don't know **her.**

(ii) When 'it' refers to an inanimate object and is governed by a preposition translate by *da-* or *dar-* + the required preposition:

> Er saß **darauf.** He was sitting on it.
> Wer sprach **davon**? Who spoke of it?
> Das Kind spielte **damit.** The child was playing with it.

These forms are equivalent to the English 'thereupon', 'thereof', 'therewith', etc. In interrogatives *wo* + the preposition is used:

> Worauf saß er? On what was he sitting?
> Wovon haben Sie gesprochen? Of what did you talk?
> Womit spielt er? With what is he playing?

(iii) Where we say 'it is I', 'it is he', etc., the German says
'I am it', 'he is it', etc.:

Ich bin es.   It is I.   Er ist es.   It is he.
Sind Sie es?   Is it you? etc.

§ 62. LITTLE, FEW:

Wenig is not declined in the singular:

Die weiße Kuh gibt wenig Milch.   The white cow gives little milk.

When inflexion is required use *gering*:

In geringer Zeit.   In a short time.

The plural *wenige* inflects according to the Adjective Rule (§ 22)
and means 'a few' (to be distinguished from *einige* meaning
'some'):

Er hat Freunde, aber wenige.   He has some friends, but only a few.

N.B. *Ein wenig* means 'a little':

Wollen Sie Milch?   Ein wenig, bitte.
Do you want any milk?   A little, please.

§ 63. MORE:

Mehr is indeclinable:

Er hat mehr Geld als ich.   He has more money than I.

Note that in English 'more' may be used in the comparison of
adjectives, but not in German:

Meine Rede war interessanter als die seinige.
My speech was **more** interesting than his.

Er wurde immer angenehmer.   He got more and more agreeable.

'More' may also be translated by *noch*:

Noch einige Minuten.   A few minutes more (see § 199).

§ 64. MUCH, MANY:

Viel generally remains uninflected in the singular:

Die schwarze Kuh gibt viel Milch.
The black cow gives a lot of milk.

When inflexion is required use *groß*:

Mit großem Vergnügen.   With much pleasure.

The plural, *viele* 'many', inflects according to the Adjective Rule:

| Er hat viele Freunde. | He has many friends. |
| Der Vater vieler Söhne. | The father of many sons. |

In English 'much' may qualify both adjectives and verbs, in German *viel* is used with adjectives, *sehr* is generally used with verbs:

| Er ist ein **viel** älterer Mann als ich. | He is a much older man than I. |
| Er bewundert mich sehr. | He much admires me. |

§ 65. ONE:

Caution must be exercised in the translation of this word. We have to choose between the Indefinite Pronoun *man* (French *on*), the Definite Article *ein* (see § 1), and a case termination:

| Das tut **man** nicht. | One doesn't do that. |
| **Einer** von uns muß gehen. | One of us must go. |

Geben Sie mir den Rock her. Welch**en**? **Den** grün**en**, bitte.
Pass me over the coat. Which one? The green one, please.

In the last sentence 'one' is translated by the case termination in *welchen* and *grünen*.

§ 66. SOME, ANY:

(i) The so-called Partitive Article 'some' (French *du, de la, des*) is either omitted in German or else *etwas* is used in the singular and *einige* in the plural; *kein* is used in the negative:

Holen Sie mir Schreibpapier und Tinte.
Fetch me some writing paper and ink.

| Geben Sie mir etwas Fleisch. | Give me some meat. |
| Haben Sie Äpfel? | Have you any apples? |

Heute speisen einige Freunde bei mir.
Some friends are dining with me to-day.

| Er trinkt keinen Wein. | He does not drink wine. |
| Sie hat keine Brüder. | She has not got any brothers. |

Note in particular that 'not any' and 'not ... a' are translated by *kein* and not by *nicht ein*.

Etwas meaning 'something' or 'some' must not be confused with *etwa* meaning 'about', 'perhaps' (see § 197).

(ii) 'Some' in the sense of the French *en* is to be rendered by *davon* or *welcher*:

Wenn Sie noch etwas Brot haben, geben Sie mir **davon**.
If you still have any bread, give me **some**.
Haben Sie Salz? Ja, ich habe **welches**.
Have you any salt? Yes, I have **some**.

(iii) When 'some' is quite indefinite and is equivalent to 'some . . . or other', use the prefix *irgend*:

Irgend jemand sagte es mir.　　Someone (or other) told me.
Leihen Sie mir irgend ein Buch. Lend me some book (or other).

Bringen Sie mir Zeitungen, irgend welche.
Bring me some papers, any you like.

§ 67. SUCH:

(i) *Solch* may either be used alone or it may be preceded or followed by the Indefinite Article:

Solcher Hund.　　⎫
Ein solcher Hund. ⎬ Such a dog.
Solch ein Hund.　 ⎭

In the first case it declines like *dieser*, in the second it follows the ordinary Adjective Rule, in the last it is invariable.

(ii) 'Such' may also be rendered by *so ein*, or *ein derartig*:

So einen　　　　　⎫
Einen derartigen ⎬ Hund habe ich noch nie gesehen.

I have never seen such a dog.

Derartig may be used adverbially, in which case it is not declined:

Einen derartig　⎫
or, Einen so　　⎬ schmutzigen Hund habe ich noch nie gesehen.

I have never seen such a dirty dog.

VIII. WORD-ORDER

§ 68. In its main outlines German word-order is not difficult. The Verb is the most important element in the sentence and the rules governing its position are hard and fast. They may be stated quite simply:

(i) In a Principal Sentence the Finite[1] Verb **always stands second**, either directly after the subject, or if some word, phrase or sentence precedes the subject directly after that:

	1	2	3
		Finite Verb	
1	Das Kind	schrieb	den Brief
2	Gestern	schrieb	das Kind den Brief
3	Auf meinen Befehl	schrieb	das Kind den Brief
	(At my order)		

If the Verb has a complement, the complement always stands **last**:

	1	2	3	4
		Finite Verb		*Complement*
1	Das Kind	hat	den Brief	geschrieben
2	Bald	wird	das Kind den Brief	geschrieben haben[2]
3	Auf meinen Befehl	ist	der Brief	geschrieben worden[2]

---

[1] The 'finite' verb is that part which shows the tense and person, e.g. in *ich* **liebe**, *ich* **liebte**, *ich* **habe** *geliebt*, *ich* **hatte** *geliebt*, *ich* **werde** *lieben*, *er* **ist** *geliebt worden*, etc. the words in heavy type are all finite.

[2] Note that the complements stand in the opposite order to that used in English:

He will **have written**	It has **been written**
= He will **written have**	= It has **written been**
= Er wird **geschrieben haben**	= Es ist **geschrieben worden**

Those who find difficulty with this word-order might do well to learn off by heart the following 'key' sequences:

gewesen sein	to have been	gelobt werden	to be praised
geworden sein	to have become	gelobt worden sein	to have been praised
gelobt haben	to have praised	gegangen sein	to have gone

(ii) In a Dependent Sentence the Finite Verb **always stands last**:

DEPENDENT SENTENCE

Subordi-nating Conj.	Rest of sentence	Verb	PRINCIPAL SENTENCE
Während	er den Brief	**schreibt,**	werde ich ausgehen
Nachdem	er den Brief	geschrieben **hat,**	kann er ausgehen
Da	der Brief	geschrieben worden **ist,**	können wir ausgehen

The complements directly precede the Finite Verb in the order already indicated.

§ 69. A Verb is **inverted in a Principal Sentence** (that is to say the subject is placed after instead of before the Verb), whenever anything other than the subject stands first in the sentence. The object of placing words before the subject is to give them greater emphasis; Adverbs of time are very commonly emphasised in this way.

N.B. (i) The Verb is inverted in a complex sentence when the Dependent stands before the Principal Clause:

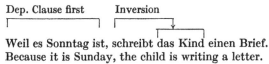

Dep. Clause first   Inversion

Weil es Sonntag ist, schreibt das Kind einen Brief.
Because it is Sunday, the child is writing a letter.

In this sentence the two clauses are grammatically dependent on each other; where two sentences have no grammatical connection there is no inversion:

Es ist Sonntag, das Kind schreibt also einen Brief.
It is Sunday, so the child is writing a letter.

(ii) The inverted order is used also in **questions**:

Schreibt er den Brief? Is he writing the letter?
Warum hast du den Brief nicht geschrieben?
Why haven't you written the letter?

§ 70.

Aber			Denn, for
Allein	}	but	Oder, or
Sondern			Und, and

are followed by the normal word-order. Sentences connected by one of these words are considered to have equal weight and are therefore both treated as principal clauses:

> Das Kind wollte den Brief schreiben, aber es war krank.
> The child wished to write the letter, but he was ill.
>
> Er konnte nicht schreiben, denn er war krank.
> He could not write for he was ill.
>
> Entweder schreibt das Kind den Brief oder seine Mutter muß
>   ihn schreiben.
> Either the child writes the letter or his mother must write it.
>
> Das Kind schrieb den Brief und der Diener trug ihn auf die Post.
> The child wrote the letter and the servant took it to the post.

N.B. *Doch*, which gives a stronger contradiction than *aber*, may be followed either by the normal or by the inverted word-order (see § 194).

§ 71. Aber, sondern and **allein** differ from each other in meaning: *sondern* is only used after negatives, *aber* is used after both negatives and affirmatives; *sondern* **contradicts** the first proposition, *aber* **concedes** it but modifies it by adding a limitation or a contrast.

Examples:

> Er ist nicht mein Freund sondern mein Feind.
> He is not my friend, but my enemy.

Sondern is used because the first proposition is negative and because a **contradiction** is expressed.

> Er ist nicht mein Freund, aber ich werde ihm doch helfen.
> He is not my friend, but I will help him all the same.

Aber concedes the first proposition and then modifies it by a contrast.

Allein has the same general sense as *aber* but is much less frequently used and is therefore more forcible; it often makes a contrast which is contrary to expectation:

Er sitzt den ganzen Tag in seinem Arbeitszimmer von Büchern umringt, allein er arbeitet nicht.

He sits the whole day in his study surrounded by books, but he does not work.

§ 72. When a Subordinating Conjunction is understood after *und* or *oder* the word-order of the sentence is the same as if the conjunction were actually there:

Nachdem Sie Ihre Schularbeit gemacht und ('nachdem' understood) einen Brief an Ihre Mutter geschrieben haben, dürfen Sie spielen.

After you have done your preparation and written a letter to your mother you may play.

Note that in this case the Auxiliary may be omitted in the first Dependent Clause.

§ 73. The above rules for the position of the Verb in the sentence should not be broken. The word-order of the rest of the sentence is, however, to a large extent fluid, and any rules which are given must on occasion give way to considerations of euphony or logic.

There is one difference in principle between German and English word-order which it is important to note. Whereas in English we can emphasise a word without altering its position in the sentence, in German when we alter the emphasis we should also alter the position. In a Principal Clause the head of the sentence is the place of greatest emphasis, otherwise the nearer a word stands to the end of the sentence the more it is stressed. The following notes should be considered in the light of the above principles.

§ 74. DIRECT AND INDIRECT OBJECTS:

Where a Verb governs two Noun Objects the indirect precedes the direct:

<pre>
            Indirect   Direct
         ┌───────────┐ ┌──────────┐
Das Kind hat seiner Mutter einen Brief geschrieben.
</pre>

The opposite, however, is the case with Pronouns:

> Das Kind hat es ihr geschickt.

§ 75. ADVERBS:

Considerable latitude is allowed in the position of Adverbs; a few hints, however, may be helpful.

(i) The Germans favour as close a connection between the subject and the verb as we do between the verb and the object. Hence in German an adverb may not stand between the subject and its verb: 'I often go there' = *Ich gehe* **oft** *hin*, or, **oft** *gehe ich hin*.

(ii) Adverbs of Time usually precede Adverbs of Manner and Adverbs of Manner Adverbs of Place:

1	2	3
TIME	MANNER	PLACE

Er reiste heute mit dem Flugzeug nach Amerika ab.

He set off for America to-day by aeroplane.

(iii) In a Principal Sentence Adverbs may either stand at the head of the sentence or they must come after the verb; two Adverbs or Adverbial Phrases may not both be placed at the head of the sentence: we cannot say, Heute mit dem Flugzeug reiste er nach Amerika ab; either *heute* or *mit dem Flugzeug* must come after the verb.

§ 76. THE PLACE OF **nicht**:

Distinction should be made between where *nicht* is used to negative a **single part** of a sentence and where it negatives the **whole sentence.** When *nicht* negatives a part of the sentence it stands directly before that part which it negatives:

> **Nicht er** gab dem Mädchen das Buch (sondern ich).
> **He** did not give the girl the book (I did).
>
> Er gab **nicht dem Mädchen** das Buch (sondern dem Jungen).
> He did not give **the girl** the book (he gave it to the boy).
>
> Er gab dem Mädchen **nicht das Buch** (sondern die Zeitung).
> He did not give the girl **the book** (he gave her the paper).
>
> Er war **nicht zu Hause.**   He was not at home.
> Er ist **nicht weit** gegangen. He has not gone far.

When *nicht* negatives the whole sentence it stands either at the end of the sentence or just before the complement:

Er gab dem Mädchen das Buch **nicht**.
Er hat dem Mädchen das Buch **nicht** gegeben.
Er sagte, daß er dem Mädchen das Buch **nicht** gegeben habe.

§ 77. ORDER OF PRONOUNS:

(i) Pronouns stand as early in the sentence as possible; they precede Adverbs:

Er hat **es** gestern dem Mädchen gegeben.
He gave it to the girl yesterday.
Er erkältete **sich** in dem Regen. He caught a cold in the rain.
Ich dachte, daß ich **es** gestern dem Mädchen gegeben hätte.
Es wundert mich nicht, daß er **sich** gestern in dem Regen erkältet hat.

(ii) In a Dependent Clause Pronouns (especially the Reflexive Pronoun) sometimes precede the subject:

Pron. Subj.

Es wundert mich nicht, daß **sich** viele gestern erkältet haben.

Pron. Subj.

Ich dachte, daß **ihr** der liebe Vater das Buch gegeben habe.

N.B. Pronouns may **not** precede if the subject is a pronoun or the impersonal *man*.

§ 78. Separable prefixes, when separated from the verb, stand at the end of the sentence.

In a principal sentence when the verb is not compound (i.e. in the Present, Imperfect or Imperative) they are separated from the verb:

(vorstellen = to introduce.)

Present Indicative: Er stellt mir das Mädchen **vor**.
Imperfect Indicative: Er stellte mir das Mädchen **vor**.
Imperative: Stellen Sie mir das Mädchen **vor**.

In Dependent Clauses or in a Principal Clause when the verb is compound the prefix is written with the verb as one word; it may be separated from its verb by *ge-* or *zu-* if the verb is in the Past Participle or the Infinitive:

Er sagte, daß er mir das Mädchen **vorstellen** würde.
Ich bat ihn mir das Mädchen **vorzustellen**.
Er hat mir das Mädchen **vorgestellt**.

IX. ADDITIONAL NOTES ON WORD-ORDER

§ 79. Dependent Clauses:

One of the most frequent sources of error in word-order is the failure to distinguish between Principal and Dependent clauses. A Dependent Clause is one which elaborates some part of a Principal Clause; there are therefore three possible types of Dependent Clause: Adjectival, Adverbial and Substantival. Relative clauses are adjectival: in the sentence 'the man who sat opposite me wore a green hat', the relative clause 'who sat opposite me' qualifies the noun 'the man'. This is clearly shown if we translate the sentence into German thus: *Der* **mir gegenüber sitzende** *Mann trug einen grünen Hut.* Adverbial clauses stand in place of an adverb, and like an adverb they can be omitted without harming the construction. In the sentence 'I will do it, whether you like it or not', 'whether you like it or not' qualifies the verb 'do' and could be omitted without harming the construction. Substantival clauses stand in place either of the subject or object of the Principal Clause. In the sentence 'He asked me how old I was', 'how old I was' is the object of 'asked' and could be replaced by a noun or a pronoun. Similarly, in the sentence 'whether you like it or not makes no difference', 'whether you like it or not' is the subject of 'makes'.

§ 80. Dependent Clauses may be introduced by three types of words. These are given below in full.

(i) Subordinating Conjunctions:

als	when	ob	whether
als ob / als wenn	as if	obgleich / obschon / obwohl	although
bis (daß)	until		
da	as, since (causal)	seit / seitdem	since (temporal)
damit	in order that		
daß	that	sobald	as soon as
ehe / bevor	before	solange	as long as
falls	in case that	soviel / soweit	as far as
indem / während	while	trotzdem	notwithstanding that
insofern	in so far as	weil	because
nachdem	after	wenn	if, when

Notes on some of the above conjunctions follow.

(ii) A Relative Pronoun:

Das Buch, das Sie mir geliehen haben, ist sehr langweilig.
The book which you lent me is very boring.

Der Bleistift, womit ich den Brief schrieb, war nicht scharf.
The pencil with which I wrote the letter was not sharp.

Alles, was in der Zeitung steht, ist nicht die genaue Wahrheit.
Everything which is in the papers is not the exact truth.

(iii) An Interrogative Adverb or Pronoun used indirectly:

Direct Questions		*Indirect Questions*
Wie alt sind Sie?		⎧wie alt er sei.
Warum gingen Sie?	Er fragte,	⎪warum er ginge.
Was hat er gesagt?		⎨was er gesagt habe.
Wer ist er?		⎩wer er sei.

§ 81. ALS, WENN, WANN:

Als = 'when', of definite past time:

> Als er mich sah, nahm er den Hut ab.
> When he saw me he took his hat off.

Wenn = (i) 'if':

> Wenn Sie mich gesehen hätten, so hätten Sie wohl den Hut
> abgenommen.
> If you had seen me you would have taken off your hat.

(ii) 'When' either in present or future time, or in past time to indicate that a thing was accustomed to happen (i.e. in the sense of 'whenever'):

> Wenn er kommt, bitten Sie ihn auf mich zu warten.
> When he comes ask him to wait for me.

> Wenn er kam, war ich nie zu sprechen.
> When (i.e. whenever) he came I was not at home.

Wann = 'when' in questions (direct or indirect):

Wann sind Sie gekommen? When did you come?
Er fragte mich, wann ich gekommen sei. He asked me when I came.

§ 82. ALS OB, ALS WENN:

There is no difference in meaning between these words. *Ob* or *wenn* may be omitted, in which case the inverted word-order is used:

He looks as if he were rich = $\begin{cases} \text{Er sieht aus, als } \begin{cases} \text{ob} \\ \text{wenn} \end{cases} \text{er reich sei.} \\ \text{or, Er sieht aus, als sei er reich.} \end{cases}$

§ 83. DA:

In English 'as' can be used both in a causal and temporal sense, in German *da* is used of **cause** only:

> Da es heute Ihr Geburtstag ist, dürfen Sie ins Kino gehen.
> As it is your birthday to-day, you may go to the cinema.

When 'as' is used of time, translate by *als*, *indem*, etc.:

> Ich sah Sie vorbeigehen, als ich am Fenster stand.
> I saw you passing as I was standing at the window.

N.B. 'As' in comparisons = *wie* (see § 33). For *da* in the sense of 'there', 'then', etc., see § 214.

§ 84. DASS:

For the sake of variation, or in order to gain clarity in a complicated piece of oratio obliqua, *daß* may be dropped; the dependent clause then has the word-order of a principal sentence:

Er behauptete, $\begin{cases} \text{daß er mir zehn Mark geliehen habe.} \\ \text{or, er habe mir zehn Mark geliehen.} \end{cases}$
He maintained that he had lent me ten shillings.

Er sagte, $\begin{cases} \text{daß ich ihm zehn Mark leihen solle.} \\ \text{or, ich solle ihm zehn Mark leihen.} \end{cases}$
He told me to lend him ten shillings.

N.B. If **daß** is dropped the Subjunctive is obligatory.

§ 85. EHE, BEVOR:

The difference between these two words is that *bevor* may only be used of time, whereas *ehe* may be used both in a temporal and a figurative sense:

> Ehe $\Big\}$ ich nach Hause kam, fing es an zu regnen.
> Bevor
> Before I came home, it began to rain.

But:

Ehe ich das glaube, müssen Sie es mir beweisen.
Before I believe that you must prove it to me.

§ 86. INDEM, WÄHREND:

(i) There is a difference between these words: *indem* 'as' limits the two actions to a short space of time and indicates that the act takes place **within** the duration of that time:

Indem er es sagte, trat ich herein. As he was saying it, I entered.

Indem is also used to indicate the means by which an act is done, and in this sense often translates the English Gerund:

Er entging dem Gefängnis, indem er einen Wächter bestach.
He escaped from prison by bribing a warder.

Während 'while' indicates the **duration** of two simultaneous actions:

Während wir bei Tisch saßen, spielte die Musik.
While we sat at table the music was playing.

(ii) *Während* and not *indem* must be used to translate 'while' in the sense of 'on the other hand':

Ein Dieb entkam, während der andere gefangen wurde.
One thief escaped, while the other was caught.

§ 87. NACHDEM:

In English 'after' may be used either as a Conjunction, a Preposition or an Adverb; in German a different word is required in each case:

Conjunction: Nachdem ich angekommen war. After I had arrived.
Preposition: Nach meiner Ankunft. After my arrival.
Adverb: Ich kam nachher an. I arrived after (or afterwards).

N.B. Similarly 'before' must be translated by *vor*, $\left.{ehe \atop bevor}\right\}$ or *vorher*:

${Ehe \atop Bevor}\Big\}$ ich angekommen war. Before I had arrived.

Vor meiner Ankunft.   Before my arrival.
Ich kam vorher an.   I arrived before (or beforehand).

§ 88. Ob:

Whenever 'if' in English is equivalent to 'whether' it should be rendered by *ob*:

> Ich wußte nicht, ob Sie kommen würden.
> I did not know if you would come.
>
> Ich fragte ihn, ob er kommen würde.
> I asked him if he would come.

§ 89. Wenn:

Variation may be obtained in conditional sentences by omitting *wenn* and using inverted word-order:

> Wenn es heute regnet, ⎫
> Regnet es heute,   ⎬ so bleibe ich zu Hause.
> Sollte es heute regnen,⎭
>
> If it rains to-day I shall stay at home.

Similar constructions are found in English:

> Were it to ⎫
> Should it ⎭ rain to-day, I should stay at home.

§ 90.
It should be noted that in German the dependent is more frequently placed before the principal clause than in English:

> Daß er das gesagt hat, glaube ich nicht.
> I don't believe that he said that.
>
> Soweit ich weiß, ist er noch nicht gekommen.
> He has not come yet, so far as I know.

§ 91.
ADVERBIAL CO-ORDINATING CONJUNCTIONS, which serve to connect two independent clauses, like real adverbs, have considerable freedom of position; if they stand at the head of the sentence they usually cause inversion (exceptions are given in § 95):

Er ist reich, daher braucht er (or, er braucht daher) nicht zu arbeiten.
He is rich, therefore he does not need to work.

Es regnet, also gehe ich (or, ich gehe also) nicht aus.
It is raining, so I am not going out.

Er ist alt, doch ist er (or, er ist doch) den ganzen Weg gelaufen.
He is old, yet he has run the whole way.

N.B. **Jedoch** 'however' and **aber** in the sense of 'however' are often placed between the subject and its verb, but strict grammarians prefer to place them after the verb:

> Er wollte gehen, ich erlaubte es jedoch (or **aber**) nicht.
> He wished to go, I, however, did not allow it.

§ 92. ENTWEDER ... ODER:

Note the word-order after these conjunctions:

> Entweder du tust es oder ich rufe deinen Vater.
> Either you do that or I call your father.
>
> Entweder er oder ich muß gehen. Either he or I must go.

§ 93. WEDER ... NOCH:

> Weder ist er selbst glücklich, noch gönnt er es anderen glücklich
>   zu sein.
> He is neither happy himself, nor does he allow others to be happy.
> Weder er noch ich war glücklich. Neither he nor I was happy.

§ 94. SO:

Principal sentences following conditional clauses are frequently introduced for the sake of form by *so* (followed by inverted word-order), especially if the dependent clause is a long one:

> Wenn er nur meinem Rat gefolgt wäre, **so** hätte er sich nicht verirrt.
> If he had only followed my advice he would not have lost the way.

So should not be used after temporal clauses.

§ 95.

Note that **Interjections** and **Exclamations** (*Ach! Ja! Mein Herr*, etc.) as well as a few adverbs (*kurzum, also*, etc.), which may be held to stand in place of a sentence, are followed by the normal, not the inverted word-order. In conversation the adverb would be emphasised if the normal order followed.

Examples:

> Ach! Ich habe mir wehgetan. Oh! I have hurt myself.
> Ja, Sie haben ganz recht.   Yes, you are quite right.
>
> Mein Herr, Sie haben Ihren Hut liegen lassen.
> You've left your hat behind, sir!

Kurzum, ich tat es.   In short, I did it.
Also Sie sind es.   So it is you.

§ 96. One sentence should not be placed inside another in German except for the sake of clarity. We should write therefore:

Ich werde dem Mädchen das Buch geben, **das ich ihr versprochen habe.**
I will give the girl the book which I promised her.

Heute hat er mir gesagt, **was er wirklich wollte.**
To-day he told me what he really wanted.

Er sagte, daß sein Haus im Wald stehe, **wo zwei Wege sich kreuzen.**
He said that his house stood in the forest where two roads cross.

But for the sake of clarity we write:

Die Frau hat mir die Zeitung, **die ich gestern sah,** gegeben.
Das Haus, **wo er wohnt,** steht im Walde.

§ 97. The above remarks apply also to infinitival clauses:

Ich habe lange gewünscht, **Ihnen einen kurzen Besuch abzustatten.**
I have long wished to pay you a short visit.

Er ging aus, **um ein Paar Schuhe zu kaufen.**
He went out to buy a pair of shoes.

Er sagte, daß es angefangen habe **in Strömen zu regnen.**
He said that it had begun to pour with rain.

But when the clause consists of one or two words only, it may for the sake of clarity be embodied inside a sentence:

Da er **mich zu besuchen** wünschte, blieb ich zu Hause.
Es fing an **zu regnen,** or, es fing zu regnen an.

So also may such infinitival clauses as are so closely connected with their verb as to form one idea with it:

Ich werde heute **viel zu arbeiten** haben.
I shall have a lot to do to-day.

Er hat **diese Frage zu beantworten** nicht vermocht.
He was not capable of answering this question.

Daß er **mich jeden Tag um zwölf Uhr zu besuchen** pflegte, wissen Sie schon.
You know already that he used to visit me every day at twelve.

N.B. A clause introduced by *um . . . zu* ('in order to') should never be embodied inside another sentence.

§ 98. If the rules governing word-order have been mastered sufficiently for correct application in short sentences, the tackling of long and complicated passages becomes merely a matter of care and attention. Often, however, the thread of the sentence is lost or some factor influencing the word-order is missed simply because in a complicated passage there are so many points to be considered that the mind, in its attempt to grapple with them all, loses sight of the construction originally used. Under such circumstances it is absolutely essential to make a fresh start, and to proceed from the beginning step by step, concentrating entirely on the word-order, and temporarily neglecting all other considerations.

X. VERBS

§ 99. There are two conjugations, the strong and the weak. The weak forms its Imperfect by adding *-te* or *-ete* to the stem, and the Past Participle by prefixing *ge-* and adding *-t* or *-et*; e.g. *loben, lob-te, ge-lob-t*; *arbeiten, arbeit-ete, ge-arbeit-et*. This class of verbs is by far the larger and is still growing, for from time to time verbs drop out of the strong conjugation and join the weak (e.g. *fragen* 'to ask' used to be strong and is now weak). Moreover, whenever a new verb is coined, e.g. *radeln* 'to ride a bicycle', or borrowed from another language, e.g. *rasieren* 'to shave', *regieren* 'to rule', *studieren* 'to study', etc., it is always weak. Strong verbs, though not nearly so numerous as weak, count among their number many of the commonest words of everyday use.

§ 100. The characteristics which distinguish strong from weak verbs are:

(i) The formation of the Past Participle in *-en*: *geben, gegeben* (there are a few exceptions like *senden, sandte, gesandt*; *denken, dachte, gedacht*, etc.).

(ii) The alteration of the root vowel: *geben, gab, gegeben*; *singen, sang, gesungen*, etc. In the 2nd and 3rd person singular of the Present Indicative the vowel of many strong verbs modifies: *ich schlafe, du schläfst, er schläft; ich werfe, du wirfst, er wirft*, etc. In the Imperfect Subjunctive the root vowel modifies if possible: *ich gab, ich gäbe; ich wurde, ich würde*; etc.

A list of strong verbs is given in the Appendix.

§ 101. The **Subjunctives** so often cause confusion both in strong and weak verbs that they are given here in full:

STRONG VERBS		WEAK VERBS	
Present Subjunctive	Imperfect Subjunctive	Present Subjunctive	Imperfect Subjunctive
Ich gebe	ich gäbe	ich lobe	ich lobte
Du gebest	du gäbest	du lobest	du lobtest
Er gebe	er gäbe	er lobe	er lobte
Wir geben	wir gäben	wir loben	wir lobten
Ihr gebet	ihr gäbet	ihr lobet	ihr lobtet
Sie geben	sie gäben	sie loben	sie lobten

Note that in weak verbs the Imperfect Subjunctive is identical with the Imperfect Indicative; the Present Subjunctive differs from the Present Indicative only in the 2nd and 3rd persons singular and the 2nd person plural.

§ 102. The **Imperfect Subjunctive** of some strong verbs is irregular: of these the only ones which should be used in prose are:

helfen	hülfe,	sterben	stürbe,
verderben	verdürbe,	werfen	würfe.

Other irregular Subjunctives (e.g. *beföhle, begönne, börste, empföhle, hübe, schölte*) should be avoided and a verb of mood used instead, e.g.

Wenn Sie mir ein gutes Wirtshaus empfehlen möchten (for empföhlen), wäre ich dankbar.

If you would recommend me a good inn I should be grateful.

§ 103. THE IMPERATIVE:

(i) The only true Imperative forms are those of the 2nd person singular and plural (used in the familiar mode of address), e.g.

Singular Sage mir. ⎫
Plural   Saget mir. ⎬ Tell me.

In polite speech the Imperative form is the same in the singular and plural:

Sagen Sie mir. Tell me.

Examples of the Imperative:

Sage mir, mein Junge, wie alt bist du?
Tell me, my boy, how old are you?

Saget mir, Jungen, was macht Ihr da?
Tell me, boys, what are you doing there?

Sagen Sie mir, bitte, wie kommt man am besten zum Bahnhof?
Tell me please, which is the best way to the station?

(ii) For the other persons of the Imperative either the Subjunctive, a verb of mood, or *lassen* is used.

Examples:

3rd person singular:

Er sage mir was er wünscht.
Er möge mir sagen, was er wünscht. } Let him tell me what he wants.
Er soll mir sagen, was er wünscht.

1st person plural:

Sagen wir, daß es möglich ist.
Wir wollen sagen, daß es möglich ist. } Suppose we say, let us say, etc. that it is possible.
Laßt uns sagen, daß es möglich ist.

3rd person plural:

Sie mögen sagen, was sie wollen. } Let them say what they like.
Sie sollen sagen, was sie wollen.

(iii) Naturally, different modal verbs will give different shades of meaning, e.g.

Er möge mir sagen. I should like him to tell me (polite suggestion).
Er soll mir sagen. He shall tell me (strong command).

Reference to the meaning of the verbs of mood will make these differences clear (see § 125 *sq.*).

§ 104. THE CONDITIONAL:

The Conditional is formed with the Imperfect Subjunctive of *werden*, e.g.

Ich würde loben.	I would praise.
Ich würde gelobt haben.	I would have praised.
Ich würde gehen.	I would go.
Ich würde gegangen sein.	I would have gone.

But in accordance with modern usage the Conditional is replaced in strong verbs by the Subjunctive:

(1) Wenn es schön wäre, so ginge ich (rather than 'so würde ich gehen').
　　If it were fine I should go.
(2) Wenn es schön gewesen wäre, so wäre ich gegangen (rather than 'so würde ich gegangen sein').
　　If it had been fine I should have gone.

For the Present Conditional therefore use the Imperfect Subjunctive, for the Past Conditional use the Pluperfect Subjunctive:

CONDITIONAL	SUBJUNCTIVE
For ich würde haben	use ich hätte.
„ ich würde gehabt haben	„ ich hätte gehabt.
„ ich würde sein	„ ich wäre.
„ ich würde gewesen sein	„ ich wäre gewesen.
„ ich würde sprechen	„ ich spräche.
„ ich würde gesprochen haben	„ ich hätte gesprochen.
„ ich würde gehen	„ ich ginge.
„ ich würde gegangen sein	„ ich wäre gegangen.

In the weak verbs the **Present** Conditional is not replaced by the Subjunctive:

> Ich würde loben.   I should praise.
> Ich würde folgen.   I should follow, etc.

But the **Past** Conditional should, as in strong verbs, be replaced by the Pluperfect Subjunctive:

Ich würde gelobt haben = Ich hätte gelobt, I would have praised.
Ich würde gefolgt sein = Ich wäre gefolgt, I would have followed, etc.

§ 105. THE PASSIVE:

It is not necessary in German to imitate the use of the French *on* and avoid all Passives. *Man*, it is true, is very frequently used to replace the Passive, especially where the agent is not clearly stated, but this is by no means invariably the case; the use of any one construction should be dictated, not by a hard and fast rule, but by a sense of style and by a desire for variety.

§ 106. The Passive form is made up in German as in English by combining the Past Participle with an auxiliary verb. But whereas we use the Past Participle + the various tenses of 'to be', the Germans use the Past Participle + the various tenses of **werden** 'to become'.

Present	*Imperfect*	*Perfect*
I **am** praised	I **was** praised	I **have been** praised
= I **become** praised	= I **became** praised	= I **have become** praised
= Ich **werde** gelobt	= Ich **wurde** gelobt	= Ich **bin** gelobt **worden**[1]

Future	*Future Perfect*
I **shall be** praised	I **shall have been** praised
= I **shall become** praised	= I **shall have become** praised
= Ich **werde** gelobt **werden**	= Ich **werde** gelobt **worden sein**

Remember that *werden* is conjugated with *sein* and not *haben*:

| Ich **bin** geworden. | I have become. |
| Ich **war** geworden. | I had become, etc. |

Therefore:

| Ich **bin** gelobt worden. | I have been praised. |
| Ich **war** gelobt worden. | I had been praised, etc. |

§ 107. Though *werden* is normally used with the Passive, its place is taken by *sein* when **state**, not **action**, is to be expressed. When the exact meaning of *sein* 'to be' and *werden* 'to become' is considered, this differentiation will be readily understood.

Die Rosen **wurden** vom Gärtner gepflückt, als ich im Garten war.
The roses were being plucked by the gardener, when I was in the garden.
(Action: the gardener was plucking the roses.)

Die Rosen **sind** jetzt alle gepflückt. The roses are now all plucked.
(State: the roses are in the state of having been plucked.)

Das Haus **wurde** im Jahre 1860 niedergebrannt.
The house was burnt down in the year 1860.

Das Haus **ist** niedergebrannt. The house is burnt down.

[1] After a Past Participle *geworden* becomes *worden* for the sake of euphony.

§ 108. PASSIVE WITH VERBS REQUIRING THE DATIVE:

It should be noted that only the direct object of a verb may be used as its subject in the Passive:

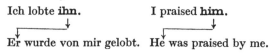

We must be careful to avoid the use of the **personal** Passive with verbs taking the Dative in German, particularly when in English they take the Accusative (as for example in the verbs 'to thank', 'to meet', 'to help', etc.).

In such sentences as 'He was met by me at the station', or, 'I was heartily thanked for my present', we can either turn the sentence and avoid the Passive: *Ich begegnete ihm am Bahnhof,* or use an impersonal construction: *Man dankte mir herzlich für mein Geschenk; Mir wurde für mein Geschenk herzlich gedankt.* The personal passive must also be avoided with verbs having two objects: 'I was given the book' must be rendered either *Mir wurde das Buch gegeben,* or *Man gab mir das Buch.*

§ 109. VERBS CONJUGATED WITH **sein**:

In German a number of verbs are conjugated with *sein* instead of *haben*. Though this is easy to understand in theory it is extremely difficult not to use *haben* in practice, and those who wish to be sure of avoiding this mistake will do well to make up sentences for themselves on these verbs, using the proper auxiliary.

Sein is used with:

(i) *Werden* and *sein*:

Ich **bin** geworden. **I have** become.   Ich **war** gewesen. **I had** been.

(ii) Verbs of Motion: *gehen, fahren, kommen, fallen, reisen, steigen, schwimmen,* etc.

(iii) Some Verbs indicating a change of state: *einschlafen* 'to go to sleep', *erscheinen* 'to appear', *erwachen* 'to awake', *gelingen* 'to succeed', *genesen* 'to recover (from an illness)', *geschehen* 'to happen', *sterben* 'to die', *verschwinden* 'to disappear', *wachsen* 'to grow'. Also the one verb of rest: *bleiben* 'to remain'. N.B. For the use of **gelingen** see § 152.

§ 110. REFLEXIVE VERBS are conjugated like ordinary Active Verbs. Mistakes are often made through imitating the French usage; note particularly that in German the Auxiliary is **haben** not **sein**, and that the Reflexive Pronoun in a principal clause is placed after and not before the Verb:

> Ich lobe mich.   I praise myself, etc.
> Du lobst dich.
> Er lobt sich.
> Wir loben uns.
> ⎰Ihr lobet euch.
> ⎱Sie loben sich.
> Sie loben sich.

§ 111. Selbst and its alternative **selber** (both indeclinable) should be distinguished from the Reflexive Pronoun; these words are added to nouns or pronouns for emphasis:

Er selbst hat mich gelobt.   He **himself** has praised me.
Der Vorsitzende selber hat es gesagt. The president **himself** said it.

N.B. *Selbst* standing in front of the noun means 'even':
Selbst der König ist sterblich. Even the king is mortal.

§ 112. Einander is indeclinable and means 'each other' (reciprocal). Distinguish from the Reflexive Pronoun:

Sie tadelten sich.   They blamed themselves (i.e. each person blamed himself).
Sie tadelten einander.   They blamed each other.
Wir wissen uns zu helfen.   We know how to take care of ourselves.
Wir müssen einander helfen.   We must help each other.

§ 113. Whereas in English we use the **Personal Pronoun** after prepositions, in German, when the subject of the sentence is referred to, the Reflexive Pronoun is used:

> Haben Sie kein Kleingeld bei **sich**?
>
> Have you no change on you?
> Sie sah ihren Freund neben **sich** stehen.
>
> She saw her friend standing near her.

§ 114. Prefixes fall into three classes:

(1) Those that are always inseparable.

(2) Those that are always separable.

(3) Those that may be either separable or inseparable.

(1) Inseparable are: *be-, ge-, er-, emp-, ent-, ver-, zer-, miß-* and *wider-*. These prefixes are never separated from their verbs; in the Past Participle *ge-* is omitted:

> Ich habe es nicht verstanden. I have not understood it.
> Wer hat den Teller zerbrochen? Who has broken the plate?

(2) Separable are all other prefixes except the seven in section (3).

(3) Either separable or inseparable are: *durch, hinter, über, um, unter, voll* and *wieder.*

§ 115. These prefixes are separable or inseparable according to their accent. If the accent falls on the prefix, the prefix is felt to be the more important element of the compound and is therefore **separable**; if the accent falls on the verb, the prefix has less prominence and is **inseparable.** The prefix is generally accented and separable when it retains its full literal force and unaccented and inseparable when it is used figuratively. In the following table examples of verbs which have both a separable and an inseparable form have been given first, for in them the difference of meaning may best be appreciated.

§ 116.

Meaning	Separable *Literal sense*	Inseparable *Figurative sense*

durch, through
Figuratively
=through
and through,
thoroughly
	1. Der Zug fuhr durch
	  The train passed through
	2. Er setzte seinen Willen durch
	  He had his own way
	3. Er strich das Wort durch
	  He crossed out the word
	4. Er hat seinen Plan durch-
	  geführt
	  He has carried out his plan
		1. Wir durchfuhren die ganze Stadt
		  We drove all over the town
		2. Der Kuchen war mit Rosinen durchsetzt
		  The cake was filled through and through with raisins
		3. Der Beamte durchsuchte meinen Koffer
		  The official searched my trunk
		4. Ich durchblätterte das Buch
		  I skimmed the book

MEANING	SEPARABLE	INSEPARABLE
	Literal sense	*Figurative sense*
hinter, behind In a literal and separable sense rare	1. Er ist hintergegangen He went behind	1. Der Schurke hat mich hinter- gangen The villain has deceived me 2. Er hat dem Staat alles hinter- lassen He left everything to the State
über, across, over The majority are insepar- able	1. Der Fährmann setzte mich über The ferryman ferried me across 2. Das Wasser ist übergelaufen The water overflowed (or boiled over)	1. Wer hat diesen Roman über- setzt? Who translated this novel? 2. Es überlief ihn ein kalter Schauder A cold shudder ran over him 3. Ich übergab ihm den Brief I delivered the letter to him 4. Er überzeugte mich davon He convinced me of it
unter, under Cf. English 'go under' and 'undergo' The majority are insepar- able	1. Da es regnete, standen wir unter As it rained we took shelter 2. Das Schiff ging mit Mann und Maus unter The ship sank with all hands	1. Ein Leutnant untersteht einem Obersten A lieutenant ranks lower than a colonel 2. Unterschreiben Sie, bitte, hier Please sign here 3. Er hat eine lange Reise unternommen He has undertaken a long journey
um, round Separable in a literal sense or in the sense of 'change' In the sense of 'all round', inseparable	1. Er baute sein Haus um He rebuilt his house (change) 2. Wir stiegen in Hamburg um We changed in Hamburg 3. Ich habe mich umgezogen I have changed my clothes 4. Er kehrte um He turned round	1. Er umbaute sein Haus mit einem Garten He built a garden round his house 2. Die Mutter umarmte ihr Kind The mother embraced her child 3. Das Heer umgab die Stadt The army surrounded the town
voll, full Cf. English 'fill full', and 'fulfil'	1. Er füllte das Glas voll He filled the glass to the brim	1. Er vollfüllte meinen Befehl He fulfilled my order 2. Er hat das Werk vollendet He has completed the work
wieder, again, back	1. Er holte das Buch wieder He fetched the book back 2. Er ist noch nicht wieder- gekommen He has not come back yet	1. Er wiederholte seine Frage He repeated his question N.B. This is the only ex- ample of an inseparable verb with *wieder*

§ 117. Nearly all inseparable verbs are **Transitive** and conjugated with **haben**:

Er **hat** die Stadt durchfahren.   He has driven all over the town.

Most separable verbs are **Intransitive** and conjugated with **sein**:

Der Zug **ist** durchgefahren.   The train passed through.

XI. THE VERBS OF MOOD

§ 118. The Verbs of Mood are important in any language, and in German especially it is essential for anyone who hopes to become a competent scholar, or even to pass the simpler examinations, to have a good understanding of them. They have therefore been dealt with here in detail.

§ 119. CONJUGATION:

	can	will	ought	must	may	be allowed
	können	*wollen*	*sollen*	*müssen*	*mögen*	*dürfen*
Present:						
ich	**kann**	**will**	**soll**	**muß**	**mag**	**darf**
du	kannst	willst	sollst	mußt	magst	darfst
er	**kann**	**will**	**soll**	**muß**	**mag**	**darf**
wir	können	wollen	sollen	müssen	mögen	dürfen
ihr	könnt	wollt	sollt	müßt	mögt	dürft
sie	können	wollen	sollen	müssen	mögen	dürfen
Imperfect:						
	konnte	wollte	sollte	mußte	mochte	durfte
Present Subjunctive:						
	könne	wolle	solle	müsse	möge	dürfe
Imperfect Subjunctive:						
	könnte	**wollte**	**sollte**	müßte	möchte	dürfte
Past Participle:						
	gekonnt	gewollt	gesollt	gemußt	gemocht	gedurft
	or	or	or	or	or	or
	können	wollen	sollen	müssen	mögen	dürfen

§ 120. The six verbs of mood and a few others (see § 187) are followed by a direct Infinitive **without** '**zu**':

Ich kann es tun. I can do it.

Do not confuse this with the case where the verb of mood is itself governed by a verb requiring *zu*:

Ich **hoffe** es tun **zu können**. I hope to be able to do it.

§ 121. The Past Participles of the verbs of mood (*gekonnt, gewollt,* etc.) are only used absolutely, i.e. when there is no Infinitive dependent on them:

Ich habe nicht gekonnt.   I have not been able to.
Ich habe nicht gewollt.   I did not wish to.

If they are accompanied by a dependent Infinitive they are themselves attracted into the Infinitive form:

I habe es nicht tun können (for gekonnt).
I have not been able to do it.
Ich habe es nicht tun wollen (for gewollt).
I have not wished to do it.

§ 122. The Imperfect and Pluperfect Subjunctive are used for the Present and Past Conditional:

Ich könnte (for, ich würde...können).
I should be able to.
Ich hätte...können (for, ich würde...können haben).
I should have been able to.

Since the Imperfect Subjunctive of **wollen** is the same as the Imperfect Indicative, confusion would arise if it were used instead of the Conditional: 'I should be willing to do it' = *ich würde es tun wollen* and not *ich wollte es tun* (which means, 'I was willing to do it').

The Pluperfect Subjunctive, however, is used for the Past Conditional:

Ich hätte es tun wollen. I should have been willing to do it.

N.B. The Imperfect Subjunctive of *wollen* is used in the sense of the French *je voudrais*:

Ich wollte, er käme heute. Would that he came to-day.

§ 123. Position in Sentence:

The verbs of mood have the same position in a sentence as a finite verb, that is to say in a principal sentence they stand second, and in a dependent clause, last:

> Er **wollte** mich besuchen. He wished to visit me.
>
> Ich weiß, daß er mich besuchen **wollte**.
> I know that he wished to visit me.

§ 124. (i) When the verb of mood is divided into Auxiliary and Past Participle or Infinitive, in a principal sentence the Auxiliary stands second, and the Past Participle last:

> Er **hat** mich besuchen **wollen**. He has wished to visit me.

(ii) But in dependent clauses the Auxiliary, instead of being placed at the end of the sentence, stands immediately before the two Infinitives:

> Er kam, weil er mich **hat** besuchen wollen.
> He came because he wished to visit me.
>
> Wenn er mich **hätte** besuchen wollen, hätte er es gekonnt.
> If he had wished to visit me, he could have done so.

Similarly we must say:

> Ich muß mein Buch im Zug **haben** liegen lassen.
> I must have left my book in the train.

§ 125. The Meaning of the Verbs of Mood:

A wrong attitude is often adopted when learning the meaning of verbs of mood; it is not advisable to think, for example, of *ich muß* as meaning simply 'I must', and *ich kann* as 'I can', for, whilst the English verbs of mood are defective, the German verbs can be fully conjugated and therefore may be rendered in English in many different ways. It is far better to take a wider view, to regard *müssen* as denoting necessity in whatever form that may be expressed in English (e.g. 'am bound to', 'am obliged to', 'cannot but', 'must needs', 'have to', etc.), to regard *wollen* as denoting 'volition', *sollen* as 'obligation', and so on. By adopting this attitude and by thoroughly mastering the underlying idea before proceeding to the different idiomatic uses a much firmer grasp and a far greater freedom in the handling of the verbs of mood can be obtained than would be the case if they were regarded merely as translating one or two stereotyped phrases.

§ 126. KÖNNEN:

(i) Actual physical or mental ability:

Ich kann schwimmen.	I can swim.
Er konnte nicht kommen.	He was not able to come.

(ii) Possibility:

Er kann schon heute kommen.	He may come to-day.
Das kann sein.	That may be.

(iii) **Idioms**:

Er kann Deutsch.	He knows German.
Er kann nichts dafür.	It is not his fault.
Kann ich herein?	May I come in?

§ 127. WOLLEN:

(i) Volition, intention:

Er will mit Ihnen gehen.
He wishes to go with you (and means to).
Er wollte nicht mit mir kommen.
He did not wish to come with me.
Ich habe es nicht sagen wollen.　I did not mean to say it.

(ii) Used instead of the Imperative:

Wir wollen gehen.　Let us go.

(See also § 103.)

(iii) **Idioms**:

Er will es getan haben.	He asserts that he did it.
Er wollte eben sprechen.	He was about to speak (i.e. he was meaning to speak).
Was wollen Sie damit sagen?	What do you mean by that?

N.B. When the English word 'will' expresses a wish it should be translated by *wollen* not *werden*:

Will you come to tea to-day (i.e. do you wish to)?
Wollen Sie heute zum Tee kommen?

Will you take a seat?　Wollen Sie Platz nehmen?

§ 128. SOLLEN:

(i) **Moral** necessity and obligation. In the Imperfect and Pluperfect Subjunctive it corresponds to the French *je devrais* and *j'aurais dû*:

> Er sollte Deutsch lernen.   He ought to learn German.
>
> Er hätte Deutsch lernen sollen.
> He ought to have learnt German.

In the Present Indicative *sollen* is generally used for a strong Future or command:

> Er soll fortgehen!   He is to go!
> Du sollst nicht stehlen! Thou shalt not steal!

(For its use in the Imperative, see § 103.)

(ii) Denotes conjecture:

> Die Gäste sollten schon hier sein.
> The guests should be here already.

(iii) *Sollen* is also used to form a Conditional (in the Imperfect only):

> Wenn er krank sein sollte, }
> Sollte er krank sein,   } so wird er nicht ausgehen.
> Should he be ill, he will not go out.

(iv) **Idioms**:

> Er soll reich sein.   He is said to be rich.
>
> Er soll nach Deutschland gereist sein.
> He is said to have gone to Germany.
>
> Was soll das heißen?   What does that mean?
> Wer soll hin?   Who is to go there?

N.B. *Der Junge soll brav sein* may mean (1) 'The boy is to be good' (command), (2) 'The boy is said to be good'.

§ 129. MÜSSEN:

Denotes **necessity**:

> Ich muß sofort abreisen. I must be off at once.
>
> Er hat gestern in aller Eile abreisen müssen.
> He was obliged to leave yesterday in a great hurry.
>
> Ich mußte lachen.   I had to laugh.

Er muß reich sein, weil er immer erster Klasse fährt.
He must be rich because he always travels first class (logical necessity).

Es muß gestern im Gebirge schön gewesen sein.
It must have been lovely yesterday in the mountains.

N.B. The English 'must not' and 'cannot' may mean 'not allowed to' and they should then be translated by *dürfen*:

Baden Sie heute? Nein, ich darf nicht.
Are you going to bathe to-day? No, I mustn't.

Ein König darf sein Wort nicht brechen.
A king cannot break his word.

§ 130. MÖGEN:

(i) Possibility with the idea of indifference, usually translated by 'may':

Sie mögen sagen, was Sie wollen.
You may say what you like (I don't care).

Das mag sein. That may be (for all I care).

Er mag es getan haben. He may have done it (I don't know).

Was auch geschehen mag. Whatever happens.

(ii) Denotes fondness, liking (see also § 144):

Ich mag gern rudern.
I like rowing.

Ich mag ihn nicht. I do not like him.

Früher mochte ich gern schwimmen.
I used to like swimming.

Ich möchte heute reiten. I should like to ride to-day.

N.B. The Imperfect Subjunctive of *mögen* often translates the English 'want', 'would', etc.:

Was möchten Sie heute tun?
What do you want to do to-day?

Ich möchte lieber zu Hause bleiben.
I would rather stay at home.

§ 131. Dürfen:

(i) Denotes permission, lawfulness:

> Darf man in diesem Abteil rauchen?
> Is one allowed to smoke in this compartment?
> Warum sind Sie nicht gekommen? Ich durfte nicht.
> Why did you not come? I was not allowed.

(ii) *Dürfen* also translates the polite 'may':

> Darf ich Ihnen eine Zigarette anbieten?
> May I offer you a cigarette? (literally, am I allowed to).
> Darf ich um diesen Tanz bitten? May I have this dance?
> Dürfte ich Sie um Feuer bitten?
> Might I trouble you for a match?

(iii) Possibility (only in the Imperfect Subjunctive), e.g.

> Das dürfte sein. That may be.

§ 132. The word 'may' is used in English in different senses. 'He may come' can be rendered:

> Er kann kommen (there is a possibility that he may come).
> Er mag kommen (he is at liberty to come, I don't mind).
> Er darf kommen (he is allowed to come).

§ 133. *Können, mögen, dürfen* all express possibility; *dürfen* is stronger than *mögen*, and *mögen* stronger than *können*:

Er kann es getan haben. He may have done it (I don't know).
Er mag es getan haben. He may have done it (a probability).
Er dürfte es getan haben. He may have done it (a polite agreement).

N.B. We may also use the Imperfect Subjunctive of *können*, in which case the probability is stronger than if we used the Present Indicative:

> Das kann wahr sein.   That may be so (a possibility).
> Das könnte wahr sein.   That may be so (a probability).

§ 134. Distinguish carefully between the Imperfect Subjunctive and the Imperfect Indicative:

Er durfte kommen.　　　　He was allowed to come (and did come).
Dürften wir morgen kommen?
Should we be allowed to come to-morrow?
Er mußte gehen.　　　　He was obliged to go (and went).
Er müßte gehen.　　　　He would have to go.
Ich mochte reiten.　　　　I liked riding (a fact).
Ich möchte reiten.　　　　I would like to ride.
Er konnte mich nicht sehen. He could not see me (fact).
Könnten Sie mich sehen, wenn ich morgen käme?
Could you see me if I came to-morrow?

Particular care must be taken with *können*, since the English 'could' is used both in the sense of 'would be able to' (Conditional) and 'was able to' (Imperfect Indicative).

§ 135. PLUPERFECT SUBJUNCTIVE:

There is still one difficulty in the use of verbs of mood which requires explanation: the translation of such sentences as, 'I ought to have gone', 'I could have done it', etc. If we render the latter sentence literally the German would be *Ich könnte es getan haben*. But in fact the German translation is *Ich hätte es tun können*.

The explanation of the difference lies not in the German but in the English and is due to the fact that the verb 'can' has no past tense; since in English we are unable to say 'I would have "can" do it', we say 'I could have done it', i.e. we use the PRESENT CONDITIONAL ('could') + the PAST INFINITIVE ('have done') instead of the PAST CONDITIONAL ('would have "can"') + PRESENT INFINITIVE ('do'). That the Past Conditional is the tense we should use if it existed becomes clear when we replace the defective 'can' by the fully conjugated 'to be able to'. We should then say: 'I should have been able to do it' (i.e. PAST CONDITIONAL + PRESENT INFINITIVE), which is exactly what the Germans do in saying, *ich hätte es tun können*. The same difficulty occurs with 'ought', which has no past tenses. Hence 'I ought to have done it' = *ich hätte es tun sollen*, not *ich sollte es getan haben*.

We have then, in translating such sentences, to make the following rearrangement of Tenses:

English: PRESENT CONDITIONAL + PAST INFINITIVE.
German: PAST CONDITIONAL + PRESENT INFINITIVE.

§ 136. Those who already know French may find the following translations helpful:

Je pourrais.	Ich könnte.
J'aurais pu.	Ich hätte...können.
Je voudrais.	Ich möchte.
J'aurais voulu.	Ich hätte...mögen.
Je devrais.	Ich sollte.
J'aurais dû.	Ich hätte...sollen.

§ 137. The verbs of mood have many common synonyms (followed generally by the Infinitive with *zu*); these may sometimes be used with advantage to give variety or to avoid an awkward series of Infinitives. Among the commonest are: *gezwungen sein, genötigt sein* for *müssen*; *vermögen* or *imstande sein* for *können*; *beabsichtigen, gewillt sein* for *wollen*. In translating 'he wished to send me his greetings' we should for example prefer *er hat beabsichtigt, mich grüßen zu lassen* to *er hat mich grüßen lassen wollen,* similarly *er ist nicht imstande gewesen, mir einpacken zu helfen* is better German than *er hat mir nicht einpacken helfen können.*

XII. NOTES ON SOME VERBS

In forming a vocabulary it is important to notice differences in usage between the two languages. Many cases arise, for example, where in English one verb is used in several senses but where in German a different verb is required for each meaning.

§ 138. ASK:

Distinguish between *fragen* and *bitten*:

Fragen = 'to ask for information': *fragen* is usually followed by a Dependent Clause introduced by a subordinating conjunction but it may also have a Noun Object with a preposition:

> Er fragte mich, wieviel es koste.
> He asked me how much it cost.
>
> Er fragte mich, wohin ich ginge.
> He asked me where I was going.
>
> Er fragte mich, ob ich ihn gesehen hätte.
> He asked me if I had seen him.
>
> Er fragte mich nach dem Preis, dem Weg, etc.
> He asked me the price, the way, etc.

Bitten = 'to ask', in the sense of 'to make a request' (it can therefore always be replaced by 'to request'); *bitten* is usually followed either by an Infinitive Clause (with *zu*), or by a Noun Object (with preposition **um**):

> Er bat mich ihm zwei Mark zu leihen.
> He asked me to lend him two marks.
>
> Er bat mich es nicht zu vergessen.
> He asked me not to forget it.
>
> Er bat mich um Geld, Verzeihung, Erlaubnis, etc.
> He asked me for money, forgiveness, permission, etc.

Note that *bitten* and *fragen* both take the Accusative of the person addressed and that the preposition used with *bitten* is *um*, whereas *fragen* is followed by *nach*:

> Er bat mich **darum.** He asked me for it.
> Er fragte mich **danach.** He asked me about it.

§ 139. CALL:

Heißen is an Intransitive word and means 'to be called':

> Er heißt Schmidt. He is called Smith.
> Wie heißt er? What is his name?

Nennen is Transitive and means 'to call', 'to name':

> Er nannte mich seinen Freund. He called me his friend.

Heißen can be used transitively, in which case it means 'to bid' and takes an Infinitive without *zu* (§ 187):

> Ich hieß ihn fortgehen.   I bade him go.

Both *heißen* and *nennen* should be distinguished from *rufen* 'to call out':

> Haben Sie mich gerufen?   Did you call me?
> Ich rief ihn zu mir.   I called him to me.

§ 140. Go:

(i) Distinction must be made between **gehen** and **fahren**: strictly speaking *gehen* means 'to go on foot' only, but in conversation it is also frequently used in a more general sense:

> Bitte, gehen Sie nicht so schnell. Please do not walk so fast.
> Ich gehe bald nach London.   I am going to London soon.

If it is desired to emphasise the fact of walking *zu Fuß* can be added:

> Wie gehen Sie hin? Ich gehe zu Fuß.
> How are you getting there? I am walking.

Spazieren gehen = 'to go for a walk' (French *se promener*):

> Ich gehe spazieren.   I am going for a walk.
> Er ist spazieren gegangen. He has gone for a walk.

Spazieren is an Infinitive governed by *gehen* and can be used also with *fahren* and *reiten*:

> Wir reiten gern spazieren.   We like going for rides.
> Er ist spazieren gefahren.   He has gone for a drive.

(ii) **Fahren** should always be used in translating 'to go' where the method of travel is a vehicle or a ship:

> Er fährt mit der Eisenbahn nach London.
> He is going to London by train.
> Er ist mit dem Dampfer nach Amerika gefahren.
> He went to America by ship.
> Das Auto fuhr 100 Kilometer die Stunde.
> The car was going at sixty miles per hour.

(iii) 'To go' is often to be translated by *sich begeben, ziehen* or *treten*. *Sich begeben* is a synonym of *gehen*. *Ziehen* is used more of movement in a collective sense and gives the idea of procession:

Die Soldaten ziehen durch die Stadt.
The soldiers are marching through the town.

Treten means literally 'to step' and expresses a brief movement:

Er trat ins Zimmer.   He went into the room.
Er trat auf die Straße.   He went into the street.

§ 141. HANG:

This word is used both transitively and intransitively in English; in German there are two words, *hangen*, strong and intransitive, and *hängen*, weak and transitive:

Das Bild hing an der Wand.   The picture hung on the wall.
Er hängte das Bild an die Wand. He hung the picture on the wall.

Hängen, which is formed from *hangen*, is known as a **factitive verb** (i.e. 'to make to hang'); other such verbs are: *fällen* 'to make to fall' (from *fallen*), *drängen* 'to press into' (from *dringen*), *ertränken* 'to drown' (from *ertrinken*), and *setzen*, *legen* and *stellen* (see § 148). Factitive verbs are transitive and conjugated weak.

§ 142. KNOW:

No confusion should arise over the difference between *kennen* and *wissen* if the student already knows French: *kennen* = *connaître*; *wissen* = *savoir*.

Kennen 'to be acquainted with' is always followed by a Noun or Pronoun Object: *Ich kenne den Mann, die Stadt, die Gegend*, etc., 'I know (I am acquainted with) the man, the town, the district', etc.

Wissen = 'to know mentally', to have grasped in the mind as a fact. Its object is usually a sentence:

Ich weiß, daß der Mann kein Geld hat.
I know that the man has no money.

Er wußte nicht, ob ich in der Gegend wohnte.
He did not know whether I lived in the district.

Wissen may also be followed by a Noun Object standing in place of a sentence: *Kennen Sie ihn? Ja, aber ich weiß seinen*

Namen nicht, 'Do you know him? Yes, but I do not know his name' (i.e. what his name is), or by a Pronoun: *Ich weiß es, manches, alles,* etc., 'I know it, much, everything', etc. (not merely 'am acquainted with' but 'apprehend').

§ 143. LEAVE:

Distinguish between:

(i) *Verlassen* 'to leave' (Transitive): *Ich verließ die Stadt, das Haus, meinen Freund,* etc., 'I left the town, the house, my friend', etc.

(ii) *Liegen lassen* or *stehen lassen* 'to leave an object behind by mistake':

Das Mädchen hat die Flasche in der Küche stehen lassen.
The maid left the bottle in the kitchen.

Die Kinder ließen ihr Spielzeug auf dem Grase liegen.
The children left their toys on the grass.

(iii) *Lassen,* which is more often used in the sense of the French verb *faire* (see § 188), 'to have a thing done', than of the English 'to leave'. But note the expressions:

Lassen Sie mich in Ruhe.   Leave me alone.
Lassen Sie das.   Leave it alone.

Er hat die Tür zu und das Fenster offen gelassen.
He left the door shut and the window open.

N.B. 'To leave' (motion) used intransitively should be rendered by *abfahren* when speaking of vehicles and by *abreisen* when speaking of human beings:

Der Zug fuhr um 6 Uhr ab. The train left at six o'clock.
Erst heute ist er abgereist. He did not leave until to-day.

§ 144. LIKE:

Gefallen, mögen, gern haben: (i) *Gefallen* = 'to like the look of': *Dieses Zimmer, dieses Bild, das Buch gefällt mir,* 'I like this room, this picture, this book'; *gefallen* is also used impersonally:

Es gefällt mir in der Stadt. I like the town (I feel at home in it).

(ii) *Mögen,* 'to care for', is a little stronger than *gefallen* and is very frequently used in a negative sense:

Zuerst gefiel mir der Mensch, aber jetzt mag ich ihn nicht.
At first I liked the look of the fellow, but now I do not care for him.

(iii) *Gern haben* = 'to be fond of' (usually persons or animals):

Mögen Sie Hunde? Ja, ich habe sie sehr gern.
Do you like dogs? Yes, I am very fond of them.

Gern is an adverb meaning 'with pleasure' and has a comparative *lieber* and a superlative *am liebsten*:

Ich habe Hans gern aber Fritz lieber und am allerliebsten habe ich Karl.
I am fond of Jack but I prefer Fred and I like Charles best of all.

The other word for 'to prefer'—*vorziehen*—should only be used where there is no question of affection:

Beim Bridgespielen ziehe ich Fritz vor, weil er niemals streitet.
When I'm playing bridge I prefer Fred, because he never quarrels.

N.B. *Gern, lieber, am liebsten* can be used in conjunction with any verb to translate 'like': *Ich lese, schreibe, reite, schwimme gern*, 'I like reading, writing, riding, swimming'.

§ 145. Look:

Sehen and *schauen* are synonyms (*sehen* is used more in North, *schauen* in South Germany):

Sehen Sie (or, schauen Sie) dahin! Look over there!

'To look' (used of outward appearance) = *aussehen*:

Sie sehen sehr wohl aus. You look very well.
Wie schön sehen heute die Berge aus!
How beautiful the mountains are looking to-day!

'To look at' = *ansehen* or *anschauen* + Accusative:

Er sah (or, schaute) mich an. He looked at me.

§ 146. Marry:

Care must be taken to distinguish in German between *heiraten, sich verheiraten* and *trauen*: *heiraten* (intransitive and transitive) = 'to marry'; *verheiraten* (transitive) = 'to give in marriage'; *sich verheiraten mit* = 'to marry'; *trauen* (transitive) = 'to perform the marriage ceremony' (French *marier*):

Er wollte die Tochter heiraten.   ⎱ He wished to marry
or, Er wollte sich mit der Tochter verheiraten. ⎰ the daughter.

Der Vater wollte seine Tochter nicht an ihn verheiraten.
The father did not wish to give his daughter to him in marriage.
Auch der Pfarrer verweigerte sich sie zu trauen.
The parson too refused to marry them.
Deshalb konnten sie nicht heiraten (or, sich nicht verheiraten).
For that reason they were not able to marry.

§ 147. MEET:

(i) *Begegnen* (conjugated with *sein* and followed by the Dative) has a narrower sense than *treffen* (conjugated with *haben* and followed by the Accusative). *Treffen* may be used for any sort of meeting, accidental or intentional: *Ich habe meinen Freund auf der Brücke, im Theater, auf dem Ball*, etc. *getroffen*, 'I met my friend on the bridge, in the theatre, at the ball', etc.

But *begegnen* should only be used when two people are meeting face to face. In contrast to the English 'meet', the **object** of *begegnen* rather than the **subject** is taken to be the agent of the meeting: *Ich bin meinem Freund auf der Brücke begegnet* implies that the friend was coming towards me rather than that I was going towards him and should therefore be translated 'My friend met me on the bridge'. A similar transposition of subject and object should be made when translating from English into German: 'She met the young man while out for a walk' = *Der junge Mann begegnete ihr bei einem Spaziergang*.

(ii) 'To meet' used intransitively = *sich treffen (se rencontrer)*:

Wollen wir uns in dem Schloßgarten treffen?
Shall we meet in the castle grounds?

§ 148. PUT:

(i) *Legen* (factitive of *liegen*) = 'to make to lie, to lay':

Das Buch liegt auf dem Tisch.	The book is lying on the table.
Wer legte das Buch auf den Tisch?	Who put the book on the table?
Er legte sich auf das Bett.	He lay down on the bed.

(ii) *Setzen* (factitive of *sitzen*) = 'to make to sit, to seat':

Das Kind sitzt auf dem Stuhl.
The child is sitting on the chair.
Wer hat das Kind auf den Stuhl gesetzt?
Who has put the child on the chair?

Ich setzte den Fuß auf die Leiter.
I put my foot on the ladder.
Wir setzten uns zu Tisch.   We sat down at table.

(iii) *Stellen* (factitive of *stehen*) = 'to make to stand, to put in an upright position':

Die Flasche, das Glas, etc. steht auf dem Tisch.
The bottle, the glass, etc. stands on the table.

Das Mädchen hat die Flasche, das Glas, auf den Tisch gestellt.
The maid has put the bottle, the glass, on the table.

Der Gärtner stellte die Leiter an die Mauer.
The gardener put the ladder against the wall.

Er stellte sich an die Tür.   He stationed himself at the door.

N.B. 'Put the book on the table' = *Legen Sie das Buch auf den Tisch*; but, 'Put it on the shelf' = *Stellen Sie es in das Regal*.

(iv) *Stecken*, literally 'to stick', may translate 'to put' only in the sense of 'to place **inside**':

Er steckte die Hand in die Tasche. He put his hand in his pocket.

§ 149. START:

Anfangen and *beginnen* are synonyms; 'it began to rain' = either *es fing an*⎱ *zu regnen.*
or   *es begann*⎰

For 'to start' used intransitively (e.g. on a journey) use *abreisen, abfahren,* or *aufbrechen* (for *abreisen* and *abfahren* see above, § 143):

Wir brachen früh morgens auf.
We started very early in the morning.

'To start' in the sense of 'to set in motion' = *in Gang setzen*:

Er setzte sein Auto in Gang und fuhr ab.
He started his car and set off.

§ 150. STOP:

(i) *Aufhören* is the opposite of *anfangen*:

Das Kind fing an zu weinen und wollte nicht mehr aufhören.
The child began to cry and would not stop.

(ii) *Stehen bleiben* denotes the cessation of a motion:

Meine Uhr ist stehen geblieben.   My watch has stopped.
Ich blieb auf der Schwelle stehen. I stopped on the threshold.

(iii) *Anhalten* is used of vehicles and **innehalten** of people:

Ich befahl dem Führer am Hotel anzuhalten.
I ordered the driver to stop at the hotel.

Er machte noch einige Schritte und hielt dann inne.
He took a few more steps and then stopped.

(iv) For 'to stop' in the sense of 'to stay at', 'to spend the night at', use *absteigen* (French *descendre*) or *übernachten*.

In welchem Hotel steigen Sie ab?
At which hotel are you stopping?

Ich übernachte im Hotel Schönblick.
I am stopping the night in the Hotel Schönblick.

§ 151. TELL:

Erzählen means 'to tell' only in the sense of 'to narrate' a story (French *raconter*); for other uses of 'to tell' use *sagen*:

Die Mutter erzählte den Kindern die Geschichte von Reineke Fuchs.
The mother told (related) to the children the story of Reynard the Fox.

But:

Sagen Sie mir wohin Sie gehen.   Tell me where you are going.

'To tell' in the sense of 'to command' or 'to bid' is best translated by *heißen*, though *sagen* may also be used: 'He told me to go' may be rendered, *Er hieß mich gehen*, or, *Er sagte mir, ich solle gehen*.

§ 152.

The correct use of some verbs in German causes difficulty because their construction differs from that of their English equivalents. The following are a few examples:

abhängen:

Das hängt von dir ab.   That depends upon you.
Von wem hat es abgehangen?   On whom did it depend?

anklagen:

Er klagte mich des Diebstahls (or, wegen des Diebstahls) an.
He accused me of theft.

Wer hat ihn des Vergehens angeklagt?
Who accused him of the crime?

auffallen:

Es fiel mir sofort auf, daß er etwas hinkte.
It struck me at once that he limped a little.
Dieser Mann fiel mir sofort auf.   I was at once struck by this man.

berauben:

Er beraubte mich meines Geldes.   He robbed me of my money.

But note the construction after *rauben* and *abnehmen*:

Er raubte **mir** das Geld, or, Er nahm **mir** das Geld ab.
He took my money.

einfallen:

Es fiel mir plötzlich ein, daß ich eine Verabredung hatte.
It suddenly occurred to me that I had an appointment.
So etwas wäre mir niemals eingefallen.
Such a thing would never have occurred to me.

eintreten:

Bitte, treten Sie ein.   Please step in.
Er ist ins Zimmer eingetreten.   He entered the room.

An alternative to *eintreten* (+ *in*) is *betreten* (+ Acc.):

Er betrat das Zimmer.   He entered the room.

Compare *steigen* (+ *auf*) and *besteigen* 'to mount'.

Er stieg auf das Pferd, or, Er bestieg das Pferd.
He mounted the horse.

gelingen:

Es gelang ihm dem Gefängnis zu entkommen.
He succeeded in escaping from prison.
Ist es Ihnen gelungen das Examen zu bestehen?
Did you succeed in passing the examination?

mangeln:

An Geld mangelt es mir nicht.   I don't lack money.
Woran mangelt es Ihnen denn?   What are you in want of then?

mitteilen:

Er teilte mir die Stunde seiner Ankunft mit.
He informed me of the hour of his arrival.
Er hat es mir nicht mitgeteilt.   He did not inform me of it.

vorbeigehen:

Er geht jeden Tag an meinem Fenster vorbei.
He passes my window every day.

Er ist an mir vorbeigegangen ohne den Hut abzunehmen.
He passed me without raising his hat.

Similar to the above are *vorbeischreiten* 'to stride past', *vorbeireiten* 'to ride past', etc.

vorwerfen:

Ich warf ihm seine Habsucht vor.
I reproached him with his avarice.

Ihnen habe ich nichts vorzuwerfen.
I have nothing to reproach you with.

zuhören:

Hören Sie mir zu.	Listen to me.
Er hat mir nicht einmal zugehört.	He did not even listen to me.

Compare *zurufen* 'to call **to**', *zuwinken* 'to wave **to**', etc.:

Er rief mir zu.	He called to me.
Er hat mir zugewinkt.	He waved to me.

zuschreiten:

Er schritt auf mich zu.	He walked up to me.
Er ist darauf zugeschritten.	He has walked up to it.

Similar to the above are *zugehen auf* 'to go up to', *zulaufen auf* 'to run up to', etc.

XIII. PREPOSITIONS

§ 153. Only the commonest meanings of the Prepositions have been given here. A knowledge of their more idiomatic uses must be built up gradually. Many examples will be found in the passages for translation and they should be noted as they occur; as much help as possible has been given in the Notes and the Vocabulary to show where the German usage differs from the English.

Prepositions may govern either: (1) the Accusative only; (2) the Genitive only; (3) the Dative only; (4) the Accusative or Dative.

§ 154. Prepositions governing the Accusative only:

durch,	through	ohne,	without
für,	for	um,	round
gegen,	towards, against	wider,	against

Examples:

Ich ging durch den Garten.	I went through the garden.
Dieser Apfel ist für dich.	This apple is for you.
Er hielt es gegen das Licht.	He held it against the light.
Er tat es gegen meinen Willen.	He did it against my will.
Er kam ohne seinen Regenschirm.	He came without his umbrella.
Er wanderte um die Stadt.	He wandered round the town.
Wir segelten wider den Wind.	We sailed against the wind.

§ 155. Prepositions governing the Genitive only:

anstatt,	instead of	während,	during
trotz,	in spite of	wegen,	on account of
um...willen,	for the sake of		

N.B. *Wegen* sometimes and *willen* always follow the word they govern.

Examples:

Anstatt einer Lampe nahm ich eine Kerze.
Instead of a lamp I took a candle.

Trotz der Hitze ging er spazieren.
In spite of the heat he went for a walk.

Sei ruhig um der Kinder willen.
Be quiet for the children's sake.

Während des Regens blieb ich zu Hause.
During the rain I stayed at home.

Seiner Krankheit wegen darf er nicht ausgehen.
On account of his illness he must not go out.

§ 156. Prepositions governing the Dative only:

aus,	out of	nach,	after, to (of places)
außer,	except	seit,	since
bei,	near	von,	of, from, by
gegenüber,	opposite	zu,	to (of persons)
mit,	with		

Note that *gegenüber* follows the word it governs.

Examples:

Er ging aus dem Zimmer.	He went out of the room.

Es war niemand dort außer ihm.
There was no one there except him.

Das Rathaus befindet sich bei der Kirche.
The Town Hall is to be found near the church.

Er saß meinem Bruder gegenüber. He sat opposite my brother.
Gehen Sie mit ihr.   Go with her.

Nach zwei Stunden klärte sich das Wetter auf.
After two hours the weather cleared up.

Er ist nach London gefahren.   He has gone to London.

Seit Ihrer Ankunft sind wir alle froh.
Since your arrival we are all happy.

Keiner von ihnen ist gekommen. Neither of them has come.

Von der Kirche bis zum Bahnhof ist eine kurze Strecke.
From the church to the station is a short distance.

Der Hirsch wurde von dem Wilddieb erschossen.
The stag was shot by the poacher.

Er kam zu mir.   He came to me.
Wir sprachen zu ihnen.   We were speaking to them.

§ 157. Prepositions governing the Accusative of 'motion to' and the Dative of 'rest or motion at':

an,	up to, at	über,	over, about
auf,	upon	unter,	under, among
hinter,	behind	vor,	in front of, before
in,	in, into	zwischen,	between
neben,	near		

Examples:

Er ging ans Fenster.	He went up to the window.
Er stand am Fenster.	He stood at the window.
Stellen Sie die Lampe auf den Tisch.	Put the lamp on the table.
Die Lampe steht auf dem Tisch.	The lamp is on the table.
Er lief hinter einen Baum.	He ran behind a tree.
Er stand hinter einem Baum.	He stood behind a tree.

Ich steckte meine Pfeife in die Tasche.
I put my pipe in my pocket.

Die Pfeife ist in meiner Tasche.	The pipe is in my pocket.

Setzen Sie sich neben mich.   Sit down near me.
Er saß neben mir.   He was sitting near me.

Er hängte das Bild über den Kamin.
He hung the picture over the fireplace.

Das Bild hing über dem Kamin.
The picture hung over the fireplace.

Der Hund legte sich unter den Stuhl.
The dog lay down under the chair.

Der Hund liegt unter dem Stuhl. The dog is lying under the chair.

Das Kind lief vor das Auto.   The child ran in front of the car.
Das Auto wartet vor der Tür.   The car is waiting before the door.

Vor meiner Ankunft waren alle froh.
Before my arrival everybody was happy.

Er nahm Platz zwischen mich und meine Schwester.
He took a seat between me and my sister.

Zwischen ihnen war ein leerer Stuhl.
Between them was an empty chair.

§ 158. In the above examples the use of the Accusative for 'motion to' and the Dative for 'rest at' should be quite clear. But the use of the Dative for 'motion at' requires some explanation; a few examples will help to make this clear:

Er ging ins Zimmer.
He went into the room (motion into the room).

Er ging auf und ab im Zimmer.
He walked up and down the room (motion inside the room).

Ich ließ den Übeltäter vor mich kommen.
I had the evildoer brought before me (motion towards).

Die Sklavin tanzte vor dem König.
The slave danced before the king (motion at).

Er fiel durch das Fenster auf die Straße.
He fell through the window into the street.

Er fiel auf der Straße.
He fell in the street (he fell when in the street).

It will be seen that whenever the motion takes place at or on a stationary element, the Dative and not the Accusative is used. A few more examples follow:

Er rudert auf dem Teiche.	He is rowing on the lake.
Der Adler schwebte in der Luft.	The eagle hovered in the air.
Wir kamen spät in der Stadt an.	We arrived at the town late.
Jemand ging am Fenster vorbei.	Someone went past the window.
Er kehrte im Wirtshaus ein.	He turned in at the inn.
Der Hund lief hinter mir her.	The dog ran along behind me.

§ 159. Owing to the fact that the German conception of 'motion to' differs from the English the Dative is often used wrongly instead of the Accusative in the following cases:

Er ging über die Brücke.	He went over the bridge.
Er warf es über die Mauer.	He threw it over the wall.

Er schrieb seinen Namen auf das Papier.
He wrote his name on the paper.

Er klopfte auf die Tür.	He knocked on the door.

Der Bergsteiger hielt sich an einen Stein fest.
The climber clung to a stone.

§ 160. In German the idea of 'motion to' is not confined to physical or material motion; the Accusative therefore is also used in the following examples:

Er wollte in die Armee eintreten.	He wished to enter the army.
Er nahm mich in seinen Dienst.	He took me into his service.
Er flüsterte es mir ins Ohr.	He whispered it into my ear.

Ich habe es ins Deutsche übersetzt.
I have translated it into German.

Er ist närrisch in sie verliebt.	He is madly in love with her.

§ 161. Similarly the Accusative is used after such verbs as 'to think of', 'to believe in', etc., the idea being that we direct our thoughts towards an object:

Denk' an mich in meiner Abwesenheit.
Think of me in my absence.

Erinnerst du dich an jenen Tag?	Do you remember that day?

Ich erinnerte ihn an sein Versprechen.
I reminded him of his promise.

Glauben Sie an Gespenster?	Do you believe in ghosts?

Man gewöhnt sich leicht an die Aussprache.
One soon gets used to the pronunciation.

N.B. The adjective *gewohnt* takes the Accusative:

Ich bin die Aussprache schon gewohnt.
I am already used to the pronunciation.

§ 162. When Prepositions governing either the Accusative or the Dative are used **metaphorically,** they are followed by **the Dative** except for *auf* and *über*, which are generally followed by the Accusative.

Examples:

An Ihrer Stelle.	In your place.
Er starb an der Pest.	He died of the plague.
Im Gegenteil.	On the contrary.
In zwei Tagen.	In two days.
Vor allem.	Above all.
Vor zwei Tagen.	Two days ago.
Er fürchtete sich vor dem Tod.	He was afraid of death.

But:

Auf diese Weise.	In this way.
Er kommt auf zwei Tage.	He is coming for two days.
Er wartet auf Sie.	He is waiting for you.
Über alle Maßen schön.	Incomparably beautiful.
Heute über acht Tage.	This day week.
Er sprach über den Völkerbund.	
He spoke about the League of Nations.	

§ 163. Many German Verbs require different Prepositions from those used with the corresponding English verb; these should be carefully noted as they occur (the Prepositions are shown in the Vocabulary). Other Verbs require a Preposition in German where the English verb has a direct object, e.g.

Es handelt sich **um** seine Ehre.	It concerns his honour.
Er hielt mich **für** einen Narren.	He considered me a fool.
Erinnern Sie sich **an** den Tag?	Do you remember the day?
Daran zweifle ich.	I doubt it.

There are also a few which have different meanings when used with different Prepositions, e.g.

Er freut sich auf die Ferien. He is looking forward to the holidays.
Er freut sich über das Geschenk. He is pleased with the present.
Er freut sich an Ihrem Erfolg. He takes pleasure in your success.

XIV. ADDITIONAL NOTES ON PREPOSITIONS

§ 164. An, auf, bei: *Auf* indicates contact with the top surface of a thing, *an* contact with any other part:

Er saß auf dem Stuhl.	He was sitting on the chair.

Er stand am Tisch, am Kamin, an der Tafel, etc.
He was standing at the table, at the fireplace, at the blackboard, etc.

Bei differs from *an* in that it does not imply contact:

Er saß bei dem Baum.	He sat near the tree (not far off).
Er saß am Baum.	He sat near the tree (touching it).

Bei can only express rest; for motion *an, neben* or *zu* must be used.

§ 165. Bei has no Preposition which corresponds to it in English and its use in German is therefore often found difficult. A few common meanings are given here:

(i) 'At the house of' (French *chez*):

Er wohnt bei seiner Tante.	He lives with his aunt.
Er speist heute bei mir.	He is having dinner with me to-day.

(ii) 'On the occasion of':

Bei seiner Abfahrt.	On his departure.
Beim Abschied.	On taking leave.
Beim Essen.	While eating.

In the above sense it often takes the place of an English sentence.

(iii) 'Amongst', 'with':

Bei uns hat er keinen guten Ruf.
Amongst us he has a bad reputation.

Bei Gott ist alles möglich.	Everything is possible with God.

§ 166. Bis (+ Accusative) 'until', 'as far as', denotes a limit or boundary and is used of time and place:

Er bleibt bis Ostern, Mittwoch, morgen, zwei Uhr, etc.
He is staying till Easter, Wednesday, to-morrow, 2 o'clock, etc.
Wieweit fahren Sie? Bis Wien.
How far are you going? As far as Vienna.

Bis is more commonly used in conjunction with other Prepositions to give the idea of 'right up to':

Er füllte mein Glas bis an den Rand.
He filled my glass to the brim.
Wir arbeiteten bis tief in die Nacht.
We worked till late at night.
Sie starben alle bis auf drei. All but three died.
Von seiner Jugend bis zu seinem sechzigsten Jahre.
From his youth up to his sixtieth year.

§ 167. Nach, zu, in: (i) *Nach* indicates the direction in which you are going: *Er fährt nach Süden*, 'He is travelling south'; *nach* should **always** be used with the names of **places** and **countries:** *Ich fahre nach Paris, Frankreich*, etc. *Zu* indicates a purpose as well as a direction; *zu* should always be used with **people:** *Er ging zu seinem Vater, zum Bahnhof, zur Stadt, zum Berg*, etc. Frequently either *zu* or *nach* might be used, but there is a slight difference in meaning: *Er ging zur Stadt*, 'He went to the town' (with some object in view); *Er ging nach der Stadt*, 'He went to the town' (i.e. in the direction of).

(ii) When 'to' implies the entering of a building, it is often to be translated by *in*: *Er ging in die Kirche, in die Schule, in die Oper, ins Theater*, 'He went to church, to school, to the opera, to the theatre'.

In is also used with the names of countries which are feminine: *Er reiste in die Schweiz, in die Türkei*, etc., 'He travelled to Switzerland, to Turkey', etc.

§ 168. Note that **nach Hause** = 'home' (motion), but **zu Hause** = 'at home' (no motion):

Er blieb zu Hause.   He stayed at home.
Wollen wir nach Hause gehen? Shall we go home?

§ 169. Vor:

(i) After verbs expressing 'fear', 'warning', etc. the English 'of' is translated by *vor*:

Ich fürchte mich vor dem Tod. I am afraid of death.
Hüte dich vor ihm.   Beware of him.
Er warnte mich vor der Gefahr. He warned me of the danger.

(ii) *Vor* also translates the English 'with', 'for', 'from' in such phrases as:

Er lachte vor Freude.	He laughed for joy.
Er heulte vor Schmerzen.	He howled with pain.
Wir zittern vor Kälte.	We tremble with cold.
Er stirbt vor Erschöpfung.	He is dying from exhaustion.

§ 170. Zu, in: 'at' with the names of towns usually = *in*: *Er wohnt in Paris*, 'He lives at Paris'; but *zu* is used in phrases like: *der Dom zu Köln*, 'the cathedral at Cologne'; *die Universität zu Heidelberg*, 'the University at Heidelberg', etc.; where it is a question of a building or an institution; an alternative to the latter would be to use the adjective formed from the name of the town: *der Kölner Dom*, *die Heidelberger Universität*, etc.

XV. NOTES ON SYNTAX

§ 171. Duration of time and definite time are both put in the **Accusative**:

Er arbeitete den ganzen Tag.	He worked the whole day (duration).
Er besucht mich jeden Tag.	He visits me every day (definite).

Die Ferien fangen den zweiten September an.
The holidays begin on the 2nd of September (definite).

But indefinite time is put in the Genitive:

Eines Tages, Morgens, Abends, etc. werde ich wieder vorbeikommen.
One day, morning, evening, etc. I will call again.

In imitation of the above expressions is formed *eines Nachts*, 'one night', although *Nacht* is feminine.

§ 172. Expressions both of time and space may be qualified by an Adverb, in which case the Noun stands in the **Accusative**:

Das ganze Jahr hindurch.	Throughout the whole year.
Sechs Monate lang.	For six months on end.
Er ging den Weg hinauf.	He went up the street.
Wir segelten den Strom hinab.	We sailed down the stream.

§ 173. Two **Accusatives** are used with *lehren* and *nennen*:

Er lehrte mich Deutsch.　　He taught me German.

Das nenne ich Betrug.　　I call that cheating.

§ 174. *Von* may be used instead of the **Genitive** where the Genitive cannot be shown by a case termination:

Die Ursache dieses Krieges.　　The cause of this war.

But:

Die Ursache von drei Kriegen.　　The cause of three wars.

Von may also be used instead of the Genitive after numerals and with titles: *einer von uns, sechs von ihnen, Tausende von Menschen, der König von England*, etc.

§ 175. In § 173 two verbs are given which take two Accusative objects, all other verbs in German having two objects require the indirect (usually the personal) object to be in the **Dative**, e.g.

Er kaufte mir das Buch.　　He bought me the book.

Ich schrieb ihm einen Brief. I wrote him a letter.

The difference between the Dative of an indirect object and *zu* (+ Dative) should be recognised. In the sentence 'he gave the book to the girl', 'to the girl', being the indirect object, is put in the Dative and requires no *zu*. Where, however, the English 'to' expresses something more, as for example motion towards, either *zu* or some other preposition is required in German, e.g. *er kam zu mir, er sprach zu mir*. In practice we can usually discover whether *zu* is required or not by turning the English sentence. If by so doing we can avoid using the 'to' in English the Dative alone is used in German, e.g. 'I gave the book to the girl' can be turned to 'I gave the girl the book' (therefore no *zu* in German). But 'he came to me', 'he spoke to me' cannot be turned (therefore use *zu*). There are a few exceptions to this rule, such as *gehören* 'to belong to', *entsprechen* 'to correspond to', etc.

Das gehört mir.　　　　That belongs to me.

Es entspricht dem, was Sie eben sagten.

It corresponds to what you were just saying.

§ 176. Verbs of **speaking** are commonly followed by a direct and indirect object, the indirect (or personal) object being in the Dative:

> Er befahl es **mir.**   He ordered me to do it.
>
> Ich habe es **Ihnen** nicht vergeben.
> I have not forgiven you for it.
>
> Antworten Sie **ihm.**   Answer him, etc.

Exceptions are *bitten* and *fragen* 'to ask' (see § 138), *entschuldigen* 'to excuse' and *warnen* 'to warn', which are followed by the Accusative:

> Ich habe **Sie** gewarnt.   I have warned you.
> Entschuldigen Sie **mich.**   Excuse me.

§ 177. The verb *sagen* may take either the Dative of the indirect object or the preposition *zu*. *Zu* is used to introduce direct speech:

> Was haben Sie ihm gesagt?   What have you told him?
> Er sagte mir, ich solle nachfolgen.   He told me to follow.

But:

> Er sagte **zu** mir: 'Du sollst zu Hause bleiben'.
> He said to me: 'You are to stay at home'.

§ 178. The **Subjunctive** is used in oratio obliqua:

Der Reichskanzler hob in seiner Rede hervor, die Regierung **sei** fest entschlossen den Weg weiterzugehen, den sie bisher beschritten hat. Deutschland **habe** Ruhe notwendig und die Regierung **werde** es sich zur Aufgabe stellen die Ruhe wiederherzustellen. Ohne die Mitwirkung der anderen Parteien **könne** aber dieses Ziel nur schwer erreicht werden und deswegen **hoffe** er, daß, u.s.w....

The German Prime Minister emphasised in his speech that the government was absolutely determined to continue on the road it had followed up till now. Germany needed quiet and the government would make it its task to restore quiet. Without the co-operation of the other parties this goal could be attained only with difficulty and for that reason he hoped that, etc....

§ 179. Similarly the Subjunctive is used in indirect questions and commands:

In dem zweiten Teil seiner Rede fragte der Reichskanzler, wer Deutschland im Jahre 1918 gerettet **habe**, und was aus dem Vaterland ohne Hindenburg geworden **wäre**. Deutschland **solle** dafür dankbar sein, daß....

In the second part of his speech the Chancellor asked who had saved Germany in 1918 and what would have become of Germany but for Hindenburg. Germany must be thankful that....

§ 180. The Tense used in reported speech is that of the original speaker. The Minister's words were: 'I **am** determined ..., Germany **needs** rest..., who **saved** Germany', etc. In each case the corresponding tense of the Subjunctive is used: the Present in the first two and the Perfect in the last. Supposing, however, the Chancellor had said: 'I maintain that my opponents **have** made a grave mistake', the reported speech would be: *Er behauptete, seine Gegner* **hätten** *einen großen Fehler gemacht*, the Imperfect Subjunctive being used instead of the Present. The reason for this is that in the third person plural the Present Subjunctive is the same as the Present Indicative.

A comparison of the Indicative and Subjunctive of *haben* will show where such change is necessary:

Present Indicative	*Present Subjunctive*
ich habe	**ich habe**
du hast	du habest
er hat	er habe
wir haben	**wir haben**
ihr habt	ihr habet
sie haben	**sie haben**

This alteration of tense should be made with verbs having an Imperfect Subjunctive which differs from the Imperfect Indicative (i.e. *haben* and *sein* and strong verbs); with weak verbs whose Imperfect Subjunctive is the same as the Imperfect Indicative no alteration of tense need be made.

§ 181. Where oratio obliqua takes the form not of a long speech but of short sentences, the use of the Subjunctive depends on the opinion of the speaker. The Subjunctive expresses doubt and uncertainty, and if the speaker wishes to cast doubt on what he is reporting he uses the Subjunctive; if, however, in his opinion the report is true, he uses the Indicative:

Er sagte, er habe den Zug versäumt.
He said he missed the train (but I don't believe him).

Er sagte, er hatte den Zug versäumt.
He said he missed the train (and I believe him).

§ 182. Since, however, we must be certain of what we ourselves say or think, the Indicative is used after a verb in the 1st person singular of the Present Indicative:

Ich glaube, daß es wahr ist.   I believe that it is true.

Ich finde, daß er heute besser aussieht.
I think that he looks better to-day.

As soon, however, as we use the negative or a past tense, the Subjunctive may be used to show that there is doubt or uncertainty in what we say:

Ich glaube nicht, daß es wahr sei.
I do not believe that it is true (but of course it may be).

Ich fand, daß er besser aussähe.
I thought that he was looking better (I may be wrong, my memory may deceive me).

§ 183. The Subjunctive is used in **Conditional sentences**. We may distinguish between three types of Conditional sentences:

(1) Wenn du mir dein Taschenmesser **gibst**, schenke ich dir einen Apfel.
    If you give me your pocket knife, I will give you an apple.

(2) Wenn du mir dein Taschenmesser **gäbest**, könntest du den Apfel haben.
    If you gave me your pocket knife, you could have the apple.

(3) Wenn du mir dein Taschenmesser **gegeben hättest**, hätte ich dir den Apfel gegeben.
    If you had given me your pocket knife, I would have given you the apple.

The first sentence is a simple condition: if the condition is fulfilled, then the rest follows automatically. Nothing is said about the likelihood of fulfilment. In the second it is implied that there are difficulties in the way of the exchange: the owner of the knife does not want to part with it, and the speaker knows this; his implied afterthought is: 'Of course, I know you won't really make the exchange'. In the third sentence it is emphasised that the condition was not fulfilled: the speaker's implied afterthought is: 'But I don't want to make the exchange at all now'. It will be seen from this that the Subjunctive is used as soon as doubt is cast on the likelihood of the fulfilment of the condition.

A few more examples of the three types are given:

(1) Wenn das Wetter nicht umschlägt, mache ich morgen eine Bergtour.
If the weather doesn't change, I shall go for a tour in the mountains to-morrow.

Wenn du spät in die Schule kommst, wirst du bestraft werden.
If you are late for school, you will be punished.

(2) Wenn du so alt **wärest** wie ich, würdest du auch langsam gehen.
If you were as old as I am, you would walk slowly too.

Wenn die Steuern nicht so hoch **wären**, könnte ich mir ein Auto leisten.
If the taxes were not so high, I could afford a car.

(3) Wenn du mich nicht eingeladen **hättest**, wäre ich böse gewesen.
If you had not invited me, I should have been angry.

Wenn mir dieser Plan gelungen **wäre**, hätte ich viel Geld verdient.
If my plan had succeeded, I should have made a lot of money.

§ 184. The **Present** and **Past Participles** are both used as Adjectives. The Present Participle has an active or intransitive sense, e.g. *der beißende Hund*, 'the dog which bites', *das laufende Kind*, 'the child who is running'. The Past Participle has a passive meaning with transitive verbs, e.g. *der gebissene Hund*, 'the dog which was bitten', but not with intransitive verbs, e.g. *der eingeschlafene Hund*, 'the dog which has gone to sleep'. No verb conjugated with *haben* can have a Present Participle with a passive meaning or a Past Participle with an active meaning; therefore 'a dog that is being bitten', 'a dog that has bitten', 'a dog that has run' cannot be rendered in German by a Participle.

§ 185. In German the Present or Past Participle frequently takes the place of a Relative Sentence in English:

> Die aus 6 Mann bestehende Mannschaft.
> The crew which consisted of 6 men.
>
> Der mit Äpfeln gefüllte Korb.
> The basket which was filled with apples.
>
> Der in vielen Kriegen verwundete Held.
> The hero who had been wounded in many wars.

Note that the Participles stand at the end of their own clause.

§ 186. The varied and frequent use of the Verbal Noun and the Present Participle in English cannot be imitated in German. The termination '-ing' should be a danger signal: the cases where it may be rendered by the corresponding German form *-end* are rare.

The following examples should show how the difficulty may be avoided:

(1) He lay on the ground **sleeping**.
Er lag auf dem Boden **und schlief**.

(2) The policeman **standing** at the corner took out his notebook.
Der Polizist, **der** an der Ecke **stand**, nahm sein Notizbuch heraus.

(3) **On thinking** it over I changed my mind.
Als ich darüber **nachdachte**, besann ich mich.

(4) **Being hungry**, I bought a loaf of bread.
Da ich hungrig **war**, kaufte ich ein Brot.

(5) She was surprised **at** my **knowing** it.
Sie erstaunte, **daß** ich es **wußte**.

(6) You will oblige me **by coming** early.
Wenn Sie früh **kommen**, werden Sie mir einen Gefallen tun.

(7) He escaped from prison **by bribing** the warder.
Er entkam dem Gefängnis, **indem** er den Wächter **bestach**.

(8) I insist **on** your **coming** with me.
Ich bestehe darauf, **daß** Sie **mitkommen**.

(9) I came in the hope **of seeing** you.

Ich kam in der Hoffnung Sie **zu sehen.**

(10) The thought **of seeing** you brought me here.

Der Gedanke Sie **zu sehen** hat mich hierher gebracht.

§ 187. Verbs which are followed by an **Infinitive without 'zu'** are:

(i) The verbs of mood: *dürfen, können, mögen, müssen, sollen, wollen.*

(ii) The following verbs: *lehren, lernen, lassen, helfen, heißen, sehen, fühlen, hören, bleiben.*

Er lehrte mich singen.	He taught me to sing.
Sie lernt jetzt tanzen.	She is learning to dance.
Wo ließen Sie das Buch liegen?	Where did you leave the book?
Ich half ihm den Rock abziehen.	I helped him to take off his coat.
Er hieß mich schweigen.	He bade me be silent.
Wir sahen das Kind fallen.	We saw the child fall.
Er fühlte seine Hand zittern.	He felt his hand tremble.
Wer hörte ihn weinen?	Who heard him cry?
Er blieb vor der Tür stehen.	He stopped in front of the door.

Note also the expression *spazieren gehen*, 'to go for a walk'.

After other verbs **zu** must be used:

Er wünschte mich zu besuchen.	He wished to visit me.
Er vermochte nicht aufzustehen.	He was not able to get up.
Du brauchst es nur zu sagen.	You only need to say so.
Das ist schwer zu verstehen.	That is hard to understand.

§ 188. Lassen, like the French *faire*, has many shades of meaning. As in *faire* the underlying idea is to cause a thing to be done:

Er ließ eine Brücke bauen.	He ordered the bridge to be built.
Lassen Sie den Zahn ausziehen!	Have the tooth drawn!
Ich werde ihn kommen lassen.	I will summon him.
Er hatte mich warten lassen.	He had kept me waiting.
Wer hat das Buch fallen lassen?	Who dropped the book?

§ 189. It will be seen from the last example above that the Past Participle of *lassen*, when it follows an Infinitive, is itself attracted into the Infinitive form (cf. verbs of mood, § 121). Other verbs which behave thus are *helfen, hören,* and *sehen*:

> Er hat mir das Zimmer aufräumen helfen.
> He helped me clear the room.

§ 190. **Um ... zu** means 'in order to':

> Wir arbeiten, um Geld zu verdienen.
> We work in order to earn money.

Frequently in English 'to' is equivalent to 'in order to', and when this is the case *um ... zu* should be used:

> Ich fahre in die Stadt, **um** meinen Freund **abzuholen.**
> I'm going to town to fetch my friend.

Um ... zu may only be used when the subject of the two sentences is the same: 'I am sending my son to school to learn German' may be turned:

> Ich schicke meinen Sohn auf die Schule, um ihn Deutsch lernen **zu lassen,**

or,

> Ich schicke meinen Sohn auf die Schule, damit er Deutsch lerne.

§ 191. The Prepositions **ohne** and **anstatt** may be used with an Infinitive:

> Er verließ das Hotel, **ohne** die Rechnung **zu** bezahlen.
> He left the hotel without paying the bill.
> **Anstatt** eine Woche **zu** bleiben, blieb er sieben.
> Instead of staying one week he stayed seven.

When the subject of the two sentences is not the same *ohne daß* and *anstatt daß* must be used:

> Er verließ das Hotel, ohne daß ihn jemand bemerkte.
> He left the hotel without anyone noticing him.
> Anstatt daß er mich einlud, mußte ich ihn einladen.
> Instead of his inviting me I had to invite him.

§ **192.** Note the use in German after *es ist* and *es gibt* of the active Infinitive where we use the passive:

Es ist kaum zu glauben.	It is hardly to be believed.
Er ist nirgends zu finden.	He is nowhere to be found.
Es gab viel zu tun.	There was much to be done.

XVI. SOME PARTICLES

The difficulty of such words as *ja, doch, einmal, schon*, etc. is due partly to the fact that they have no exact equivalents in English and must often, therefore, either be rendered by phrases which do not exactly correspond to them, or be left altogether untranslated. A few of the commonest uses are given here.

§ **193.** DENN:

(i) Usual meaning 'for':

Er wollte nicht kommen, denn er war müde.
He did not wish to come, for he was tired.

(ii) Often used to give emphasis to questions:

Sind Sie denn so dumm, daß Sie mich nicht verstehen können?
Are you really so stupid that you cannot understand me?
Wo sind Sie denn gewesen?   Where on earth have you been?

§ **194.** DOCH:

Has many different shades of meaning according to the context, accent and place in the sentence, but the fundamental idea is always **adversative**. We can distinguish the following meanings according to whether *doch* is accented or not:

A. Accented.

(i) *Doch* gives a **firm** contradiction; it may be placed either before or after the verb; if placed before the verb it may be followed either by the normal or by the inverted word-order:

Er ist ein geschickter Kerl, doch traue ich (or, doch ich traue) ihm nicht.
He is a clever fellow, yet I do not trust him.

Er mag recht haben, doch kann ich (or, doch ich kann) es kaum
    glauben.
He may be right but I can hardly believe it.

Er suchte lange nach dem Pfad, aber er konnte ihn doch nicht finden.
He looked for the path a long time, but could not find it all the same.

(ii) When placed after the verb *doch* frequently contradicts
an idea which is not expressed but merely implied:

Sie sind also doch gekommen.   So you have come after all.
    (The implied idea is 'I thought you wouldn't'.)

(iii) Similarly *doch* is used like the French *si* to give an
affirmative answer to a question expecting a negative one:

Sehen Sie ihn nicht? Doch, ich sehe ihn.
You don't see him, do you? Yes, I see him.

Sind Sie niemals in Deutschland gewesen? Doch, doch!
Have you never been in Germany? Oh yes!

B. Unaccented.

(i) The adversative force of *doch* is not felt so strongly:

Er hat mich im Stich gelassen, nachdem ich doch für ihn so viel
    getan habe.
He left me in the lurch even after I had done so much for him.

Er erntet, was er doch nicht gesät hat.
He reaps what he has not sown.

(ii) Frequently the contrast is with an idea that is not expressed; in this case the adversative force very often gives the
idea of contrary to expectation, surprise, etc. and may be translated by the English 'really', 'surely', etc.:

Es ist doch schön hier.
It really is beautiful here (I did not think it would be so beautiful).

Haben Sie doch niemand gesehen?
Have you really seen no one (surely you must have)?

Sie wissen doch, daß er fort ist.   You surely know that he has gone.

(iii) *Doch* is also used to emphasise Imperatives and wishes.
With Imperatives *doch* implies that the person addressed is
unwilling:

Essen Sie doch noch etwas.	Do eat some more.
Warten Sie doch bis ich fertig bin.	Do just wait until I'm ready.
Wäre er doch hier!	If only he were here!

§ 195. EINMAL:

(i) Usual meaning 'once':

Ich werde es nur einmal sagen. I shall only say it once.

Dieser Palast war einmal die Wohnung eines Königs.
This palace was once the dwelling of a king.

(ii) Used to give emphasis (in conversation often shortened to *mal*); it is most frequently found in commands and often corresponds to the English '**just**', '**do**', etc.:

Kommen Sie einmal her!	Do come here.
Warten Sie einmal bis ich fertig bin!	Just wait until I'm ready.
Schauen Sie einmal dahin!	Do look over there.

§ 196. ERST:

'Not until', 'only', etc.:

Er kam erst spät nach Hause. He did not come home till late.

Erst vor zwei Tagen habe ich ihn kennen gelernt.
I only met him three days ago.

Erst may be distinguished from *nur*, in that the latter marks the final limit of a progress whereas the former merely marks a stage which is likely to continue:

Ich hatte erst zwei Briefe geschrieben.
I had only written two letters (I was going to write some more).

Ich habe nur zwei Briefe erhalten.
I have received only two letters.

§ 197. ETWA:

(i) 'About':

Es waren etwa 300 Leute anwesend.
There were about 300 people present.

(ii) Suggests a possibility, especially in questions; the nearest English equivalent is 'perhaps':

Hat er etwa recht? Is he perhaps right?

Könnten Sie mir etwa 5 Mark leihen?
Could you possibly lend me 5 shillings?

§ 198. Ja:

(i) Emphasises an affirmative statement; since it has no direct equivalent in English it may be rendered in many different ways:

Ich bin hungrig, geben Sie mir ja etwas zu essen.
I'm hungry, do give me something to eat.
Er ist ja mein Freund.   He is my friend, you know.
Er kommt ja immer zu spät. He always comes too late.
Du weißt ja schon, was ich sagte.
You know exactly what I said.

(ii) In the above cases *ja* is unaccented; in strong commands and to give a strong contradiction to an expressed doubt *ja* is accented:

Er soll **ja** zu Hause bleiben. He is to stay at home.
Machen Sie das Fenster zu, bitte. Ich habe es **ja** getan.
Please shut the window. I have already done so.

§ 199. Noch:

(i) Indicates the continuation of an action up to a certain point: 'still', 'yet', 'up till', 'now', etc.:

Das alte Schloß steht heute noch.
The old castle still stands to-day.
Noch vor einem Jahr studierte er auf der Universität.
Up till a year ago he was studying at the University.
Er wird noch heute kommen. He will come before the day is out.

The negative of *noch* = *noch nicht*:

Er hat sich noch nicht erholt. He has not recovered yet.

(ii) From the idea of continuation has developed that of intensity, multiplication, etc.:

Sagen Sie es, bitte, noch einmal. Please say it once more.
Er ist noch größer als ich. He is still taller than I am.

Wir haben nur noch zwei Kilometer.
We only have another two kilometres.

(For the difference between *noch ein* and *ein ander* see § 59.)

§ 200. Schon:

(i) Usually means 'already', 'as early as':

Ich bin mit meiner Arbeit schon fertig.
I have already finished my work.

Schon gestern, am Montag, vor zwei Jahren bin ich nach Deutschland gekommen.
I came to Germany two years ago yesterday, on Monday.

Note that *schon* is often inserted in German where 'already'
is omitted in English:

Wie lange sind Sie schon hier? Ach, schon längst.
How long have you been here? Oh, for a long time.

(ii) *Schon* may be used without reference to time and often
translates the English 'surely', 'never fear', etc.:

Sie wird schon kommen.   She will come, I am sure.
Er wird mich schon bezahlen.   He will pay me, never fear.

It may also often translate 'quite':

Das ist schon gut.   That is quite all right.
Das ist schon etwas anderes.   That is something quite different.

Note the difference between:

Er ist schon angekommen.   He has already arrived.

and

Er wird schon kommen.   He is sure to come.

§ 201. Überhaupt:

Indicates that a statement is made **without limitation**:

Er ist überhaupt sehr liebenswürdig.
He is altogether very obliging (not merely on one occasion but
always).

Bei uns gibt es überhaupt keine solche Tiere.
Such animals do not exist at all in our country.

Du hättest es überhaupt nicht tun sollen.
You should not have done it at all.

§ 202. Wohl:

(i) When accented = 'well', 'good':

Ich freue mich, Sie wohl zu sehen.
I am glad to see you well.

Das tat mir wohl.　　　　　　That did me good.

(ii) *Wohl* unaccented makes a **tentative** statement and frequently translates the English 'I should think', 'I suppose', etc.:

Es ist wohl zehn Tage seitdem ich Sie gesehen habe.
It must be ten days, I should think, since I saw you.

Er kommt wohl heute noch.　　I think he will come to-day.

Das mag wohl sein.　　　　　That may well be.

It is similarly used in questions:

Sind Sie wohl fremd hier?　I suppose you must be a stranger here?

§ 203. Zwar (= *zu Wahr*, 'in truth') has no English equivalent:

(i) It generally defines something which has preceded:

Er hat drei Kinder und zwar zwei Töchter und einen Sohn.
He has three children, two daughters and one son.

Er ist ein Verrückter und zwar ein gefährlicher.
He is a madman and a dangerous one too.

(ii) *Zwar* is also used in concessive clauses:

Sie ist zwar sehr nett, aber hübsch ist sie doch nicht.
She is certainly very nice, but she isn't pretty.

Zwar sind wir arm, aber wir sind doch nicht unglücklich.
It is true we are poor, but we are not unhappy.

§ 204. Note the following differences:

Erst vor einem Jahre wollte ich Deutschland besuchen.
Not till a year ago did I wish to visit Germany.

Noch vor einem Jahre wollte ich Deutschland besuchen.
Up till a year ago I wished to visit Germany.

Schon vor einem Jahre wollte ich Deutschland besuchen.
For the last year or more I have wished to visit Germany.

XVII. DETACHED REMARKS

§ 205. The real subject may be postponed in German and its place taken by **es**; this often corresponds to the English use of 'there':

Es lebte einmal ein König.   There was once a king.

Es blühen keine Rosen in meinem Garten.
There are no roses flowering in my garden.

Es kamen zwei Ritter hergezogen.
Two knights were riding along.

Es speist niemand bei uns heute. No one is dining with us to-day.

This use of *es*, which is very common in Poetry, is also permissible in Prose, especially in short sentences and at the beginning of narratives.

Note that when the verb is inverted or the real subject stands first the **es** drops out (except in the case of *es gibt*, § 206):

Einmal lebte ein König.
Zwei Ritter kamen dahergezogen, etc.

§ 206. Distinguish between **es ist** and **es gibt**; *es gibt* means 'there is' in the sense of 'there exists' (no narrow limits being expressed); *sein* should be used when definite circumscribed limits are given:

Es gibt noch Löwen in Afrika. There still are (exist) lions in Africa.

Es gibt Menschen, die daran glauben.
There are people who believe in that.

Es gibt überhaupt nichts Schöneres als gute Musik.
There is nothing more beautiful than good music.

Es gibt keine Autos im Dorfe. There aren't any cars in the village.

But:

Es sind viele Autos auf dem Marktplatz.
There are plenty of cars in the market place.

Es ist Tinte im Tintenfaß.   There is some ink in the inkpot.

Es ist kein Feuer im Zimmer.   There is no fire in the room.

N.B. Sein always agrees with the **real object,** and its grammatical subject *es* is omitted in Dependent Sentences:

Es **waren** 20 **Leute** im Zimmer.   There were 20 people in the room.
   (*Waren* agrees with the real subject *Leute*.)
Er sagte, daß 20 Leute im Zimmer seien.
   (*Es* omitted in dependent sentence.)

Es gibt is used in the singular only and is followed by the Accusative; *es* is never omitted:

Er sagte, daß **es** hier keinen Menschen gebe, der Englisch spricht.
He said there was no one here who speaks English.
Hat **es** jemals etwas Schöneres gegeben?
Was there ever anything more beautiful?

§ 207. Except when the verbs 'to be', 'to have', 'to hear', 'to see', 'to make' are used in a strictly literal sense, we should avoid translating them by the German 'Mutterwörter' *sein, haben, hören, sehen* and *machen*; we may easily find more descriptive substitutes.

   For **sein** we may use *sitzen, stehen, wohnen, sich befinden,* etc.:

Es sitzt ein Vogel auf dem Dach.   There is a bird on the roof.
Wer steht dort an der Ecke?   Who is at the corner there?
Jetzt wohnt er in London.   He is in London now.
Er befindet sich auf einer Reise.   He is on a journey.

   For **haben** we may use *tragen, besitzen,* etc.:

Wieviel Geld tragen Sie bei sich?   How much money have you on you?
Er besitzt ein schönes Gut.   He has a lovely estate.

   For **hören** we may use *vernehmen, erfahren,* etc.:

Ich vernehme, daß er tot ist.   I hear that he is dead.
Wo haben Sie das erfahren?   Where did you hear that?

   For **sehen** we may use *bemerken, verstehen, begreifen,* etc.:

Hast du es bemerkt?   Did you see it?
Verstehen Sie, was ich meine?   Do you see what I mean?
Können Sie das nicht begreifen?   Can't you see that?

   (*Begreifen* is stronger than *verstehen*.)

For **machen** we may use *verfertigen, bereiten*, etc.:

Dort werden Stühle und Tische verfertigt.
Chairs and tables are made there.
Sie bereitete mir ein gutes Essen.
She made me a good dinner.

§ 208. In elevated style the Auxiliary is sometimes omitted from Dependent Clauses. This omission should not be imitated by beginners except to avoid the clashing of two similar words and even then only if the sentence cannot be otherwise turned. We might for example write: *Was es gekostet, hat er mir nicht gesagt* (omitting *hat*); but better would be: *Er hat mir nicht gesagt, was es gekostet hat.*

§ 209. One Auxiliary may serve two or more verbs; in a principal sentence it stands before the first, in a dependent clause after the last verb:

Ich habe ihn zwar gesehen aber nicht gehört.
I have certainly seen him but I have not heard him.
Die Bremen, von der Sie gewiß gehört und die Sie vielleicht auch gesehen haben, ist heute nach Neu-York abgefahren.
The Bremen, of which you have certainly heard and which you perhaps have even seen, sailed to-day for New York.

§ 210. Hin and **her**: these two adverbs are used with verbs of motion; *hin* describes motion away from the speaker or spectator, *her* movement towards him (*hin, her*). The following short passage may help to make this clear:

Fritz wollte hinein (motion away) und klopfte an die Tür. 'Herein!' (motion towards speaker) rief ich, worauf er eintrat. 'Darf ich zu Ihrer Mutter hinaufgehen (motion away)?' bat er. 'Selbstverständlich', antwortete ich, 'und wenn Sie herunterkommen (motion towards speaker), bringen Sie ja die Zeitung mit', etc.

Fred wished to come in and knocked at the door. 'Come in!', I cried, whereupon he entered. 'May I go up to your Mother?' he requested. 'Naturally', I answered, 'and when you come down, mind you bring the paper with you', etc.

N.B. **Wo, da, dort, hier,** when they imply motion, must have one of these suffixes:

Wohin gehen Sie?	Where are you going?
Woher kommt er?	Where does he come from?
Er geht dorthin (or, dahin).	He is going there.
Kommen Sie hierher!	Come here!

§ 211. Distinguish between *einsteigen* and *herein-* or *hinein-steigen*; between *ausgehen* and *hinausgehen*, etc. In conjunction with one of these words, verbs of motion imply movement in a **definite direction**; without their addition the motion has no definite direction.

Ausgehen = 'to go out' (for a walk, etc.):

Sind Sie heute ausgegangen?   Have you been out to-day?

Hinausgehen = 'to go out' (away from the spectator):

Er ging hinaus, um mit dem Gärtner zu sprechen.
He went out to speak to the gardener.

Similarly:

Er stieg in den Wagen ein.   He entered the carriage.

But:

Steigen Sie schnell in meinen Wagen herein.
Get into my carriage quickly.

§ 212. Hin and **her** are frequently used figuratively, especially with verbs of seeing and in expressions of time:

Er sah zum Fenster herein (or, hinein).
He looked in at the window.

(*Herein* if the spectator is inside, *hinein* if the spectator is outside.)

Das ganze Jahr hindurch.   Throughout the whole year, etc.

§ 213. In **herum** and **umher** there is no motion towards the speaker: *herum*, 'round about' (in a circle); *umher*, 'this way and that', 'up and down', 'about':

Zuerst ging ich um das Rathaus herum.
First I went round the Town Hall.

Dann ging ich im Rathaus umher.
Then I walked about inside the Town Hall.

§ 214. Da may be used of time and circumstance as well as of place. In the latter meaning it is equivalent to *dort* and means 'then', 'in that place', etc.; in the former it may be rendered by 'then', 'thereupon', 'so', etc.:

Da sagte er.   Then he said.

Da lachte ihn jeder aus.   Thereupon everyone laughed at him.

Da nahm ich Hut und Mantel und verließ das Haus.

So I took my hat and coat and left the house.

Distinguish *da* in the above sense from *da* meaning 'since', 'as' (§ 83).

§ 215. Some abstract nouns which are used in the plural in English have no direct plural in German and have to borrow forms, e.g. *der Tod,* 'the death'; *die Todesfälle,* 'the deaths'. Frequently, however, the singular form will serve equally well. 'My acknowledgments' for example = *meine Anerkennung* (not *meine Anerkennungen*). So also we may use *der Unterricht* for 'lessons', *das Almosen* for 'alms', *die Entschädigung* for 'damages', *das Gefolge* for 'attendants', etc. On the other hand there are some words which are used in the plural in German when the singular is used in English. Two examples are:

Die Fortschritte, 'progress':

Er hat gute Fortschritte gemacht. He has made good progress.

Die Kenntnisse, 'knowledge' (in the sense of wide knowledge):

Er ist ein Mann von vielen Kenntnissen. He is a man of much learning.

§ 216. Some nouns have two plurals with different meanings. A list of such words may be found in most Grammars; note particularly the difference in meaning between *Worte* and *Wörter*:

Wörter = 'single words' (French *les mots*):

Das Wörterbuch.   The dictionary.

Der Satz bestand aus 10 Wörtern. The sentence consisted of 10 words.

Worte = 'words in a sentence' (French *les paroles*):

Er sprach einige Worte.   He spoke a few words.

Auf seine Worte lege ich viel Wert.

I value his words very much.

§ 217. If experience did not prove the contrary it would have seemed unnecessary to caution any except beginners against inventing tenses in German to correspond to such English forms as 'I am working', 'I do work', etc. The following compound tenses in English have no direct parallel in German and must be rendered by the Present, Imperfect, Future, Perfect and Pluperfect:

I am working, I do work	= ich arbeite
I was working, I did work	= ich arbeitete
I shall be working	= ich werde arbeiten
I have been working	= ich habe gearbeitet
I had been working	= ich hatte gearbeitet

§ 218. The difference between the Perfect and the Imperfect in German is often not properly understood.

The Imperfect (i) is the tense of **narrative** (French *passé historique*):

Napoleon starb auf St Helena. Napoleon died on St Helena.

Ich ging spazieren, da traf ich einen Freund, der mich zum Tee einlud, so begleitete ich ihn, etc.

I went for a walk, and met a friend who invited me to tea, so I accompanied him, etc.

(ii) expresses **duration of time** or **simultaneous action**:

Ich saß zwei Stunden im Garten.
I sat for two hours in the garden.

Als er hereintrat, schrieb ich einen Brief.
I was writing a letter when he entered.

The Perfect (i) is the tense used in **ordinary conversation** (as in French):

Gestern ist ein Kind ins Wasser gefallen und ertrunken.
A child fell into the water yesterday and was drowned.

Ich habe ihn heute gesehen.   I saw him to-day.
Ich habe Sie Donnerstag erwartet.   I expected you on Thursday.

(ii) refers also to past events which still have results in the present:

Marconi hat die drahtlose Telegraphie erfunden.
Marconi invented Wireless Telegraphy.
   (Perfect tense because the invention remains.)

Goethe hat den *Faust* geschrieben.
Goethe wrote *Faust* (we can still read *Faust*).

Goethe schrieb den Faust means that Goethe (and no one else) wrote *Faust*.

§ 219. German punctuation is the same as English except in the following particulars:

(i) A comma is used at the beginning and end of all dependent sentences:

Das Kind, dem ich das Buch gegeben habe, ist jung.
Er sagte mir, daß er reich sei.

(ii) A colon is used after a verb introducing direct speech:

Er sagte: 'Wie alt bist du?'

(iii) The first pair of inverted commas is written below, not above, the line.

INDEX TO SYNTAX

PASSAGES FOR TRANSLATION

SECTION I

MODEL LESSON I

(1) After one of Peter the Great's wars, some officers were relating their brave deeds, when the imperial jester interrupted them, crying, 'I too have a story to tell and a better one than any of yours'. (2) 'Let us hear it then', said the officers, and the fool began: 'I never liked to fight in a crowd, and therefore always went out to fight alone. (3) One day, going close to the enemy's lines, I suddenly discovered a Swedish soldier lying on the ground just before me. (4) There was not a moment to lose. I drew my sword, and at one blow cut off his right foot'. (5) 'You fool!' exclaimed one of the officers, 'you should rather have cut off his head.' (6) 'So I would', answered the jester laughing, 'but somebody else had done that already.'

(1) 'After one of Peter the Great's wars, some officers were relating their brave deeds, when the imperial jester interrupted them, crying, "I too have a story to tell and a better one than any of yours".'

'After one of Peter the Great's wars.' There are three words in German for 'after', according as it is an adverb, a conjunction or a preposition (see § 87); here it is a preposition: use therefore *nach* (followed always by the dative): *nach einem*. *Peter der Große* is declined according to the ordinary rule of adjectives (§ 22) and its genitive is therefore *Peters des Großen*; 'wars' too is in the genitive, and in order to show this in German we should place it before, not after, *Peters des Großen* and write: *nach einem der Kriege Peters des Großen*. It would also be possible to use *von* here: *nach einem von den Kriegen*, but *von* should be avoided if possible, and its use cannot be justified here, since the case of *Kriege* is clearly shown by the definite article (see § 174).

'some officers were relating their brave deeds.' Since the expression 'nach einem der Kriege Peters des Großen' has been placed before the subject, the verb inverts; we must therefore say: 'were relating some officers their brave deeds'. In English 'some' may be used partitively both in the singular and the plural, e.g. 'some bread', 'some people'; in German there is no word to serve this double purpose, in the singular *etwas* is used, in the plural *einige*: *etwas Brot, einige Leute*. So here we shall say 'einige Offiziere'.

'were relating their brave deeds.' *Erzählen*, in the sense of 'to tell **of**' or '**about**', may be followed either by **von** or **über**. It may also, as here, govern a direct accusative, e.g. *er erzählte die Geschichte*, 'he related the story'. 'their brave deeds': 'brave' is *tapfer*; *kühn*, which might be used as an alternative, means rather 'bold': *Karl der Kühne* = 'Charles the Bold'. The word for 'the deed' is *die Tat*, derived from *tun*, 'to do' (past tense *ich tat*), and so: 'erzählten einige Offiziere ihre tapferen Taten'.

'when the imperial jester interrupted them, crying.' This is a dependent clause, so the verb 'interrupted' will come at the end. *Als*, *wenn* and *wann* are all used to translate 'when'; the differences between their meanings have been discussed earlier (see § 81). Here we require *als*, which is used of **definite past** time only. 'the imperial jester': 'imperial' = *kaiserlich* (formed from *der Kaiser*, 'the emperor'); 'the jester' = *der Hofnarr* (*der Hof*, 'the court'; *der Narr*, 'the fool'); so: 'der kaiserliche Hofnarr'. The word for 'to interrupt' is *unterbrechen*, which requires the accusative, and, since it is used in a figurative sense, is inseparable (§ 115), so we have: 'als der kaiserliche Hofnarr sie unterbrach'. We have still to translate 'crying'. In a grammatical note (§ 186) the learner has been cautioned against imitating the English use of the present participle in German; we cannot in fact write *ausrufend*. The present participle, here as frequently, is to be avoided by the use of a finite verb or of a preposition and noun; we can either say 'and cried', *und rief aus*, or 'with the cry', *mit dem Ausruf*. The phrase is preferable to the finite verb and so we shall have: 'als der kaiserliche Hofnarr sie mit dem Ausruf unterbrach'.

'I too have a story to tell and a better one than any of yours.' If this anecdote were spoken, not written, the infinitive 'to tell' might occupy the same position in German as in English; in writing, however, we should observe the formal rule and postpone it to the end. 'I too': in German *auch* should in strict grammar be placed before not after the word it qualifies, so we shall write: 'Auch ich'. The idiom for 'to have to' is the same in German as in English: 'I have a lot to do' = *ich habe viel zu tun*. It will be noticed that the infinitive with *zu* is required; *zu*, as has been emphasised, may only be dropped after verbs of mood and a few others (see § 187). 'to tell' may frequently be rendered by *sagen*, e.g. 'can you **tell** me the time' = *können Sie mir* **sagen**, *wieviel Uhr es ist*; but when 'tell' = 'to tell about', i.e. 'to relate', we must use *erzählen*; so: 'Auch ich habe eine Geschichte...zu erzählen'. 'and a better one than any of yours': comparatives decline in German exactly like any other adjective: 'a better book' = *ein besseres Buch*. Here we are referring to the feminine noun *die Geschichte*, so 'a better one' will be *eine bessere*, the English 'one' being rendered by the case termination in German (see § 65). 'than any of yours': 'any' in the indefinite sense is rendered by *irgend*: *irgend etwas* = 'anything', *irgend ein Buch* = 'any book', etc. *Irgend* cannot be used alone, and here therefore we must say *irgend eine* (*eine* being in agreement with **die** *Geschichte*). 'of yours': we must distinguish between possessive **adjectives** (my, your, his house, etc.) and possessive **pronouns** (whose house? mine, yours, his, etc.). Here we require the pronoun; three forms are possible in German, all of which conform to the ordinary rule for the adjective: 'my house and yours' = *mein Haus und* **das** *Ihrige*, **das** *Ihre* or *Ihres*. If we were using the polite form of address here we might write then *der Ihrigen* (genitive plural). But in the seventeenth century the normal mode of address was *Ihr*, not *Sie* (which did not come into use until the middle of the nineteenth century), and we should use therefore the pronoun formed from *Ihr—Eurig*; so: 'der Eurigen'.

The rendering for section (1) is: 'Nach einem der Kriege Peters des Großen erzählten einige Offiziere ihre tapferen Taten, als der kaiserliche Hofnarr sie mit dem Ausruf unterbrach: "Auch ich habe eine Geschichte und eine bessere als irgend eine der Eurigen zu erzählen"'.

(2) '"Let us hear it then", said the officers, and the fool began: "I never liked to fight in a crowd, and therefore always went out to fight alone."'

'Let us hear it then.' The various different forms which may be used for the imperative in German have been commented on (see § 103); here we may conveniently use that form which corresponds closest to the English and write: *laß uns...hören*. Note that a person in authority would use *du* to his inferiors, and that we therefore write *laß* and not *lassen Sie* or *laßt*; *lassen* is followed by the same construction as verbs of mood and hence *hören* is not preceded by *zu*. 'it' refers to *die Geschichte*, and is therefore rendered by *sie* not *es*. For 'then' we might use the inferential particle *denn* (see § 193 (ii)) and write: *laß uns sie denn hören*. This would sound better German if we placed the emphatic adverb *so*, which expresses curiosity, impatience, etc., at the head of the sentence: 'So laß uns sie denn hören'.

'said the officers, and the fool began.' Since the direct speech 'so laß uns sie denn hören' stands before the subject the verb inverts (as in English), so: 'sagten die Offiziere'. *Beginnen* and *anfangen* are synonyms; if we use the latter we must recollect that the prefix is separable and write: *und der Hofnarr fing* an (for the position of separable prefixes see § 78).

'I never liked to fight in a crowd.' The German for 'never' is either *nie* or *niemals*; for 'to fight' we shall find *kämpfen* and *fechten* in the Vocabulary; *fechten* means to fight with a sword (in a duel, for example); use here the more general word *kämpfen*. 'the crowd' = *die Menge*, and 'in a crowd' = *in einer Menge*. 'to like' is often translated by *gefallen*: 'how do you like this house?' = *wie gefällt Ihnen dieses Haus?* (literally 'how does this house please you?'). But 'to like' followed by another verb is more idiomatically rendered by the use of *gern*: 'I like reading' = *ich lese gern*; so here, 'I like fighting' = *ich kämpfe gern*. All that now remains is to place the words in the right order; we must remember first that *nie*, being an adverb, cannot separate the subject from the verb. We may write either *nie kämpfte ich* or *ich kämpfte nie*. *Gern*, since it is a predicate of the verb, would ordinarily be placed at the end of the sentence, but in this case *in einer Menge* is so much more important that we should do well to place it at the end. The sentence then runs: 'Ich kämpfte nie gern in einer Menge'.

'and therefore always went out to fight alone.' In German, adverbs either stand at the head of the sentence or must follow the verb; as the conjunction 'therefore' opens the sentence we must place 'always' after the verb and say: 'and therefore went I always out'; since the word-order is inverted the subject 'I' must be expressed. The verb for 'to go out' is separable in

German as in English; the prefix will stand here at the end of the sentence. The German word-order is then: 'and therefore went I always alone out'; the position of 'to fight' will depend on whether we use a verb or a noun in translating. 'therefore' = *daher* or *darum*, 'to go out' = *ausgehen*, 'always' = *immer* and 'alone' = *allein*; the only difficulty is the translation of 'to go out **to fight**'. *Gehen* by itself is used with an infinitive without *zu*, e.g. *spazieren gehen*, 'to go for a walk', but as *gehen* is compounded here we cannot use this construction. We might write: *er ging aus* **um zu** *kämpfen*, 'he went out **in order to** fight', but this is somewhat clumsy and we should do better to use instead of a verb a noun and a preposition: 'he went out into the fight' = *er ging in den Kampf aus*. This is correct German, but we could improve on it by using *ausziehen* for *ausgehen*; the latter is the general word, the former has a military nuance, e.g. *Georg zog gegen den Drachen aus* = 'George went out to fight the dragon'; *das Heer zog in den Krieg aus* = 'the army marched out to battle'.

The suggested rendering of section (2) is: '"So laß uns sie denn hören", sagten die Offiziere, und der Narr fing an: "Ich kämpfte nie gern in einer Menge, und daher zog ich immer allein in den Kampf aus"'.

(3) 'One day, going close to the enemy's lines, I suddenly discovered a Swedish soldier lying on the ground just before me.'

'One day, going close to the enemy's lines.' We can avoid the present participle here by a dependent clause: 'when I one day close to the enemy's lines went'. 'When' of past time we know is *als*; since 'one day' is **indefinite** time we must use the genitive (see § 171); so: 'als ich eines Tages'. A literal rendering of 'the enemy's lines' would be *die Linien des Feindes*; but we should simplify this phrase by using the adjective formed from *der Feind, feindlich*: *die feindlichen Linien*. 'close' = *nahe*, and 'to go close to' = *nahe an* (+ Acc.) *kommen*; we might therefore write: *als er nahe an die feindlichen Linien kam*. Simpler, however, would be the use of the verb formed from *nahe, sich nähern* (+ Dat.) = 'to approach'. The reflexive pronoun, following the rule that pronouns stand as early in the sentence as possible, will come directly after the subject: 'Als ich mich eines Tages den feindlichen Linien näherte'.

'I suddenly discovered a Swedish soldier lying on the ground just before me.' Since the dependent clause 'when I went close to the enemy's lines' stands before the subject the verb inverts, and as only one word or phrase may precede the subject 'suddenly' must be placed after the verb: 'discovered I suddenly'. The word-order of the rest of the sentence depends on the translation of 'lying'. We have noted that the present participle is to be avoided; here we might use either a relative sentence, 'who on the ground just before me lay', or an infinitive, 'discovered I suddenly a Swedish soldier on the ground just before me **to lie**'. We should prefer the latter rendering on the grounds of simplicity. 'suddenly' = *plötzlich*, 'to discover' = *entdecken* (*decken* = 'to cover', *ent* gives the idea of 'out of'), 'to lie' = *liegen*; so using the same construction after *entdecken* as we would after *finden* (i.e. a direct infinitive; see § 187) we shall have: 'entdeckte ich plötzlich...liegen'. 'a Swedish soldier lying on the ground just before me.' 'a Swedish soldier': Sweden is in German *Schweden* and the adjective formed from this is *schwedisch* (spelt with a small letter); 'the soldier' is *der Soldat* (declined weak); so here: 'einen schwedischen Soldaten'. For 'ground' we might use either *die Erde* or *der Boden*; since there is no question of motion, *auf* will be followed by the dative and we shall say either *auf dem Boden* or *auf der Erde*. 'just before me': the remarks made above about 'after' apply to 'before'; here it is not the conjunction *bevor* or the adverb *vorher* but the preposition *vor* that is required; 'just' may be rendered by *gerade*, 'exactly', and the phrase will therefore be: 'gerade vor mir'.

The rendering for the whole of section (3) is: 'Als ich mich eines Tages den feindlichen Linien näherte, entdeckte ich plötzlich einen schwedischen Soldaten gerade vor mir auf dem Boden liegen'.

(4) 'There was not a moment to lose. I drew my sword, and at one blow cut off his right foot.'

'not a' in German = 'none', *kein*: 'I have **not a** single penny' = *ich habe* **keinen** *einzigen Pfennig*. 'The moment' = *der Augenblick*, 'to lose' = *verlieren*; we have therefore so far: *kein Augenblick zu verlieren*. The nominative case will be correct only if we use *sein* in translating 'there was': *es war kein*

Augenblick zu verlieren'. If *geben* were used we should write: *es gab keinen Augenblick zu verlieren.* The differences in meaning between *geben* and *sein* need not concern us now, since we shall do well here to avoid both and to use the more idiomatic *gelten*: 'Es galt keinen Augenblick zu verlieren', '**It was important** not to lose a moment.' (In this latter sentence *keinen Augenblick* is governed by *verlieren*, in the previous one it was governed by *geben*.)

'I drew my sword, and at one blow cut off his right foot.' 'to draw the sword' = *das Schwert ziehen*, so write: *ich zog mein Schwert.* 'and at one blow cut off his right foot': 'at one blow' is in German '**with** one blow', **mit** *einem Schlag*; for 'to cut off' we should use *abhauen* rather than *abschneiden*; *schneiden* gives the idea of cutting a thing off neatly, *hauen* means 'to hew' or 'to hack'. If we render 'his right foot' literally by *sein rechter Fuß*, we might write: *und mit einem Schlag hieb er seinen rechten Fuß ab*; this is correct, but two improvements might be made: in the first place the rather clumsy inversion and the consequent repetition of the subject would be avoided by placing *mit einem Schlag* after instead of before the verb: *und hieb mit einem Schlag.* In the second place the Germans, like the French, avoid, in prose at least, the use of the possessive pronoun: 'I shook his hand' = 'I shook to him the hand', *ich schüttelte ihm die Hand.* So here we should write: 'und hieb **ihm** mit einem Schlag **den** rechten Fuß ab'.

The German for section (4) runs: 'Es galt keinen Augenblick zu verlieren. Ich zog mein Schwert und hieb ihm mit einem Schlag den rechten Fuß ab'.

(5) '"You fool!" exclaimed one of the officers, "you should rather have cut off his head."'

'"You fool!" exclaimed one of the officers.' 'You fool!' may be rendered literally, 'du Narr!' When *ein* stands alone it is declined according to the ordinary rule of the adjective (i.e. strong if nothing precedes); since we are referring here to **der** *Offizier*, we will write: *einer der Offiziere.* 'to exclaim' = *ausrufen*, so we have: 'rief einer der Offiziere aus'.

'you should rather have cut off his head.' 'rather' here is not the adverb *ziemlich*, but *lieber*, the comparative of *gern*: 'he is rather ill' = *er befindet sich ziemlich unwohl*; but 'I would rather come to-morrow' = *lieber möchte ich morgen kommen.* For 'his head' we should, as in the previous sentence, avoid the possessive adjective and write: **ihm den** *Kopf.* Where English says 'you should have...cut off', putting the **infinitive** in the past tense the German says 'you should have *oughted* to cut off', more logically putting the **Verb of Mood** into past time (see § 135). 'to ought' = *sollen,* 'you should have *oughted'* = *du hättest...gesollt;* but the past participle of modal verbs when it follows an infinitive is itself attracted into the infinitive form, so we write here: 'du hättest...abhauen sollen'.

The translation for section (5) is then: '"Du Narr!" rief einer der Offiziere aus, "du hättest ihm lieber den Kopf abhauen sollen"'.

(6) '"So I would", answered the jester, laughing, "but somebody else had done that already."'

'So I would.' In German the verb may not be omitted from a sentence for the sake of brevity, as it is in English; so here we must say: 'So I would **have done**'. In this and similar expressions 'so' is to be rendered by *es* or *das,* not by *so,* e.g. 'I said so' = *ich sagte* **es,** 'I thought so' = *ich dachte es,* etc. The past conditional of 'to do' is *ich würde getan haben,* or, to use its more common form, *ich hätte getan* (see § 104); so we may write: *ich hätte es getan.* This, though grammatically correct, is not sufficiently emphatic; we should use *das* for *es* and place it at the head of the sentence: *Das hätte ich getan.* We may further improve the sentence by inserting one of those particles so frequently used in German to 'fill out' sentences (see § 193 *sq.*); here either *schon* or *auch* is possible: 'Das hätte ich auch getan'.

'answered the jester, laughing.' It has been emphasised that the present participle is employed less frequently in German than in English; it may, however, be used adverbially or as a predicative adjective, e.g. *sie stürzte* **schluchzend** *aus dem Zimmer,* 'she rushed sobbing out of the room'; *die Katze saß* **schnurrend** *auf seinem Schoße,* 'the cat sat purring in his lap'; so here using *antworten* for 'to answer' (*erwidern* is an alternative word) we may say: 'antwortete der Hofnarr, lachend'.

'but somebody else had done that already.' If we use *aber* the word-order will be as in a principal clause, if, however, we

prefer *doch* 'yet', on the grounds that it makes a stronger contradiction, the verb should be inverted (though *doch* may also
be followed by the normal word-order; see § 70): 'somebody
else' = *jemand anders* (*anders* is the adverb from *ander*, 'other'),
so we might write: *doch hatte das schon jemand anders getan*.
Schon might also be placed after *jemand anders*; for *getan*, which
we have already used once, we can substitute the more general
word *besorgen*, 'to see to', 'to settle', e.g. *Wollen Sie, bitte, die
Billets kaufen? Jawohl, ich werde es besorgen*, 'Will you buy the
tickets? Yes, I'll do it'.

Section (6) runs: '"Das hätte ich auch getan", antwortete
der Hofnarr, lachend, "doch hatte das schon jemand anders
besorgt"'.

The suggested rendering for the whole is:

Nach einem der Kriege Peters des Großen erzählten einige
Offiziere ihre tapferen Taten, als der kaiserliche Hofnarr sie mit
dem Ausruf unterbrach: 'Auch ich habe eine Geschichte und
eine bessere als irgend eine der Eurigen zu erzählen'. 'So laß
uns sie denn hören', sagten die Offiziere, und der Narr fing an:
'Ich kämpfte nie gern in einer Menge, und daher zog ich immer
allein in den Kampf aus. Als ich mich eines Tages den feindlichen Linien näherte, entdeckte ich plötzlich einen schwedischen
Soldaten gerade vor mir auf dem Boden liegen. Es galt keinen
Augenblick zu verlieren. Ich zog mein Schwert und hieb ihm
mit einem Schlag den rechten Fuß ab'. 'Du Narr!' rief einer
der Offiziere aus, 'du hättest ihm lieber den Kopf abhauen
sollen.' 'Das hätte ich auch getan', antwortete der Hofnarr,
lachend, 'doch hatte das schon jemand anders besorgt.'

In the notes attached to the following passages for translation
references have been made to the grammatical sections. In order
to avoid their use becoming merely a matter of habit, it would
perhaps be better to attempt a translation before looking at
the notes. For the same reason passages have been inserted at
intervals without any notes.

Few notes have been given on the ordinary rules for word-
order and those who find difficulty with word-order should refer
to chapters VIII and IX.

1. THE FLY AND THE OX

The ox was returning home one evening[1] tired out by his day's work[2], and when he turned into[3] the yard he met the horse, who had been standing the whole[1] day in the stable and[4] was now going to[5] the paddock for his evening's walk[2]. When he[6] saw the ox, who was so tired that he could hardly stand, he asked: 'Where have you been all this time[7]?' Then the thin small voice of a fly, which was sitting on one of the ox's horns, was heard[8]: 'We have been ploughing[9]'.

[1] Genitive or Accusative? § 171.   [2] 'day's work', 'evening walk', *die Tagesarbeit, der Abendspaziergang*; see p. 2.   [3] This implies motion; case? § 157.   [4] The Relative is understood after *und*; word-order? § 72.   [5] Use *auf* (+Acc. or Dat.?).   [6] Refers to das *Pferd*, therefore *es*; see § 61 (i).   [7] 'all this time', *so lange*.   [8] Avoid the Passive by using *ertönen* w. 'to resound'.   [9] Tense? § 217.

2. THE PEASANT'S MISTAKE

One day an old peasant brought a basket of[1] fine apples to[2] the castle of a certain count. On the[3] staircase he met two monkeys, dressed[4] like children, who flung themselves on his[3] basket and emptied it[5]. The peasant respectfully[6] took off his hat. When he came before the[3] count, the latter asked him, 'Why do you bring me[7] an empty basket?' 'My lord[8],' the peasant replied, 'it is not my fault. My basket was quite full, but your two sons have emptied it[5].'

[1] Use the Genitive, not *von*.   [2] Use *in*, 'into'; see § 167 (ii).   [3] Accusative or Dative? § 158.   [4] Translate 'two like (*als*) children dressed monkeys'; termination of the Adjective? § 22, III.   [5] Refers to der *Korb*; see § 61 (i).   [6] Position of Adverbs? § 75 (i).   [7] Case? § 175.   [8] *Herr Graf*.

3. TOO LATE

A father had strictly forbidden his children to[1] speak at meals[2]. Young[3] Jack, however, cried[4] out one day at table: 'Papa, I must tell[1] you[5] something important[6]'. The parents gave[7] the boy such a stern look that he did not dare to[1] speak. After a while the father, who was curious, said: 'Well[8], what did you wish to say to[9] me?' Jack answered, 'It is too late now. I wanted[10] to tell you that you had a large snail in your salad; but[11] you have already eaten it'.

900 Anekdoten

[1] Infinitive with or without *zu*? § 187.   [2] 'at meals', *beim Essen.*
[3] Say 'the young Jack'; when Proper Names are preceded by an Adjective the Definite Article must be inserted, e.g. das *schöne England*, etc.   [4] 'to cry out', *aus-rufen* st.; Position of Separable Prefix? § 78.   [5] *Du* or *Sie*? § 5.   [6] 'something important', *etwas Wichtiges*; see § 28.   [7] 'to give a look', *einen Blick zu-werfen* (+ Dat.).   [8] *also.*   [9] *zu*? § 177.
[10] Use *wollen*, 'to wish'.   [11] Word-order after *aber*? § 70.

4. THE STUDENT FROM[1] PARADISE. i

A poor student, who was walking through a village, came to the house of a rich farmer. The farmer was not[2] at home, but his wife, who was standing at the door, saw the student and asked[3] where[4] he came from. 'I am a poor student', answered the youth, 'and I come from[1] Paris.' The woman, who was very simple-minded, thought that he had[5] said Paradise, and since she wished[6] to have news of her dead brother she asked[3] him to come in[7]. 'If you come from Paradise', she said, 'I wonder[8] if you know my brother Jack; while he lived he was[9] always a pious man.'

Old Fable

[1] *aus*, 'out of'.   [2] Since 'not' qualifies 'at home', *nicht* should precede *zu Hause*; see § 76.   [3] *fragen* or *bitten*? § 138.   [4] 'where...from', *woher*; since the original words were 'where do you come from?' the **Present** Subjunctive must be used, see § 180.   [5] Since he had not said it, the Subjunctive must be used; see § 181.   [6] Position of Verb of Mood? § 123.   [7] *ein* is not sufficient; should we use *herein* or *hinein*? § 210.
[8] Say 'you will probably (*wohl*) know (*kennen* or *wissen*? § 142) my brother'.   [9] Since this is a conversation we should use the Perfect Tense; see § 218.

5. THE STUDENT FROM PARADISE. ii

The student, who at once saw[1] with whom[2] he had to deal, asked for[3] the name of her brother. 'He was called[4] Jack Greentree and he had red hair and squinted a little', answered

HG   8 the farmer's wife. 'Then I know him well', cried the youth, 'poor fellow, he has fallen[5] upon evil times and has neither clothes nor the money to buy[6] food.' When the good woman heard this she wept bitterly. 'Oh, my poor Jack!' she sobbed, 'if only I had[7] a messenger, how gladly would I send both money and clothes.'

Old Fable

[1] Use *bemerken* w. 'to notice'; *sehen* should be used only in the literal sense; see § 207.　　　[2] *mit wem er es zu tun hatte*; for *wer* see § 17.　　　[3] Make sure of using the correct Preposition.　　　[4] 'to be called', *heißen* st.; 'I am called Smith' = *ich heiße Schmidt*.　　　[5] 'to fall upon evil times', *in schlimme Zeiten geraten* st.　　　[6] The Infinitive must stand at the end of its Clause.　　　[7] Mood of Verb? § 183 (ii).

6. THE STUDENT FROM PARADISE. iii

'As it chances[1]', said the student, 'I will be returning to Paradise myself[2] in a few days and if you give me the clothes and the money, I will carry them to[3] your brother.' So the woman fetched some shirts, a coat, a pair of[4] trousers and a few handkerchiefs and packed them up; then she fetched a bag of[5] money and gave it to[6] the student with the bundle. The latter thanked the woman and went his way[7]. When the farmer returned and heard what[8] his wife had done, he was very angry. 'You foolish woman', he shouted, 'you have been deceived[9] by a scoundrel', and he saddled his horse at once and hurried[10] after the student.

Old Fable

[1] Say 'by chance (*zufällig*) I will be returning'; for 'will be returning' see § 217.　　　[2] *selber*; see § 48.　　　[3] *zu* or *nach* with people? § 167 (i).　　　[4] Omit 'of', § 48.　　　[5] *voll*.　　　[6] Not *zu*; see § 175.　　　[7] 'to go one's way', *sich auf den Weg machen* w.　　　[8] Word-order after *was*? § 80 (iii).　　　[9] For the conjugation of the Passive see § 106.　　　[10] 'to hurry after', use *nach-eilen* w. (+ Dat.); Position of Separable Prefix? § 78.

7. THE STUDENT FROM PARADISE. iv

When the youth saw the farmer on his horse, he threw his bundle over[1] a hedge, took up a spade which was lying by the road and pretended[2] to be working. 'Have you seen a student with a bundle on his[3] back?' cried the farmer. 'Yes', came the reply, 'when he saw you he jumped over the hedge and ran into the forest.' 'Well, hold my horse until I catch him', said the farmer and hurried into the wood. The student, however, picked up his bundle, mounted the horse and rode off[4]. When the farmer on[5] his return found neither the horse nor the man he saw[6] that he too[7] had been tricked and went sadly home. When his wife asked him if[8] he had found the student he replied, 'Yes, I found[9] him, and I gave him my horse too in order that[10] he might[11] reach Paradise quicker'. *Old Fable*

[1] Is this motion? § 159.   [2] 'to pretend', *tun als ob*: 'he did as if he was working'.   [3] *sein* or *der*? § 8.   [4] *davon*.   [5] *bei*.   [6] Avoid using *sehen*, § 207.   [7] *auch er*, see p. 104.   [8] *ob* or *wenn*? § 88.   [9] Inversion? § 95.   [10] *um...zu* can only be used when the Subjects of the two Sentences are the same; see § 190.   [11] Say 'could reach'.

8. AN UNLUCKY MOUSE

During the German lesson last week, something funny[1] happened in the class. As[2] the master was standing at[3] the blackboard, an inquisitive mouse crept out[4] of its hole and wandered across[5] the classroom. The pupils forgot their work immediately and threw note-books, books and anything that[6] came to hand[7] at the unlucky animal. When the master, surprised[8] by the noise, turned round, the mouse was already lying dead on the ground. As[2] the pupils had aimed so well, he overlooked[9] their behaviour and the lesson proceeded to the satisfaction of all[10].

[1] 'something funny', *etwas Komisches*; see § 28.   [2] *da* or *als*? § 83.   [3] *an* or *bei*? § 164.   [4] *aus* (+ *hinaus* or *heraus*? § 210).   [5] Here *durch*.   [6] Translate 'everything which (*das* or *was*? § 19 (i))'.   [7] 'to come to hand', *in die Hände kommen* st.   [8] The Past Participle must stand at the end of its phrase: 'by the noise surprised'.   [9] Translate 'forgave them (Dat.) their behaviour (Acc.)'.   [10] 'to the satisfaction of all', *unter allgemeiner Zufriedenheit*.

9. THE MODEL STATE[1]

Under the elms on the south side of our garden lives[2] the small people[3] of the bees under the peaceful rule of the queen. These tiny[4], industrious, black and yellow[5] animals have their home[6] in four hives, each of which[7] forms a state in itself[8]. Woe[9] to

116 PASSAGES FOR TRANSLATION

him who disturbs them at[10] their work or even approaches too
near them. They put[11] the bravest to flight with their sharp
stings, for they wish to devote themselves quietly and undisturbed to their work, making[12] honey-combs out of the finest
wax and storing[12] up there the honey which[13] they collect with
such trouble and industry.

[1] *der Musterstaat.*   [2] *wohnen* w. should be preferred to *leben* w., where the
English 'live' = 'dwell'.   [3] 'people' in the sense of 'a nation' = *das
Volk.*   [4] Translate by using a Diminutive; see § 38 (i).   [5] 'black
and yellow' one word in German, 'blackyellow'.   [6] 'to have one's
home', *hausen* w. 'to house'.   [7] Say 'of which each'; for the
Genitive of the Relative see § 9.   [8] *für sich.*   [9] *Wehe dem, der ...*
[10] *bei*; see § 165 (ii).   [11] 'to put to flight', *in die Flucht jagen* w.
[12] Avoid the Present Participles by the use of Principal Sentences; see
§ 186 (i).   [13] Translate 'the with so much trouble and so great industry
collected honey'; see § 185.

10. A CAT

My aunt, who lives in the country, has a beautiful silver-grey
Persian cat which is the favourite of the whole house. In the
winter the animal has its particular chair near the fire, where
it sits for hours and sleeps. In summer pussy prefers to sit on
the desk in the full sun, purring with content and hardly leaving
me room to work. Now and again she creeps into the garden
to catch birds and mice, after which she sits down on the wall
in order to wash her paws.

11. THE COUNT OF[1] NEMOURS

King Louis XIV of France was explaining to[2] his guests at[3]
Versailles that the will of the king was[4] the highest law. Even
if the king said: 'Jump into the water!' one must[4] obey him
without dispute. At[5] these words the Count of Nemours got
up and walked towards[6] the exit. When the king asked him
where[7] he was going, he replied: 'Sire, I am going to[8] learn to
swim'.

900 *Anekdoten*

[1] *von?* § 174.   [2] Dative; no *zu* is required; see § 175.   [3] *zu.*
[4] Indirect Speech; Mood? § 178.   [5] Preposition? § 165 (ii).   [6] 'to
walk towards', *zu-schreiten* st. (+ Dat.).   [7] *wo* is not sufficient; see
§ 210, N.B.   [8] We may use an Infinitive without *zu* after *gehen* (e.g.
spazieren gehen); see § 187.

12. THE HUNGRY HAMBURGERS[1]

Two peasants came for the first time[2] to[3] Hamburg and entered
a restaurant at 7 o'clock in the morning[4] in order to have breakfast. After they had sat down[5], one[6] of them nudged the other
and pointed to a notice[7] which hung[8] on the wall. The other
read it. 'What?' he said in astonishment, 'breakfast from seven
till eleven, lunch from eleven till four, dinner from four till
nine!'—'Good heavens![9] when[10] shall we have time to see the
town?'

[1] *Hamburger*: formed by adding -*er* to the name of the town; cf. 'Berlin',
der Berliner; 'London', *der Londoner*; etc.   [2] *Mal* or *Zeit*? § 57.
[3] *nach* or *zu*? § 167 (i).   [4] 'in the morning' to be translated by one
word; see § 54.   [5] *sich setzen* w. not *sitzen*; see § 148 (ii).   [6] 'one of
them', say here 'the one'; termination of *ein*? § 30.   [7] Use *das
Schild* (the signboard).   [8] *hangen* or *hängen*? § 141.   [9] 'Good
heavens!' *Herrgott!*   [10] *wenn, wann* or *als*? § 81.

13. THE MILLER, HIS SON AND THEIR ASS. i

A miller and his son were driving their ass to a neighbouring
town to[1] sell him there. They had not[2] gone far, when they
met a troop of[3] girls who were returning from the town, talking
and laughing together. 'Look[4] there!' cried one[5] of them, 'have
you[4] ever seen such fools to[6] go on foot, when[7] they could[8]
ride?' The old man, when he heard this, bade his son get[9]
on the ass, and walked by his side[10]. Soon they came to a
group of old[11] men. 'There![12]' said one of them, 'it proves
what[13] I was saying. No one respects old age[14] in these days[15].
Do you see how[13] the young rascal is riding while his old father
must walk?' Thereupon the father bade his son dismount and
mounted himself.   *Old Fable*

[1] = 'in order to'; see § 190.   [2] Place of *nicht*? § 76.   [3] Omit *von*;
see § 48.   [4] Use *du* or *Ihr* throughout; 'look there', *schaut einmal hin*.
[5] Termination of *ein*? § 30.   [6] 'who go on foot (*zu Fuß*)'.   [7] *wenn*
or *als*? § 81.   [8] *könnten* or *konnten*? § 134.   [9] 'to get on', *sich
setzen* w. (*auf*).   [10] 'by his side', *neben ihm her*.   [11] Case? § 49.
[12] *Sieh da!*   [13] Word-order after 'what', 'how', etc.? § 80 (iii).   [14] 'old
age', *das hohe Alter*.   [15] 'in these days', *heutzutage*.

14. THE MILLER, HIS SON AND THEIR ASS. ii

They had not gone far in this way[1] when they met a crowd of
women and children. 'Well, you lazy old man![2]' cried several
voices at once[3], 'how can you ride on the animal while the poor
boy can hardly keep step[4] by[5] your side?' The good-natured
miller immediately took[6] up his son behind him[7] and soon they
reached the town. 'Tell me[8], my friend,' said a townsman,
'does that ass belong to[9] you?' 'Yes', replied the old man.
'Oh![10] I should not have thought[11] so[12]', said the other, 'by
the way[13] you treat him. You two are better able[14] to carry
the poor beast than he you!'

Old Fable

[1] *auf diese Weise*; for case after *auf* see § 162.   [2] *Na, du alter Faulpelz.*
[3] 'at once', *zugleich.*   [4] 'to keep step', *Schritt halten* st.   [5] *an.*
[6] 'to take up', use *setzen* w. 'to place'.   [7] This refers to the Subject of
the Sentence; should we use *sich* or *ihn*? § 113.   [8] *sage mir einmal.*
[9] *gehören* takes the Dative; no *zu* is required, § 175.   [10] Word-order
after Interjections? § 95.   [11] Use *glauben* w.; for the Past Conditional
see § 104.   [12] *das* not *so*; see p. 110 (6).   [13] Say 'according to the way
in which', *nach der Art wie.*   [14] Use the Imperfect Subjunctive, *Ihr
zwei...könntet.*

15. THE MILLER, HIS SON AND THEIR ASS. iii

'As[1] you wish', said the old man, 'we can[2] but try', and he
dismounted with his son. Then they tied the ass's legs together
and by means of a pole tried to carry him on their shoulders
over a bridge that led into the town. This was such a funny[3]
sight that the people ran out[4] in crowds[5] in order to laugh[6]
at it, till the ass, who did not like[7] the noise, freed himself by[8]
a kick from the cords and fell[9] off the pole into the river. Upon
this the old man, vexed and ashamed, made[10] his way home[11]
again. For he saw[12] that in spite of his efforts to please everyone
he had[13] pleased no one and had lost his ass into the bargain.

Old Fable

[1] *wie*; see § 33, N.B.   [2] Translate 'we need (*brauchen* w.) only try it'.
Infinitive with or without *zu* after *brauchen*? § 187.   [3] Say 'a so funny
sight (*der Anblick*)'; see § 67 (ii).   [4] Use *herbei-laufen* st. 'to run up to'.
[5] *haufenweise*, 'in heaps'.   [6] 'to laugh at', *sich darüber lustig machen* w.
[7] Use *gefallen* st.; see § 144 (i).   [8] *durch.*   [9] Place of *fallen*? 'till'

is understood; see § 72.   [10] 'to make one's way', *sich auf den Weg machen* w.   [11] *zu Hause* or *nach Hause*? § 168.   [12] Use *ein-sehen* st.; see § 207.   [13] Omission of Auxiliary? § 209.

16. WHY THE BIG ONES[1] WERE ON TOP

An old farmer was making his usual weekly call on[2] a customer. 'Potatoes are good this morning', he said, throwing an admiring look on the basket he[3] had brought.

'Oh, are they[4]?' answered the customer. 'That reminds me[5], I want to have a word[6] with you about the potatoes you[7] sold me last week. How is[8] it that the potatoes at the bottom of the basket are so much smaller than those on top[9]?'

'It comes about like this[10]', replied the old man with a sly look, 'potatoes are growing so fast now that by the time[11] I have dug a basketful the last ones are[12] twice as large as the first.'

Quotable Anecdotes

[1] Use a case termination; see § 65.   [2] *bei*.   [3] Avoid a Dependent Clause; say 'the brought basket'.   [4] *Ach wirklich?*   [5] 'That reminds me', say *hören Sie einmal*, 'just listen'.   [6] 'to have a word with', *ein Wörtchen sprechen* st. (*mit*).   [7] The Relative Pronoun cannot be omitted in German; see § 13.   [8] 'How comes it that...'.   [9] Translate 'those which lie on top (*oben*)'; for 'those which' see § 14 (i).   [10] *es kommt daher*, 'it comes from this'.   [11] 'by the time that', use *während*, 'while'.   [12] Say 'have become'; be careful about the position of the Verb.

17. THE DOCTOR'S PRESCRIPTION

A man told[1] his wife, who had not been looking[2] well for[3] some time, to see[4] the doctor. After the doctor had examined her, he said: 'It is nothing serious[5]; what you need[6] is plenty[7] of bathing, fresh air and light clothes'. When she came home her anxious husband asked, 'Well, what did the doctor order?' 'He said I must go to a coast resort, drive a car[8] and buy some new[9] clothes'.

[1] 'said to his wife she should (*sollen*) see...'; see § 151.   [2] See § 145.   [3] *seit*? § 56.   [4] Say 'to visit a doctor'.   [5] 'nothing serious', *nichts Ernstes*.   [6] Here *nötig haben*; *brauchen* = 'to need' of concrete objects.   [7] 'plenty of', *viel*.   [8] 'to drive a car', *Auto fahren* st.; in this sense *fahren* is conjugated with *haben* not *sein*.   [9] Termination of the Adjective after *einige*? § 24.

18. TWELVE FOOLISH FELLOWS. i

Once upon a time[1], twelve foolish fellows went out fishing[2]. Some stopped ashore[3], and others waded into the water; and when they went home, they said to each other[4], 'I hope that none of us are drowned'. 'Ah!' said one, 'let[5] us see; for[6] twelve of us went out.' So they counted[7], and no one could make out more than eleven[8], for each had forgotten to count himself[9]. 'Alas[10]!' they said, 'one of us is drowned.' They returned to the pond, where they had fished, and looked everywhere for the missing man[11], till a gentleman riding[12] by came up[13] and asked what they had lost.

New London Jest Book

[1] Translate 'there went once', *es gingen einst*; see § 205.   [2] 'in order to catch fish'.   [3] 'to stop ashore', *am Ufer bleiben* st.   [4] Translate 'the one said to the other'.   [5] Supply here *einmal* (see § 195); for Imperative see § 103.   [6] Word-order after *denn*? § 70.   [7] Use *ab-zählen* w. 'to count up'.   [8] Translate 'no one could bring it further than eleven'.   [9] For Reflexives see § 110.   [10] *O weh!*   [11] Use *der Vermißte*, 'the missed one'.   [12] Avoid Present Participle; see § 186 (ii).   [13] Say *auf sie zukam*, 'came up to them'.

19. TWELVE FOOLISH FELLOWS. ii

'Oh', said they, 'to-day twelve of us went fishing[1], and one of us cannot[2] be found.' 'Indeed', said the gentleman, 'how many are there of you now?' 'Eleven', said one, reckoning them up, but leaving himself out as before. 'Well', said the gentleman, enjoying[3] the joke, 'what will you give[4] me if I find the twelfth man?' 'Sir', they said, 'all[5] our money.' 'Give it me[6] then', answered he; whereupon he gave the first a smart blow[7] over the shoulders, and said, 'You are number one[8]'. Thus he treated them all[9]; and when he came to the last, he dealt him a harder[10] blow than the rest and said, 'He[11] is number twelve'. 'May God reward[12] you', exclaimed all[9] of them, 'for finding our poor comrade!'

New London Jest Book

[1] 'to go fishing', *fischen gehen* st.; cf. *spazieren gehen*, see § 140 (i).   [2] Translate 'is not to be found'; see § 192.   [3] Say 'whom the joke pleased' (*gefallen* st. § 144).   [4] Use the Present Indicative.   [5] Termination of *all*? § 58 (i).   [6] Word-order? § 74.   [7] 'to give a sharp

blow over', *einen tüchtigen Schlag versetzen* w. (*auf*). ⁸ *ein* or *eins*? § 51.
⁹ See § 58 (iii). ¹⁰ Insert *noch*; see § 199 (ii). ¹¹ Use *der*; see § 3 (i);
er is not sufficiently emphatic. ¹² *vergelte es Ihnen Gott...dafür daß...*,
'may God reward you for it that you have found...'.

20. A JAPANESE NOBLEMAN

A Japanese nobleman had thirty beautiful vases; one day a
servant broke one of them. As the nobleman valued his vases
above everything, he condemned the poor servant to death.
The next day another servant came to the nobleman and said
that he could mend the vase. They went together into the room
where the vases stood in a cupboard; the servant opened the
cupboard and with one blow broke all the vases. Then he said:
'Now you have no more vases and I shall die happy, for I have
perhaps saved twenty-nine people from death'. The nobleman
felt the justice of these words and pardoned both servants.

German Composition

21. TWO DOGS

A friend of mine¹ at² whose house I often used to stay had
two dogs. One was called Diana, the other Luxi. Diana was
the favourite of the older people in the house because she was
so affectionate; she would wag her tail with³ pleasure if you
looked at her. The younger people, however⁴, preferred Luxi
who, although he was twelve years old, was still full of life;
he could jump over a brook nearby which was 15 feet⁵ broad.
Both dogs loved⁶ going for a walk and it was a pleasure to go
with them. Luxi disappeared immediately in search of⁷ a rabbit,
while Diana would jump about or chase the shadows of butterflies, which she thought⁸ were living animals.

¹ *von mir*. ² *bei*; see § 165 (i). ³ *vor*; see § 169 (ii). ⁴ Position
of *jedoch*? § 91, N.B. ⁵ *Fuß* or *Füße*? § 47. ⁶ Use *gern*; see
§ 144 (iii). ⁷ 'in search of', *nach*. ⁸ Use *halten für*, 'to consider'.

22. ROBINSON CRUSOE

Sir T. Robinson was a tall, ungainly[1] man, and his figure looked[2] still more remarkable in his hunting dress, composed[3] of a cap, a tight green jacket and leather breeches[4]. In[5] this suit he once paid a surprise visit to his sister, who was married and lived in Paris. He arrived during[6] a large dinner party. The servant announced, 'M. Robinson!' and the latter entered the dining-room, to the great amazement of the guests. One of them, who was in the act[7] of raising his[8] fork to his[8] mouth, dropped it and, unable to restrain[9] his curiosity, he burst out with[10]: 'Pardon me, sir, are you the celebrated Robinson Crusoe?'

New London Jest Book

[1] Termination of the Adjective? § 23.   [2] Translate 'had a still more remarkable appearance (*das Aussehen*)'; for 'more' see § 63.   [3] 'which was composed of'.   [4] 'leather breeches', *die Lederhose* (Sing.).   [5] Say 'so clothed he surprised once with his visit his sister who...'; this avoids a series of Prepositional phrases.   [6] 'during', here *zu*.   [7] 'to be in the act of', *im Begriff sein* (+ Infinitive).   [8] Avoid the Personal Pronoun, see § 8.   [9] Use *bezwingen* st. 'to compel'.   [10] *platzte er heraus mit*.

23. A MISUNDERSTANDING

Father and mother were travelling by rail with their small son William. As the boy was continually leaning[1] out of the window, the father told him that he would soon be losing his hat. But William did not[2] heed the warning. Suddenly the father seized the hat and hid it. When William began to cry[3] his father said to[4] him: 'Be[5] quiet and I will whistle, then your hat will come back'. He whistled and showed the boy his hat. Soon after[6], while the parents were talking to each other[7], William seized his father's hat and threw[8] it out of the window. Then he smiled childishly and said: 'Daddy, whistle again!'

900 Anekdoten

[1] A Reflexive Verb; place of *sich*? § 77.   [2] Place of *nicht*? § 76.   [3] Position of an Infinitival Clause? § 97.   [4] *zu*? § 177.   [5] Should *du* or *Sie* be used? For the Imperative see § 103.   [6] *darauf* or *nachher*.   [7] 'each other', *einander*; see § 112.   [8] 'to throw out of the window', *zum Fenster hinaus-werfen* st.

24. THREE UNLUCKY ANSWERS. i

One of Frederick the Great's[1] best regiments consisted only of exceptionally tall men[2]. One day a very tall[3] Frenchman came to the captain and said he would like to serve the King of[4] Prussia. The captain accepted him on account of his size, and said that he must learn German as quickly as possible[5]. Meanwhile he must[6] learn off by heart[7] the answers to the three questions which the king put[6] to every new soldier. The first is[6], how old are you[8]? The second, how long have you been[9] in my service? The third, do you receive your uniform and pay punctually?

[1] See § 45. [2] Translate 'of soldiers of exceptionally big growth (*der Wuchs*)'. [3] 'very tall', *baumlang*. [4] *von*? § 174. [5] 'as quickly as possible', use *möglichst*; see § 34. [6] This is still Indirect Speech; see § 178. [7] 'off by heart', *auswendig*. [8] In the time of Frederick the Great the 3rd person was used to people of lower rank; so translate, *wie alt ist er?* etc. [9] He is still in his service, use therefore the Present, not the Perfect, Tense.

25. THREE UNLUCKY ANSWERS. ii

A short time afterwards[1] the king was reviewing the regiment. When he came to the Frenchman he stopped[2] and asked him: 'How long have you been in my service?' The Frenchman, who did not understand the question, gave the answer he had learned: 'Twenty-one years, your Majesty[3]'. 'What! how old are you then[4]?' asked Frederick astonished. 'Six months, your Majesty[3].' This answer surprised the king still more. 'Either[5] you are mad or I am[6]', he exclaimed. 'Both, your Majesty[3]', said the soldier, giving his last answer. When the king heard[7] the reason for the man's conduct he laughed heartily and ordered the soldier to learn German quickly.

[1] *kurze Zeit darauf*. [2] *stehen bleiben* or *an-halten*? § 150 (ii). [3] 'your Majesty', *Majestät*. [4] *denn*; see § 193. [5] Order after *entweder*? § 92. [6] Say 'I am it'; see § 61 (iii). [7] Here *erfahren* st. 'to learn'; *hören* = 'to hear' in the literal sense; see § 207.

26. A GOOD EXCUSE

During the Seven Years War[1] a young soldier who had not served long in the German army was placed[2] in guard of a gun. Being[3] thirsty, he left[4] his post and went to an inn to[5] drink a glass of[6] beer. Soon afterwards an officer came round[7] and found the gun deserted; he asked[8] where the sentry had gone and was directed[9] to the inn. There he called[10] the unfortunate man to account, and asked him why he had left his post. 'Captain[11]', answered the soldier, 'I tried in vain to move the gun myself. One person alone could[12] never carry it off; and if more than one were to come[13] I shouldn't be of any use[14]!'

[1] 'the Seven Years War', *der siebenjährige Krieg*.   [2] 'to place in guard of', *zum Wachtposten bei…stellen* w.   [3] Avoid Present Participle; see § 186 (iv).   [4] *lassen* or *verlassen*? § 143.   [5] = 'in order to'; see § 190.   [6] Genitive? § 48.   [7] 'to come round', *die Runde machen*, 'to make the round'.   [8] Use *sich erkundigen* w. 'to inquire'.   [9] Use an impersonal form; see § 105.   [10] 'to call to account', *sich vor-nehmen* st. (+Acc.).   [11] *Herr Hauptmann*.   [12] Indicative or Subjunctive? § 184.   [13] 'were to come'; use the Imperfect Subjunctive; see § 101.   [14] *so wäre ich dabei nichts nütze*.

27. THE PLEASURES OF THE COUNTRY. i

An Austrian was once on a visit[1] to a friend in the country. At first he enjoyed himself very much[2] and thought how much nicer it was[3] to live in the country than in a town[4]. After three days his beard was becoming unpleasantly long and he asked his friend if[5] there was[6] a barber in the village. 'A barber', said the friend, 'I don't think so[7]; all the[8] peasants shave themselves, and, as you see, I have a beard. I advise you to go to Brumbach, there they have a chemist's shop, a restaurant, and even a police station, so they are sure to have a barber.' On the next morning the Austrian saddled a horse and set off for[9] Brumbach.

[1] 'on a visit to', *zu Besuch bei*.   [2] 'much', *sehr* not *viel*; see § 64 (ii).   [3] Present or Imperfect Subjunctive? § 180.   [4] Say 'in the town'.   [5] Not *wenn*; see § 88.   [6] = 'existed'; see § 206.   [7] Say 'I believe not'.   [8] Omit 'the'; see § 58 (i), N.B.   [9] = 'to'; *nach*? § 167.

28. THE PLEASURES OF THE COUNTRY. ii

When he arrived in Brumbach he stopped[1] first at[2] the chemist's
to make some purchases for his friend. The shop, however, was[3]
shut and on the door was[3] nailed the following note: 'If anyone wants me[4], I am to be found[5] at[2] Mr Kovac's birthday
party'. The Austrian went to the barber, here too there was a
notice which read[6], 'I am shaving to-day at the police station'.
The Austrian, who was beginning to get angry, proceeded[7] to
the police station, where a policeman informed him that the
barber had gone to the count's castle and would not be back
till evening[8]. The Austrian returned home very angry, with a
beard still longer than before[9]. As he approached the house he
had a premonition that here too he would find a note, and sure
enough[10] he found one: 'We have gone to the parson in Schiel-
bach, follow[11] us'. The Austrian, whose patience was completely
exhausted, seized his pencil and wrote underneath: 'And I have
gone to Vienna—to get a shave[12]'.

[1] an-halten? § 150 (iii). [2] bei. [3] werden or sein? § 107. [4] Translate 'in case (falls) one seeks me'. [5] Use the Active not the Passive
Infinitive; see § 192. [6] Use lauten w. 'to run'. [7] Use sich begeben
st. 'to betake oneself'; see § 140 (iii). [8] 'till evening', erst am Abend;
for erst see § 196. [9] Is this an Adverb? § 87. [10] 'sure enough',
tatsächlich. [11] Use nach-kommen st. (+ Dat.). [12] Use sich rasieren
lassen, 'to have oneself shaved'; for the use of lassen see p. 3.

29. VAIN CHARITY

A rich man was travelling in his carriage in the depths of winter[1]
when he saw an old beggar-woman by the way. 'How terribly
cold it must be outside in the snow', he thought, and opened
the window in order to give alms[2] to the old woman. Only then[3]
did he notice that he had taken a piece of gold[4] out of his pocket,
and not the silver piece[4] he meant[5] to give. 'It is too much',
he said, and was about to withdraw his hand; but the cold
made[6] him drop the coin, which fell into the snow. The rich
man shut the window and drove on. 'After all[7]', he thought,
'I am rich and can afford[8] to do[9] a good deed from time to
time.' But the beggar-woman on her knees in the snow searched

in vain for[10] the piece of gold[4]; she was not only poor and old, but[11] blind into the bargain[12].

Guerber, Contes et Légendes

[1] Translate 'in the deepest winter'.   [2] Note that the Singular is used, *ein Almosen* (n.); see § 215.   [3] 'not until then'; see § 196.   [4] 'piece of gold', 'silver piece', one word in German.   [5] 'to mean to', *wollen*; see § 127 (i).   [6] Use *zwingen* st. 'to compel'; followed by Infinitive with or without *zu*? § 187.   [7] Here, *was tut's?* 'what does it matter?'   [8] Say 'have money enough to...'; *genug* must follow the noun.   [9] Use *sich leisten* w. (*sich* is in the Dative).   [10] *nach*.   [11] *aber* or *sondern*? § 71.   [12] 'into the bargain', here *noch dazu*.

30. NOT HIGH ENOUGH

It is well known that Vienna is one of the dearest towns in Europe. A traveller, who wished to stop there, went into a big hotel and asked the porter what the prices of the rooms were. The latter answered: 'A room on the first floor costs twenty shillings, on the second floor fifteen, on the third floor twelve and on the fourth floor ten shillings'. 'I am sorry', said the traveller, 'your hotel is too low for me.'

900 Anekdoten

31. LONGMAN, BROADMAN AND SHARPEYE[1]. i

A king, who wished his eldest son to marry[2], gave him a key, and told him to go[3] up into the room in the old tower and choose from the portraits he found there the princess he liked[4] best. The prince climbed up the stairs, unlocked the door and entered. On the walls hung[5] the pictures of eleven beautiful princesses; they were all so enchanting, however, that he could[6] not decide which he liked the best. While he stood lost in admiration[7], he noticed that one picture was covered by a curtain; he strode up to it[8], pulled aside the curtain and saw the picture of a girl, whose face wore such[9] a sad expression that his heart was touched. 'This one[10] will I marry[2] and none other', exclaimed the prince, 'even if I have to pay[11] for it with my life.'

Old Fable

[1] *Langmann, Breitmann und Scharfauge.*   [2] *heiraten* or *verheiraten*? § 146.   [3] Use a Verb of Mood, 'and said to him he **should** go up';

for omission of *daß* see § 84.   [4] Use *gefallen* st. 'who pleased him
(Dat.) best'.   [5] *hangen* or *hängen*? § 141.   [6] Indicative or Subjunctive?   [7] *voll Bewunderung*, 'full of admiration'.   [8] Use
zuschreiten; see § 152.   [9] For 'such' see § 67 (ii).   [10] Omit 'one'.
[11] 'even if I must pay it with the life'.

32. LONGMAN, BROADMAN AND SHARPEYE. ii

So he went to the king and informed[1] him of his decision. The
king was sad, for he knew that this princess was[2] in the power
of a magician who was in the habit[3] of turning all her suitors
into stone; but since a king cannot[4] break his word, he gave
his son permission to go out into the world to seek his bride.

The first difficulty which the prince encountered[5] was a thick
forest. Just as he began to fear that he had lost his way, he
saw a tall man, who cried to[6] him: 'Halt, prince, my name[7]
is Longman, for I can stretch myself out as long as I please[8];
and I should like to enter your service'. 'Well', said the prince,
'if you can lead me out of this horrible forest, I will certainly[9]
take you on[10].' Longman stretched himself till he could see
over[11] even the highest tree, then he grew small again and led
the prince out of the forest. Before them lay a large plain, and
in the distance[12] towered high grey cliffs.   *Old Fable*

[1] 'informed (*mit-teilen* w.) to him his decision'; see § 152.   [2] Use an
alternative to *sein*; see § 207.   [3] 'to be in the habit of', *pflegen* w.
(+ Inf.); Position of Infinitive? § 97.   [4] *können, müssen* or *dürfen*?
§ 129, N.B.   [5] Say 'which met (*begegnen* w.) the prince'; see § 147.
[6] Use *zurufen* st.; see § 152, *zuhören*.   [7] Say 'I am called'; § 139.
[8] 'as long as I please', *nach Belieben*, 'according to desire'.   [9] Here
gerne 'gladly'.   [10] Translate 'take you into my service' ('into' = *in*
+ Acc. or Dat.? § 160).   [11] 'to see over', *über* (+ Acc.) *hinweg sehen.*
[12] 'in the distance', use *jenseits*, 'on the other side'.

33. LONGMAN, BROADMAN AND SHARPEYE. iii

The first man[1] they met on the plain was very fat; he came
up to the prince and said that he was called Broadman, because
he could stretch himself[2] out as far as he pleased. To prove his
assertion he stretched himself out, until he filled[3] the whole
plain. 'That is a very remarkable feat', said the prince, and
engaged him at once. The next man they met had a bandage

over[4] his eyes; he too wanted to serve the prince. The prince, who had a kind heart, granted his request while[5] regretting the loss of his eyesight. 'On the contrary', replied the former, 'I am called Sharpeye, for my eyes are[6] so sharp that when[7] I take off this bandage everything I look at splits in pieces.' 'Oh!' said the prince, 'then just have a look at[8] that cliff, will you?' The man did so, the cliff split in pieces and a mighty castle was revealed[9] in which the prince could see the princess he loved[10]. 'Let us hurry there[11]', he said. *Old Fable*

[1] Use *der Mensch*, 'the human being'. [2] Use *sich aus-dehnen* w. [3] Say 'had filled (*aus-füllen* w.)'. [4] *vor*, 'in front of'. [5] Translate 'yet regretted'. [6] Translate 'see so sharply'. [7] Remove the sentence 'when I take off this bandage' to the end in order to avoid confusion; see § 96. [8] 'to have a look at', *sich...an-sehen* (+ Acc.); for 'just' see § 195 (ii). [9] Say 'there showed itself'; § 205. [10] Avoid a Relative Sentence. [11] *dort* is not enough; motion away is implied; see § 210, N.B.

34. LONGMAN, BROADMAN AND SHARPEYE. iv

The four travellers reached the castle shortly before sunset and, finding all the doors open, entered. As[1] they were admiring the stone statues which stood round the enormous hall, a door suddenly opened[2] and the magician came in leading the princess by[3] the hand. 'You need not introduce yourself', he said to the prince, 'I know who[4] you are and what you want[5]; but before[6] you can marry the princess, you must sit in this room with her for[7] three nights on end; I shall visit you each morning and if the princess is not there[8] each time, you will be turned into stone.' With that[9] he disappeared. The prince was determined not to go to sleep, but before long he and his companions sank into a deep sleep. At dawn they awoke and found that the princess had disappeared. The prince began to lament, but Sharpeye took off his bandage and saw the princess 100 miles off[10] in an acorn hanging on a tree in a forest. *Old Fable*

[1] Temporal or causal? § 83. [2] Reflexive, 'opened itself'. [3] *an* (+ Dat.). [4] *wer* or *der*? § 17. [5] *wünschen* is better than *wollen* here: *wünschen* = French *désirer*; *wollen* = French *vouloir*. [6] Since 'before' is used in a figurative sense *ehe* should be preferred to *bevor*; see § 85. [7] Omit 'for'; § 56. [8] Translate 'should the princess ever be absent...'; see § 89. [9] 'with that', *darauf*. [10] *entfernt*.

35. LONGMAN, BROADMAN AND SHARPEYE. v

Longman stretched himself till[1] he could cover[2] 10 miles with each stride, and fetched the acorn, which the prince threw on the floor so that it broke; and lo![3] there stood the princess just as the magician entered. The same thing[4] happened the next night; only the princess was hidden in a cliff 200 miles off. On the third morning Sharpeye saw the princess in a shell at the bottom of the Black Sea 300 miles off; this time he took Broadman with him[5], and when they arrived[6] there the latter made[7] himself as broad as possible and drank up so much of[8] the sea that Longman was able to reach the shell. They hurried home as fast as they could and succeeded[9] in reaching the castle before sunrise; when the magician saw the princess for[10] the third time, he was immediately turned into a black raven which flew away with hoarse cries[11]. The prince took the princess home and married her, and at the marriage feast[12] no one ate, drank or danced better than Longman, Broadman and Sharpeye.

Old Fable

[1] Translate 'so that'.   [2] Use *zurück-legen* w. 'to lay behind'.   [3] 'lo!' *siehe!*   [4] For 'thing' see § 29.   [5] Omit 'him'.   [6] Use *gelangen* w.; *dort* must have a Suffix, *hin* or *her*?   [7] Say 'stretched himself out...'.   [8] *von*.   [9] For construction with *gelingen* see § 152.   [10] Preposition? § 57.   [11] *mit heiserem Gekrächze.*   [12] 'marriage feast' one word in German.

36. WHEN MAY[1] ONE STEAL?

The judge was speaking to a man who stood in court for[2] theft: 'You are already over seventy years old; are you not ashamed to steal at[3] that age?' The accused replied: 'When I was fifteen years old and was had up[4] for theft the judge said to me: "Are you not ashamed to steal at[3] that age?" When I was getting on for thirty[5] years old, I was again accused of theft and again the judge said the same words[6] to me. Now tell me, judge[7], at what[8] age is one allowed to steal?' *900 Anekdoten*

[1] = 'is one allowed to'; see § 181.   [2] *wegen.*   [3] *in* (+ Acc. or Dat.? § 162).   [4] 'to have up (for)', *an-zeigen* w. (*wegen*).   [5] Translate 'as I was near (*gegen*) thirty'.   [6] *Worte* or *Wörter*? § 216.   [7] Say 'Mr Judge'.   [8] See § 21 (ii).

37. BALAAM'S[1] SWORD

A young student at Oxford[2], who had received a visit from some friends, thought that it was his duty to show them the sights of the town. He took[3] them first of all[4] to the Ashmolean Museum and saw there, among many other curiosities, a rusty old[5] sword. 'This', said he, 'is the sword with which Balaam wanted to kill the ass.' One of the company remarked that[6] he thought Balaam had[7] no sword, but[8] only wished[9] for one. 'You are right', replied the student, 'and this is the very[10] sword he wished[11] for.'

New London Jest Book

[1] 'Balaam', *Bileam*; for the Genitive see § 41. [2] Use the Adjective *Oxforder* (indeclinable). [3] Use *führen* w. 'to lead'. [4] 'first of all', *zunächst*. [5] Termination of Adjective? [6] Avoid using *daß*; see § 84. [7] Translate 'had possessed'; see § 207. [8] *aber* or *sondern*? § 71. [9] Use *sich wünschen* w. [10] 'the very sword', *eben das Schwert*. [11] Since this is a conversation we should use the Perfect; see § 218 (i).

38. THE LEGEND OF SAINT ELISABETH

Saint Elisabeth was a Landgravine of Thuringia who spent her time in[1] good works and who was known far and wide for her goodness of heart[2] and piety. She used[3] to walk down every day with a basket of provisions on her arm from the Wartburg into the valley, to bring food and consolation[4] to the poor. The Landgrave did not approve[5] of this and in the end strictly forbade her to make these visits. A few days afterwards, just as he was returning from hunting[6], he met his wife on the drawbridge as she was on her way to a sick bed[7], her basket filled with provisions[8]. He spoke to her roughly[9] and threw back the lid of the basket, expecting[10] to catch her in the act of disobeying[11] him. But what[12] was his astonishment when he found nothing in the basket but a mass of red roses.

[1] 'to spend time in', *Zeit mit...zu-bringen* st. [2] 'goodness of heart', *die Herzensgüte*. [3] Use *pflegen* w. 'to be accustomed to'. [4] 'to bring consolation to', *Trost spenden* w. (+ Dat.). [5] 'to approve of this', *damit einverstanden sein*. [6] Say 'from the hunt'. [7] Say 'to an invalid'. [8] Translate 'with her with provisions filled basket'; see § 185. [9] 'to speak roughly to', *an-herrschen* w. (+ Acc.). [10] Use *in der Meinung* + Perfect Infinitive, 'in the opinion to have caught'. [11] 'to catch in the act of disobeying', *auf verbotener Tat ertappen* w. [12] 'how great was'.

39. A DIPLOMATIC REPRIMAND

The English ambassador Prior was once attending[1] the opera in Paris and found himself in the same box as a nobleman whose acquaintance he had recently made, and who talked louder than the artist sang. Prior endured this for some time and[2] then began to criticise the singer severely[3] in[4] a still louder voice. The nobleman stopped[5] to inquire the reason for this outbreak, adding that the singer was held to be[6] one of the finest artists in France. 'Yes', replied His Excellency, 'but he makes such a noise, that I do not have the pleasure of being able[7] to listen to your lordship.'   *New London Jest Book*

[1] Here *besuchen* w. 'to visit'.   [2] In order to avoid the repetition of *und* start a new Sentence: 'then he began...'.   [3] *scharf*.   [4] Translate 'with still louder voice'.   [5] Say 'interrupted his speech'.   [6] Use *gelten* st. *als*, 'to pass for'.   [7] 'to be able to'; Infinitive with or without *zu*? § 120.

40. THE POLITENESS OF THE EAST

A king of the East spoke to his minister: 'I have a favour to ask you. Will you grant it me?' The minister replied: 'Your request is an order to me. But I too have a request, will you grant it also?' 'Your request too shall be granted', answered the king, and then revealed his wish to the minister: 'Give me, I pray you, those magnificent gardens which lie on the bank of the Euphrates'. The minister readily granted this wish and the king then asked what he wanted. 'Give me back the gardens', replied the minister.   *900 Anekdoten*

41. THE PRINCESS WHO WAS TURNED INTO STONE[1]. i

The Day King[2] once loved the daughter of the Night King[2] and wished to marry her. The latter, however, would not allow it, and forbade his daughter ever to meet him again. So the two lovers decided to fly together, and early one morning[3] the Day King carried off the princess with her attendants in his chariot.

When the Night King learnt a few hours later that his daughter
had disappeared, he flew into a rage[4] and mounted the highest
tower of his castle to look for her[5]. But since he could only see
by night, and the[6] Day King's chariot made no noise[7], he was
not able[8] to discover their whereabouts[9].

[1] *die versteinerte Prinzessin.*   [2] 'the Day King', 'the Night King',
translate *der Fürst des Tages* and *der König der Nacht.*   [3] 'early one
morning', *eines Morgens früh.*   [4] 'to fly into a rage', *in heftigen Zorn
geraten* st.   [5] 'to look for', use *aus-schauen* w. (*nach*).   [6] 'since'
is understood; word-order? § 72.   [7] Translate 'went noiselessly';
should 'go' be rendered by *gehen* or *fahren*? § 140 (ii).   [8] Use an alternative
to *können*; see § 137.   [9] 'their whereabouts', *ihren Aufenthalt.*

42. THE PRINCESS WHO WAS TURNED
INTO STONE. ii

As he was about to descend, the favourite dog[1] of the princess
began to bark with[2] joy. The Night King knew at once where
they were, and sent[3] his thunderbolt after them. The princess[4],
her attendants and the dog were all immediately turned into
stone, and to this day[5] they stand on the edge of a large plain
in the form[6] of a chain of mountains[7] with the biggest and most
beautiful mountain in the middle. The Day King, however,
could not be harmed[8] by[9] the thunderbolt, and every[10] morning
and evening, when he comes in his chariot and fixes his burning
eyes on these mountains, it seems as if they glow under his
gaze[11], and become once more for a short while alive.

[1] *der Lieblingshund*; cf. *der Lieblingssohn*, 'the favourite son', etc.   [2] *vor*;
§ 169 (ii).   [3] 'to send **after**', use **nach**-*schicken* w. (+ Dat.); compare
zu-*hören*, 'to listen **to**'; see § 152.   [4] Say 'the princess with her
attendants and dog'.   [5] 'to this day', *heute noch*; for the meaning of
noch see § 199.   [6] 'in the form of', *als.*   [7] 'the chain of mountains', *die Gebirgskette.*   [8] Use *verletzen* w. 'to injure'; for the Passive
see § 106.   [9] After a Passive **durch** translates the means, **von** the
agent: *er wurde* **durch** *den Donnerkeil verletzt*, but *er wurde* **von** *dem
König verletzt.*   [10] Accusative or Genitive? § 171.   [11] *unter seinen
Blicken*, 'under his glances'.

43. THE ONLY WAY OUT

Two old women were quarrelling in a railway carriage whether the window should be open or shut. One[1] maintained that she would certainly catch her death of cold[2] if the window was opened; the other cried that she would certainly have a stroke[3] if the window was not opened. At last the ticket-collector, who had been getting more and more impatient[4] at the quarrel, said to one of the fellow[5] travellers: 'The best thing[6] we can do is to open the window for[7] a while and then one of them[1] will die; after that[8] we can shut the window again, and then the other will die. Then we shall get some peace'.

900 *Anekdoten*

[1] Say 'the one'; see § 30.   [2] 'to catch one's death of cold', *sich zu Tode erkälten* w.   [3] Say 'a stroke (*Schlag*, m.) would certainly hit (*treffen* st.) her'.   [4] Translate 'always more impatient'; see § 63.
[5] *der Mitreisende*; cf. *der Mitgast*, 'the fellow guest', *der Mitchrist*, 'the fellow Christian', etc.   [6] Say 'at best (*am besten*) we open the window'.
[7] Omit 'for'.   [8] 'after that', *danach* or *hernach*.

44. CLOTHING

It will strike[1] every Englishman on[2] his first visit to Germany that the clothing of young people there[3] is in general different from that of[4] young people in England. While[5] in Germany suits are worn, the Englishman prefers a pair of grey flannels[6] and an old coat, which[7] is naturally cheaper and more comfortable, though perhaps less tidy. In German schools caps of different colours[8] are worn to distinguish one form from another, and similar caps are also used[9] later on at[10] the university as the badge of various clubs.

[1] 'to strike', *auf-fallen* st.; see § 152.   [2] *bei*; see § 165 (ii).   [3] Say 'of the **there** young people (*die Jugend*)'; for the use of 'there' as an Adjective see p. 144.   [4] 'that of', see § 14 (ii).   [5] *während* must be used here; see § 86 (ii).   [6] 'flannels,' *Flanellhosen* (pl.).   [7] 'which' refers to the whole of the previous Sentence; *das* or *was*? § 19 (ii).
[8] 'of different colours', use the Adjective *bunt*, 'many coloured'.   [9] 'to be used as the badge of', *als Abzeichen dienen* w. 'to serve as badge of...'.   [10] *auf* (+ Dat.).

45. ALL'S WELL THAT ENDS WELL[1]. i

An honest workman was returning to a certain city by[2] the evening train[3] after a hard day's work[3] in the country. He sat all[4] alone in the compartment, peacefully smoking his pipe. At the last station[5] before the terminus a lady came[6] in holding[7] in her arms a little dog. The strong smell of tobacco pleased neither the lady nor the dog, and she requested the workman rather sharply to stop[8] smoking. He pointed out[9] that it was a smoking compartment[10], that she had had plenty of[11] time to look for a non-smoker[10], and that in any case they would arrive at their destination in a few[12] minutes.

[1] *Ende gut, Alles gut.*　　　[2] *mit.*　　　[3] 'evening train', 'day's work'; use Compound Words in German.　　　[4] *ganz.*　　　[5] 'station', use here *die Haltestelle*; 'at' = *an*.　　　[6] Say 'climbed in'; should *ein* or *herein* be used? § 211.　　　[7] Use a Relative Sentence; should this come before or after the Separable Prefix? § 96.　　　[8] Translate 'to discontinue (*unterlassen* st.) the smoking'.　　　[9] 'to point out to someone', *jemand aufmerksam machen.*　　　[10] *ein Abteil für Raucher*; 'a non-smoker', *ein Abteil für Nichtraucher.*　　　[11] 'plenty of', *reichlich* (Adv.).　　　[12] Should *einige* or *wenige* be used here? § 62.

46. ALL'S WELL THAT ENDS WELL. ii

These remarks made[1] the lady very angry. She opened both windows, and when the little dog began to sneeze she lost[2] her temper and snatching[3] the man's pipe flung it out[4] of the window. Thereupon he too lost his temper, seized the little dog and threw[5] it after the pipe. A few minutes later the train drew[6] up in the station, and the lady and the workman were explaining matters[7] to the station-master, when suddenly they saw the little dog trotting up[8], wagging his tail[9], and proudly carrying the pipe in his mouth.

[1] 'to make someone angry', *jemand in Zorn versetzen* w.　　　[2] 'to lose one's temper', *in Wut geraten* st.　　　[3] Use *nehmen* st.　　　[4] 'out of the window', *zum Fenster hinaus.*　　　[5] 'to throw after', use *nach-werfen* st. (+Dat.); *werfen* + the Preposition *nach* = 'to throw at'.　　　[6] = 'stopped'; see § 150 (iii).　　　[7] 'matters'; *die Sache*, 'the affair'.　　　[8] Use *daherlaufen*; Construction after *sehen*? § 187.　　　[9] 'to wag the tail', use *schweifwedeln* w.; the Present Participle may be used adverbially here; see p. 110 (6).

47. RABELAIS

Three hundred years ago there[1] lived in France a famous doctor, named Rabelais, who on account of his wit was[2] often invited to meals[3]. One day he was eating[4] with[5] the Archbishop of Paris, when a dish of[6] partridges was[2] brought in. Rabelais took his knife, tapped[7] on the edge of the dish and said: 'That is very difficult to digest'. The Archbishop immediately called his servant and ordered him to carry the dish away. The latter was about to do this, when Rabelais took[8] the dish from him, and began to eat the partridges. The Archbishop was surprised: 'First you say that it is[9] difficult to digest and now you are eating it yourself'. 'Pardon me,' said Rabelais, 'I was speaking of[10] the dish and not of[10] the partridges.'

[1] Use es; see § 205.   [2] Should we use sein or werden here? § 107.
[3] zu Tisch.   [4] Use speisen w. 'to have a meal'.   [5] bei; see § 165 (i).
[6] Omit 'of'; cf. ein Glas Bier, etc., § 46.   [7] Translate 'hit on the edge of the dish with it...'; for 'with it' see § 61 (ii).   [8] 'To take from', use abnehmen; see § 152, berauben.   [9] Subjunctive? § 181.   [10] von.

48. A GLASS OF BRANDY

A man entered a railway carriage during a journey and exclaimed: 'Has anyone here a bottle of brandy? A lady has fainted in the next compartment'. A gentleman readily opened his suitcase, poured the desired brandy out of a bottle into a little glass and passed it to the stranger. The latter at once put the glass to his lips and drained it. Then he gave the glass back to the gentleman with the words: 'Now I feel better; I can't bear seeing a lady faint'.   900 *Anekdoten*

49. A GOOD REASON

Charles II asked Stillingfleet, the bishop, how it happened[1] that he usually preached extempore[2], but always read[3] the sermons which he delivered[4] before the court. The priest answered that the awe[5] of standing before so great and wise a prince[6] robbed him of his self-confidence. 'But will[7] your Majesty', continued he, 'permit me to ask a question in my turn[8]? Why do you read[3] your speeches to[9] parliament?' 'Well', replied the king, 'I will tell you candidly. I have asked[10] them so often for money, that I am ashamed to look[11] them in the face.'

New London Jest Book

[1] Translate 'how it came'; Mood? § 179.   [2] 'extempore', *aus dem Stegreife*.   [3] Use *vor-lesen*, 'to read aloud'.   [4] 'to deliver a sermon', *eine Predigt halten* st.   [5] Translate 'that the awe which he felt (*hegen* w.) before...'.   [6] Here *Fürst*, 'a ruling prince'.   [7] *Eure Majestät* requires that the Verb should be in the Plural; should *wollen* or *werden* be used? § 127, N.B.   [8] 'in my turn', *meinerseits*.   [9] This is an Indirect Object.   [10] Construction after *bitten*? § 138.   [11] Say 'to look (*schauen* w.) to them (Dat.) into (*in*) the face'; case after *in*? § 160.

50. NARCISSUS

Narcissus was dead. All the[1] flowers drooped[2] their heads and mourned for their lost favourite. They turned to the brook, which flowed[3] gently by, and said: 'How sad thou too must be, since our friend has died'. And the brook answered and said: 'Yea, truly, ye are right, for his sake I am shedding bitter tears'. 'We can well understand that', said the flowers, 'for he was so often and so long at thy side, when[4] he mirrored himself in thy waters[5].' 'Yes', answered the brook, 'but not on that account do I mourn, but[6] because I saw myself in his eyes, as[4] he bent over me.'

After Oscar Wilde

[1] Omit 'the'; § 58 (i), N.B.   [2] 'to droop', *hängen lassen*; cf. *fallen lassen*, etc., § 188.   [3] 'to flow gently by', *dort vorbei-rieseln* w.   [4] = 'whenever'; *wenn* or *als*? § 81.   [5] 'waters', use *die Fluten*.   [6] *aber* or *sondern*?

SECTION II

MODEL LESSON II

(1) Lord Chesterfield to his son.

Blackheath,
June 15th, 1759.

(2) My dear friend,
Your letter of the 5th, which I received yesterday, gave me great satisfaction, being all in your own hand, though it contains great and, I fear, just complaints of your state of ill health. (3) You have done very well to change the air, and I hope that the change will do well by you. (4) I would therefore have you write after the 20th of August to Lord Holderness, to beg of him to obtain His Majesty's leave for you to return to England for two or three months, upon account of your health. (5) Two or three months is an indefinite time, which may afterwards be insensibly stretched to what length one pleases; leave that to me. (6) In the meantime you may be taking your measures as best you can. God bless you.

(1) 'Lord Chesterfield to his son. Blackheath, June 15th, 1759.'

'Lord Chesterfield to his son.' The names of places such as Blackheath, etc., or of titles, especially those of well-known characters, should be left untranslated. It would be ludicrous to try to render Lord Chesterfield in German; there is no title which exactly corresponds to our 'Lord', the nearest equivalent in German being *Herr*, which properly speaking does not mean 'Lord' at all, but 'Mr'. The name of Lord Chesterfield is sufficiently well known in Germany to be recognised without translation.

'to his son' might be rendered by the dative, *seinem Sohn*, but far better would be the use of *an* + the accusative. Both *ich schreibe ihm* and *ich schreibe an ihn* are correct German, but in superscriptions *an* should always be used. A proclamation, for example, addressed by a king to his people would be headed *an mein Volk* not *meinem Volk*. The suggested rendering therefore is: 'Lord Chesterfield an seinen Sohn'.

'Blackheath, June 15th, 1759.' In translating dates first remember that the numeral is placed before and not after the month, and then decide whether the accusative of definite time or the preposition *an* + the dative is to be used. The use of *an* corresponds, as might be expected, to the use of the English 'on', and commonsense will tell us to avoid it here; *an* is in fact never used at the head of a letter. The translation therefore runs: 'Blackheath, den 15ten Juni, 1759'.

(2) 'My dear friend, Your letter of the 5th, which I received yesterday, gave me great satisfaction, being all in your own hand, though it contains great and, I fear, just complaints of your state of ill health.'

'My dear friend.' Though the formal modes of address, *sehr geehrter Herr*, 'Dear Sir', *sehr geehrte gnädige Frau*, 'Dear Madam', etc., are as strictly adhered to in German as in English, the liberty of expression between friends is correspondingly great and we can render 'my dear friend' quite literally by 'mein lieber Freund'.

'Your letter of the 5th, which I received yesterday.' As a rule Germans avoid using 'I' at the commencement of a letter. Lord Chesterfield has conveniently done the same, so we need make no change in word-order. 'Your letter of the 5th' may be translated straightforwardly; we must remember, however, that a father in addressing a son would use the intimate forms *Du, Dein* (spelt with a capital in letters) and not the polite forms *Sie, Ihr*; so, 'Dein Brief vom fünften': *vom fünften* and not *des fünften* is the correct idiom here.

For 'to receive' two words will be found in the Vocabulary, *empfangen* and *erhalten*. Here *erhalten* is to be preferred; *empfangen* is used of 'social' receptions: *Frau Schmidt empfing mich freundlich*, 'Mrs Smith received me kindly'. *Empfangen*, when used for the receipt of letters, expresses the idea of **welcome** reception and is then generally found in its noun form; it is frequently to be seen in this form in business communications: *hiermit bestätige ich den Empfang Ihres Geehrten vom 25.*, 'herewith I acknowledge the receipt of yours of the

25th'. If we use *erhalten* the whole phrase runs: 'Dein Brief vom fünften, den ich gestern erhielt'.

'gave me great satisfaction.' The two ordinary words for 'satisfaction', *die Befriedigung* and *die Zufriedenheit*, are not suitable here. *Befriedigung* conveys the idea of the gratification of a wish: *jetzt hast du die Befriedigung deines Wunsches*, 'now you have the satisfaction of your desire'. *Zufriedenheit* denotes a state of mind rather than a temporary satisfaction: *du hast es zu meiner Zufriedenheit getan*, 'you have done it to my satisfaction'. We must therefore look for another word. *Die Genugtuung* would be possible, but it is rather too official in tone; a word much more commonly used is *die Freude*, and 'to give pleasure' can best be rendered by *Freude geben* or by the more idiomatic *Freude bereiten*, 'to prepare pleasure'. The sentence will then be: 'hat mir große Freude bereitet'.

'being all in your own hand.' A present participle introducing a sentence must here, as always, be avoided. The sentence may be turned in this case by a dependent clause; since a reason is being given the clause will be introduced by *da*: 'since it was all in your own hand'. We must recollect that 'it' refers to **der** *Brief* and will therefore be translated by *er* not *es*. If we now render literally *da er ganz in Deiner eigenen Hand war*, we should have produced grammatically correct but not good idiomatic German; the sentence would moreover convey the idea not that the letter was written by his own hand but rather that it was actually lying in it. The sense would be clearer if we translated 'was' by 'was written', *geschrieben wurde*, or better *geschrieben ist*, since the present state rather than the past action is in question. But the phrase is still far from perfect. We should be able to improve on *ganz in Deiner eigenen Hand*; if no suitable idiom is known we might say simply, *von Dir selbst*, 'by you yourself'; but there are in fact at least two suitable phrases: *von eigener Hand* or better, because shorter, *ganz eigenhändig*. If we use the latter, the sentence will run: 'da er ganz eigenhändig geschrieben ist'.

'though it contains great and, I fear, just complaints of your state of ill health.' 'though it contains': *obgleich, obschon, obwohl* are synonyms and we may use whichever we wish; *enthalten* = 'to contain'. Since the clause is subordinate the verb must stand at the end; so: 'obgleich er...enthält'. 'to complain of' is *sich beklagen über*, 'a complaint of' will therefore be *eine Klage über*; remember that *über* is one of the two prepositions (the other is *auf*) which when used metaphorically are followed by the accusative and not the dative. 'great and just': the two obvious words, *groß* and *gerecht*, are to be avoided; *groß* means either large in size or famous and is rarely employed in any other sense; we can use here either *schwer*, the usual epithet of *Klagen*, or *manche*, 'many'. *Gerecht* is unsuitable because it implies that the justice of the complaints had been previously challenged; *wohlbegründete*, 'well-grounded', gives the required meaning. The parenthesis 'I fear' might be rendered by *ich fürchte*, but the Germans generally say *wie ich fürchte*, e.g. 'his riches run, I believe, into millions' = *sein Reichtum beläuft sich, wie ich glaube, auf Millionen.* 'your state of ill health' will, if rendered literally, be *Dein Zustand der Krankheit*, but very frequently two English nouns connected by 'of' are in German best rendered by a compound noun, e.g. 'the art of poetry' = *die Dichtkunst*, 'the love of truth' = *die Wahrheitsliebe*, etc. So here a compound word should be used, *der Krankheitszustand.*

The rendering of the whole of section (2) is as follows:

'Mein lieber Freund, Dein Brief vom fünften, den ich gestern erhielt, hat mir große Freude bereitet, da er ganz eigenhändig geschrieben ist, obwohl er manche und, wie ich fürchte, wohlbegründete Klagen über Deinen Krankheitszustand enthält.'

(3) 'You have done very well to change the air, and I hope that the change will do well by you.'

'You have done very well.' 'To do well' might be rendered by *gut tun*, but this expression is suited rather to conversational than to literary German and more often means 'to do good', i.e. 'to benefit', than 'to do well'; e.g. *meine Ferien haben mir gut getan*, 'my holidays have done me good'. *Wohl tun* corresponds more closely both to the style and the sense. So: 'Du hast wohl getan'; *sehr* has been omitted since the expression is sufficiently emphatic in German without it.

'to change the air'. The word 'change' may be translated in several different ways; of the three commonest renderings *wechseln*, *ändern* and *verändern*, *wechseln* = 'to exchange one thing for another', e.g. *darf ich mit Ihnen Plätze wechseln?*, 'may

I change places with you?; *ändern* = 'to alter', 'to become different', e.g. *er hat sich sehr geändert*, 'he has changed a lot'; *verändern* = 'to vary', e.g. *das Wetter verändert sich mit jedem Tag*, 'the weather changes every day'. The word required here is *verändern*, but the expression *die Luft verändern* is not good German. We can, however, make use of the verbal noun *die Veränderung* and turn the phrase by saying: 'you have done well to obtain (*sich verschaffen*) change of air', *Du hast wohl getan, dir Luftveränderung zu verschaffen.*

'and I hope that the change will do well by you.' There are no grammatical difficulties in this sentence, the only problem is how to render the idiom 'to do well by someone'. There is no exact equivalent for this in German, the nearest approach is *einem wohl bekommen* or, if we wish to parallel the English play on words, *einem wohl tun*, 'to do one good'. If we then render the rest of the sentence literally we shall have: *und ich hoffe, daß Dir diese Luftveränderung wohl tun wird.* A slight improvement on this would be made were we to omit *Luftveränderung*, for the Germans are less prone to repeat words for the sake of the sound of a phrase, than we are.

The German for section (3) is: 'Du hast wohl getan, Dir Luftveränderung zu verschaffen und ich hoffe, daß Dir diese wohl tun wird'.

(4) 'I would therefore have you write after the 20th of August to Lord Holderness, to beg of him to obtain His Majesty's leave for you to return to England for two or three months, upon account of your health.'

'I would therefore have you write after the 20th of August to Lord Holderness.' 'I would have you write' might be rendered in several ways: we might say, for example, 'in my opinion you ought to write', *meiner Meinung nach solltest Du schreiben*, but better than this, because it is simpler and corresponds closer to the English, is 'I should like you to write', *ich möchte, daß Du schreibest* (subjunctive); the use of an infinitive after *mögen* is impossible here, since the subjects of the two verbs are different: 'I should like to write' = *ich möchte schreiben*, but 'I should like **you** to write' = *ich möchte, daß Du schreibest*. Write then: 'Deswegen möchte ich, daß Du schreibest'. *Deswegen*, being the most emphatic word, has been placed first.

'after the 20th of August to Lord Holderness.' The position
of the numeral in dates has received comment; we must be
careful here, however, to avoid the use of *von*; where we can
say either 'the 20th of August' or 'August the 20th', the
Germans can only say *den* 20*sten August*; so: 'nach dem 20sten
August'. 'to Lord Holderness': in the dative the case would
not be shown, therefore use *an* with the accusative: 'an Lord
Holderness'. The whole sentence now runs: 'Deswegen möchte
ich, daß Du nach dem 20sten August an Lord Holderness
schreibest'.

'to beg of him to obtain His Majesty's leave for you to return
to England for two or three months, upon account of your
health.' This sentence is clearly too complicated in structure
for it to be likely that a word for word translation will be
correct; some rearrangement is necessary. In the first place a
series of short infinitival clauses must be avoided; in this passage
there are three, introduced respectively by 'to beg', 'to obtain'
and 'to return'; one of these, 'to return', may be avoided by
the use of a substantival phrase: 'leave for a return'; the other
two may remain, but we must be careful in translating them
to remember that the infinitive stands at the end of its own
clause, 'to beg' after 'of him' and 'to obtain' at the end of the
whole sentence. Even so some further rearrangement is desirable.
In German word-order we have two principles to guide us, one
that words having logical connection stand near each other, the
other that short and unimportant words should come early in
a sentence and heavy and important words late. On the second
principle we shall place the short pronoun 'for you' first in the
sentence. It would then seem to a German mind more consistent
with the train of thought to proceed immediately with 'upon
account of your health'. The rest of the sentence, 'His Majesty's
leave for you to return to England for two or three months',
might stand unless we were to say 'to obtain from his Majesty
leave for your return...'; in which case 'from his Majesty'
would have to be placed near to, i.e. directly before, 'to obtain',
and the word-order would then be: '...of him to beg for you
on account of your health the granting of a return for two or
three months from His Majesty to obtain'. 'to beg of him':
'to', since it is equivalent to 'in order to', will be rendered by
um...zu. The difference between *bitten* and *fragen* has been dis-

cussed (see § 138). Here *bitten* might be used; but *bitten* corresponds rather to the English 'to ask' than 'to beg of' and is too familiar a word to be used towards Royalty. The polite and formal tone of the English is given by the German word *ersuchen*, so: 'um ihn zu ersuchen'.

'for you...upon account of your health.' In such cases the dative rather than *für* + acc. is used, e.g. 'I will look after that **for you**' = *ich werde es* **dir** *besorgen*; 'I have bought presents **for you** all' = *ich habe* **Ihnen** *allen Geschenke gekauft*. 'upon account of your health' might be rendered by the rather pompous phrase, *mit Rücksicht auf Deine Gesundheit*, 'in consideration of your health'; alternatively we can choose between *wegen* and *willen*, which both follow the word they govern: *wegen* means simply 'because of', *willen* means 'with the intention of attending to', e.g. *meiner Krankheit wegen darf ich nicht ausgehen*, 'I cannot go out on account of my illness'; but *meiner Krankheit willen ist der Arzt gekommen*, 'the doctor has come on account of my illness'. Here, since intention is implied, *willen* should be used; being simpler it may be preferred to *mit Rücksicht auf*; so: 'Dir Deiner Gesundheit willen'.

'leave for a return to England for two or three months.' The ordinary word for 'leave', *die Erlaubnis*, would be used if we were asking leave of a father or a schoolmaster, but hardly of a king. *Die Genehmigung*, 'the assent', is the word we want here; *Genehmigung* is followed by the preposition *zu*, so 'leave **for** a return' will be 'die Genehmigung **zu** einer Rückkehr'.

'to England.' Names of towns and countries do not require the definite article unless preceded by a qualifying adjective: *das schöne England*, 'beautiful England'; but *England ist schön*, 'England is beautiful'. 'to' with names of places is always *nach*, so here: 'die Genehmigung zu einer Rückkehr nach England'.

'for two or three months.' We should not render this literally by **für** *zwei oder drei Monate*; **auf** *zwei oder drei Monate* would be possible (see § 56), or, if we wish to be more accurate, *auf die Dauer von zwei bis drei Monaten*, 'for the length of two or three months'; but both these translations have here the disadvantage that we already have several prepositional phrases in succession and shall require yet another to translate 'from His Majesty'; we had better therefore look for some expression which does not involve the use of a preposition. In § 55 we noted that from *das Jahr* was formed the adjective *jährig*, from *die Stunde* the adjective *stündig*, etc.; the use of such formations in expressions both of time and place is very common in German, e.g. *das* **dortige** *Haus*, 'the house over there'; *der* **hiesige** *Wein*, 'the wine of this district'; *die* **heutige** *Post*, 'to-day's mail'; *der* **jetzige** *Kurs*, 'the present rate of exchange', etc. If we use here the adjective formed from *der Monat* we shall have: 'zu einer zwei- oder dreimonatigen Rückkehr'; note the hyphen which indicates that *monatig* has been omitted, cf. *Feld- und Gartenfrüchte, Personen- und Schnellzüge, Haupt- und Fürwörter*, etc.

'from His Majesty to obtain'. *Bekommen*, 'to get', is too colloquial; it is probable that the required word will begin with the prefix *er-* which gives in itself the idea of obtaining, e.g. *arbeiten*, 'to work', *erarbeiten*, 'to obtain by work', *schmeicheln*, 'to flatter', *erschmeicheln*, 'to obtain by flattery', etc. There are in fact three words which might be used here, *ersuchen, erlangen* and *erbitten*. The first we have already used earlier in the sentence; of *erlangen* and *erbitten* the latter is to be preferred, since it is politer and corresponds to the idea of the English 'to obtain by asking'. So: 'zu erbitten'. 'from His Majesty' is rendered literally 'von Seiner Majestät'.

The whole sentence therefore runs: 'Deswegen möchte ich, daß Du nach dem 20sten August an Lord Holderness schreibest, um ihn zu ersuchen, Dir Deiner Gesundheit willen die Genehmigung zu einer zwei- oder dreimonatigen Rückkehr nach England von Seiner Majestät zu erbitten'.

(5) 'Two or three months is an indefinite time, which may afterwards be insensibly stretched to what length one pleases; leave that to me.'

'Two or three months is an indefinite time.' For the difference between *die Zeit* and *das Mal* see § 57; *die Zeit*, meaning time in a general sense, is required here; 'indefinite' may be rendered straightforwardly by *unbestimmt*, 'not fixed' (*bestimmen* = 'to fix' or 'appoint'); if we keep to the English order we may translate: *zwei oder drei Monate sind eine unbestimmte Zeit*; the English uses 'is', German *sind* (in stricter grammar, as the subject is plural). The rendering is now correct but not elegant;

we should improve on the German and reproduce more closely Lord Chesterfield's elevated style if we used *es* as the grammatical subject and said: 'Es sind zwei oder drei Monate eine unbestimmte Zeit'.

'which may afterwards be insensibly stretched.' The meaning of 'insensibly' is not quite clear in English; if we take it to denote 'gradually', *nach und nach* or *allmählich* can be used, if 'without being noticed', which seems more probable, *unbewußt*, or better *unmerklich*, is the correct translation. 'afterwards' is literally *nachher*; but *nachher* in German is less widely used than the English 'afterwards' and should in prose at least be reserved for sentences in which a previous action has been expressed, e.g. *erst müssen Sie essen, nachher dürfen Sie ausgehen*, 'first you must eat, you can go out afterwards'. Where no previous action has been expressed 'afterwards' may be rendered by *später*.

'may...be stretched.' The obvious word *strecken* may not be used metaphorically. We may say, *er streckte die Hände gegen den Himmel aus*, 'he stretched his hands to heaven', but not *er streckte die Zeit aus*. We might use *verlängern*, 'to lengthen', but *ausdehnen*, which means to stretch elastically (metaphorically or actually), is nearer to the English. 'may' might be rendered by the imperfect subjunctive of *können* followed by the passive infinitive, *könnte ausgedehnt werden* (the subjunctive giving the idea of contingency or potentiality). The above rendering, however, is rather clumsy and looks like English German. As an alternative we might use the impersonal *man*: *man könnte ausdehnen*; but better, because more idiomatic, would be the use of *sich lassen* + the **active** infinitive, which exactly corresponds to the English 'may' followed by the **passive**: e.g. 'this sentence may best be translated by the use of an infinitive' = *dieser Satz läßt sich am besten durch den Gebrauch eines Infinitivs übersetzen*. If we use *sich lassen*, the sentence runs: 'Es sind zwei oder drei Monate eine unbestimmte Zeit, die sich später unmerklich ausdehnen ließe'.

'to what length one pleases.' We might attempt to translate this on the same lines as the English, using as in the original a dependent clause. If we do this we shall have to be careful not to render 'to what length' word for word into German; *zu welcher Länge* is quite impossible. We should turn the phrase by saying 'as much as', *so viel*, or 'as long as', *solange*. For 'to please', *gefallen* is not suitable; *solange es einem gefällt* is clumsy and would not be used by a German; much better here would be the use of *mögen* and the impersonal *man*: *solange man möchte*, 'as long as one would like', and this, were no shorter or more idiomatic expression available, would be a reasonable rendering of the English. But there are in fact two expressions in German which render the English equally well and which are preferable on account of their brevity; these are *nach Belieben*, 'according to desire', and *beliebig*. If we use the former the rendering is: 'die sich später nach Belieben unmerklich ausdehnen ließe'.

'leave that to me.' Some different words which may be used to translate 'to leave' have been discussed in § 143, here we must use *überlassen*; *über* is a prefix which may either be separable or inseparable. Since *überlassen* is used metaphorically here we shall say 'überlaße das mir', and not 'laße das mir über' (for a note on prefixes see § 115).

The rendering for the whole of the section is then: 'Es sind zwei oder drei Monate eine unbestimmte Zeit, die sich später nach Belieben unmerklich ausdehnen ließe; überlaße das mir.'

(6) 'In the meantime you may be taking your measures as best you can. God bless you.'

The first sentence is quite straightforward in construction. 'In the meantime' might be translated in a variety of ways: *indessen, unterdessen, in der Zwischenzeit* all give the meaning correctly, but *mittlerweile* may be preferred to them because it corresponds better to 'in the meantime' as opposed to the more usual 'meanwhile'. 'you may be taking your measures': 'you may' might be translated either by *Du kannst* or *Du magst*; *Du magst*, which is rather politer, is the better of the two. The idiomatic expression 'to take measures' is commonly *Maßregeln* or *Maßnahmen treffen*; but both of these mean to take precautionary rather than preparatory measures, e.g. *die Polizei hat strenge Maßnahmen* or *Maßregeln gegen Taschendiebe getroffen*, 'the police have taken severe measures against pickpockets'. A word which has no precautionary idea is *die Anstalt*, 'the preparation', and here the correct phrase is *Anstalten treffen*. The sentence then runs: 'Mittlerweile magst Du Deine Anstalten treffen'.

'as best you can.' Here, as in the expression 'to what length one pleases', a literal translation is possible; there is nothing grammatically incorrect with *wie Du es am besten kannst*, but the sentence is obviously a word for word rendering of an English phrase and we should do well to avoid it for that reason, as well as on the general principle that short sentences should always if possible be replaced by adverbial phrases, e.g. 'when I arrived' = *bei meiner Ankunft*, not *als ich ankam*, etc. A clue to a possible alternative here is given by the phrase *am besten*; upon reflection we may remember that 'best' can be translated in two ways, either by *am besten* or *aufs beste*; *am besten* makes a comparison with the performance of others, *aufs beste* does not, e.g. *von den drei Schwestern tanzte die jüngste am besten*, 'of the three sisters the youngest danced best' (comparison with the performance of others): *sie tanzte aufs beste*, 'she danced extremely well'. *Aufs beste* would therefore be a possible translation here; but 'as best you can' is rather more emphatic in English than *aufs beste* is in German. We could obtain a more exact balance by using the word *vorteilhaft*, 'advantageous'— *aufs vorteilhafteste*. Alternatively to this we might abandon the use of *auf* altogether and say *so vorteilhaft wie möglich*, 'as advantageously as possible'; if we use the last rendering, which may be preferred to the others on the grounds of style, the whole sentence will run: 'Mittlerweile magst Du Deine Anstalten so vorteilhaft wie möglich treffen'.

'God bless you.' As in French the intimate mode of address is used towards the Deity. We must be careful then to use the correct imperative form (see § 103). The ordinary word for 'to bless' is *segnen*, and *Gott segne Dich* would be correct German, but an expression which is much commoner and which would probably be used here by a German is: *behüte Dich Gott*, 'God watch over you'.

The suggested rendering for the whole is:

Lord Chesterfield an seinen Sohn.

Blackheath,

den 15ten Juni, 1759.

Mein lieber Freund,

Dein Brief vom fünften, den ich gestern erhielt, hat mir große Freude bereitet, da er ganz eigenhändig geschrieben ist, obwohl er manche und, wie ich fürchte, wohlbegründete Klagen

über Deinen Krankheitszustand enthält. Du hast wohl getan,
Dir Luftveränderung zu verschaffen und ich hoffe, daß Dir diese
wohl tun wird. Deswegen möchte ich, daß Du nach dem 20sten
August an Lord Holderness schreibest, um ihn zu ersuchen, Dir
Deiner Gesundheit willen die Genehmigung zu einer zwei- oder
dreimonatigen Rückkehr nach England von Seiner Majestät zu
erbitten. Es sind zwei oder drei Monate eine unbestimmte Zeit,
die sich später nach Belieben unmerklich ausdehnen ließe;
überlaße das mir. Mittlerweile magst Du Deine Anstalten so
vorteilhaft wie möglich treffen. Behüte Dich Gott.

51. THE MAD TEA PARTY. i

The table was a large one, but the three were all crowded[1]
together at one corner. 'No room! No room!' they cried out
when they saw Alice coming[2]. 'There's[3] plenty[4] of room', said
Alice indignantly, and she sat down in[5] a large armchair at[5] one
end of the table.

'Have[6] some wine', the March Hare[7] said in an encouraging
tone.

Alice looked all round the table[8], but there was[3] nothing on
it[9] but tea.

'I don't see any wine', Alice remarked.

'There isn't[3] any', said the March Hare.

'Then it wasn't very civil of you to offer it', said Alice
angrily.

'It wasn't very civil of you to sit down without being invited[10].'

'I didn't know it was your table', said Alice, 'it's laid[11] for
a great many more than three[12].'

Alice in Wonderland

[1] 'crowded at', use *drängen* w. *in* (+ Dat.).   [2] Infinitive? § 187.
[3] Should *sein* or *geben* be used? § 206.   [4] Say 'still much room'.
[5] 'in', 'at'; the motion should be shown by the first Preposition, not the
second.   [6] Use *nehmen* st. not *haben*; for 'some' see § 66 (i).   [7] 'the
March Hare', *der Märzhase*.   [8] *Alice blickte um den Tisch herum*.
[9] See § 61 (ii).   [10] 'without being invited', *ungeladen*.   [11] 'to lay
the table', *den Tisch decken* w.   [12] Supply 'persons'.

52. THE MAD TEA PARTY. ii

'Suppose[1] we change the subject', the March Hare interrupted[2], yawning. 'I'm getting tired of this[3]. I vote[4] the young lady tells us a story.'

'I'm afraid[5] I don't know[6] one', said Alice, rather alarmed at the proposal.

'Then the Dormouse shall[7]', they both cried. 'Wake up, Dormouse!' And they pinched it on both sides at once[8].

The Dormouse opened his eyes. 'I wasn't asleep', he said in[9] a hoarse, feeble voice: 'I heard every word you were saying'.

'Tell us a story!' said the March Hare. 'Yes, please do[10]!' pleaded Alice. 'And be quick about it[11]', added the Hatter, 'or[12] you'll be asleep again before it's done[13].'

Alice in Wonderland

[1] For 'suppose we' see § 103 (ii); 'to change the subject', *von etwas anderem reden* w.   [2] When transitive 'to interrupt' = *unterbrechen*, when intransitive, as here, use *dazwischen-werfen* st.   [3] Translate 'I am beginning to have enough of it (*davon*)'.   [4] Use *vor-schlagen* st. 'to propose'.   [5] 'I am afraid'; use the Adverb *leider*, 'unfortunately'.   [6] *wissen* or *kennen*? § 142.   [7] Supply 'relate one'; this is a strong command; see § 103 (iii).   [8] Translate 'in both sides at once (*zugleich*)'.   [9] 'with hoarse, feeble voice'.   [10] Translate 'please do that'.   [11] 'to be quick about it', use *sich beeilen* w. 'to hurry up'.   [12] *sonst*, 'otherwise' (followed by inversion).   [13] *fertig*, 'finished'.

53. THE MAD TEA PARTY. iii

'Once upon a time[1] there were three little sisters', the Dormouse began in a[2] great hurry, 'and their names[3] were Elsie, Lacie and Tillie, and they lived at the bottom of a well—'

'What did they live on[4]?' said Alice, who always took a great interest[5] in questions of[6] eating and drinking.

'They lived on Treacle', said the Dormouse, after thinking[7] a minute or two.

'They couldn't have[8] done that, you know[9]', Alice gently remarked, 'they'd have been[10] ill.'

'So[11] they were', said the Dormouse, 'very ill.'

Alice tried a little to fancy to herself what[12] such an extra-ordinary way of living[13] would be like, but it puzzled her too much[14], so she went on: 'But why did they live at the bottom of the well?'

Alice in Wonderland

[1] Use *es*; see § 205.   [2] Omit 'a'; for the omission of the Article in a short phrase cf. *in kurzer Zeit*, 'in a short time'; *mit lauter Stimme*, 'in a loud voice', etc.   [3] Use *heißen* st.; see § 139.   [4] 'to live on', *leben* w. *von*; for 'on what' see § 18 (i).   [5] 'to take an interest in', *sich interessieren* w. *für*.   [6] Omit 'questions of'; for 'eating and drinking' use Nouns formed from Verbs; Gender of such Nouns? § 38 (ii). [7] Say 'after short thought (*die Überlegung*)'.   [8] Tense of *können*? § 135.   [9] 'you know', translate by *doch*; § 194 B (ii).   [10] Use *werden*, 'to become'; for the Past Conditional see § 104.   [11] *das wurden sie auch.*   [12] Translate 'how such an extraordinary way of life would be'.   [13] 'way of living', *die Lebensweise*.   [14] Translate *aber es machte ihr zu viel Kopfzerbrechen*; *sich den Kopf zerbrechen* = 'to wrack one's brains'.

54. THE MAD TEA PARTY. iv

The Dormouse again took[1] a minute or two to think about it, and then said, 'It was a treacle-well'.

'There's no such thing[2]!' Alice was beginning very angrily, but the Hatter and the March Hare went[3] Sh! Sh! and the Dormouse sulkily remarked, 'If you can't be civil you'd better[4] finish the story for yourself[5]'.

'No, please go on', Alice said very humbly. 'I won't interrupt you again. I dare say[6] there may be *one*.'

'One, indeed[7]!' said the Dormouse indignantly. However, he consented[8] to go on. 'And so these three little sisters—they were learning to draw, you know—'

'What did they draw?' said Alice, quite forgetting her promise.

'Treacle', said the Dormouse, without[9] considering[10] at all[11] this time.

Alice in Wonderland

[1] Say 'the Dormouse again reflected (*sich besinnen* st.) for a few minutes'. [2] *So was gibt es nicht!*   [3] *machen* w.   [4] Say 'so finish the story preferably (*lieber*) yourself'; for the use of *so* see § 94.   [5] Use *selber*, § 111.   [6] 'I dare say', translate by *wohl*; see § 202 (ii).   [7] *Wieso, eine!*   [8] 'to consent'; use *sich überreden lassen*, 'to allow oneself to be persuaded'.   [9] Construction after *ohne*? § 191.   [10] = 'reflecting'. [11] 'at all', *überhaupt*; see § 201.

55. A GOOD LESSON

A gentleman sent a salmon as a present to Swift; the servant
who carried it entered the doctor's study without[1] knocking and,
laying down the fish, said, 'My Master has sent you this salmon'.
'What! young man,' exclaimed the Dean, 'is this the way[2] you
always behave yourself? Let me teach you better[3]. Sit down
on this chair and I will show you how to[4] deliver such a message.'
The boy sat down and the Dean came up to the table and
making a low bow said, 'Sir, my Master presents his compliments[5] and begs your acceptance of this salmon'. 'Does he[6]?'
answered the boy, 'Here, John (after ringing[7]), take this honest
lad down to the kitchen and let[8] him have as much as he can
eat and drink; then send him up to me and I'll give him five
shillings[9].'

New London Jest Book

[1] Construction after *ohne*?   [2] 'do you always behave yourself thus
(*so*)?'   [3] 'to teach someone better', *jemand eines Besseren belehren* w.
[4] Translate 'how you should (*sollen*) deliver...'; *wie* + an Infinitive is
impossible.   [5] 'to present one's compliments', *vielmals grüßen lassen*;
see p. 3.   [6] 'Does he?' *Wirklich?*   [7] 'after he had rung'.   [8] 'let
him have as much...'; *lassen Sie ihm so viel geben...*, 'let give to him as
much...'.   [9] Use *die Mark*; Singular or Plural? § 46 (ii).

56. A CLEVER CONJURING TRICK

Two thieves were once having dinner with[1] a friend. One of
the thieves, who noticed that the other had secretly concealed
a silver spoon in his boot, said to his host as he was taking his
leave[2]: 'I must inform you that I am a conjurer; I should like[3],
before I go, to perform[4] one trick for you'. Thereupon he took
a silver spoon from the table, put it in his coat pocket and
cried: 'One[5], two, three!' Then he clapped his hands[6] and said:
'Now, you will find the silver spoon in the left boot of my friend
there'. And sure enough a spoon was found there. The conjurer
then departed with the other spoon in his pocket.

900 Anekdoten

[1] Preposition? § 165 (i).   [2] 'as he was taking his leave', use a Prepositional Phrase; see § 165 (ii).   [3] Verb of Mood? § 130 (ii).   [4] 'to
perform', here *zum besten geben*; 'for you', use the Dative, see p. 143.
[5] Not *ein*; see § 51.   [6] 'to clap hands', *in die Hände klatschen* w.

57. WHAT I SAID TO THE MILKMAN

One afternoon I heard a knock[1] at the door and found it was
the milkman. Mrs Doncaster (the laundress) was not there[2], so
I took in[3] the milk myself. The milkman is a very nice man,
and, by way of[4] making himself pleasant, said, rather com-
plainingly[5], that the weather kept[6] very dry. I looked at him
significantly and said, 'Ah, yes, of course[7] for your business you
must find it very inconvenient', and laughed.

He saw he had been caught[8] and laughed too. It was a very
old joke, but he had not expected it at that particular moment,
and on the top[9] of such an innocent remark.

S. Butler, *Notebooks*

[1] Translate 'I heard knocking (Infinitive? § 187) at the door'.   [2] *zugegen*,
'present'.   [3] 'to take in', use *an-nehmen* st. 'to accept'.   [4] 'by
way of', say 'in order to'.   [5] Translate 'in rather complaining tone'.
[6] Use *bleiben* st.   [7] 'of course' and 'for your business' should not both
precede the Verb; see § 75 (iii).   [8] *erwischt*.   [9] Translate 'and
after such an innocent remark into the bargain'.

58. A NEW MOVEMENT IN GERMANY

In the last ten years there has been founded among young
people in Germany a new movement which devotes itself in
summer to walking tours[1]. These so-called 'Wandervögel',
rucksack on back and lightly clad[2], wander in small or large
parties through the whole country. Every age and degree is
represented among them. As it is one of the chief objects[3] of
this movement to combine as many tours as possible with the
smallest possible[4] expense, there[5] have been built in most towns
inns[6] where dinner and bed[7] can be had in exchange for[8] a
small sum. The young German thus becomes well acquainted[9]
with his country and certainly gathers much useful experience.

[1] 'walking tours', *der Wandersport*.   [2] 'lightly clad', *leichtbekleidet*.
[3] 'the chief object', *der Hauptzweck*; cf. *die Hauptstraße*, 'the main street';
die Hauptsache, 'the essential thing', etc.   [4] Use *möglichst*; see § 34.
[5] Use *so*; see § 94.   [6] The German word is *die Jugendherberge*.
[7] 'Dinner and bed', *Abendessen nebst Nachtquartier*.   [8] 'in exchange
for', *gegen*.   [9] 'to become acquainted with', *kennen lernen* w.

59. THE UNLUCKY PROFESSOR

A professor at the University of Cologne used in his spare time to lay down rules for the weather. In this, however, he was very unfortunate, for the weather almost always turned out otherwise than he had prophesied. This annoyed him greatly. When therefore he learnt that a shepherd, who lived in a nearby village, always prophesied the correct weather, he determined to visit him and ask for his secret. The shepherd said to him without further ado: 'In Cologne there is a professor who also prophesies what the weather will be. I always say the opposite to what he prophesies and my prophecy turns out correctly'.

900 *Anekdoten*

60. A GOOD BARGAIN

An American who was touring in[1] Scotland took a fancy[2] to a handsome dog and tried his best[3] to persuade the owner to sell[4] it. The owner asked some questions, and on learning that it was the gentleman's intention to take 'Jock' to America, he decidedly refused to part with the dog. They were still arguing the matter when an Englishman came along[5], and he also made a bid for the dog, which, though less than the American's[6] offer, was at once accepted. After the Englishman had departed with the dog he had acquired[7], the Yankee turned to[8] the Scot and said, in a tone of annoyance[9]: 'Why[10], you said just now you wouldn't sell your dog'. 'I beg your pardon[11]', replied the canny Scot, 'my words were: I cannot part with him. Jock will be back sure enough in a day or two, but he could never swim[12] the Atlantic.'

[1] 'to tour in', *durchreisen* w.; Separable or Inseparable? § 116.   [2] 'to take a fancy to', *Gefallen* (m.) *finden an* (+Acc.).   [3] 'his best'; *mit allen Kräften*, 'with all his might'.   [4] Say 'to the sale of the same'.   [5] *daher*.   [6] 'than that of the American'; for 'that of' see § 14 (ii).   [7] *mit dem erstandenen Hund*, 'with the acquired dog'.   [8] *an*.   [9] Say 'in annoyed (*ärgerlich*) tone'.   [10] Use *ja*; see § 198 (i).   [11] *ich bitte um Verzeihung*.   [12] Use *durch-schwimmen* st.; *schwimmen* is intransitive.

61. THE PASSION PLAY IN OBERAMMERGAU

In the middle of the Thirty Years War the plague broke out in Germany, and those whom[1] war had spared fell victims[2] to this pestilence. Finally, Oberammergau, which lies deeply buried in the mountains, fell[3] a prey to it likewise and the inhabitants[4] hastened into the church, where they vowed to represent the life and sufferings of Christ if God would only free them from this terrible scourge. According to[5] the legend no further case of the plague occurred in the village and in the year 1631 the first passion play was performed there[6] in the churchyard. When, later on, passion plays in every country were banned by the pope, the people of Oberammergau[7] alone were allowed[8] to continue[9] their performances for the sake of the vow they had made[10].

[1] 'those whom', *wen*; § 14 (i), N.B.   [2] Translate 'fell a victim to...'.
[3] Translate 'Oberammergau also was afflicted (*heim-suchen* w.) by it'.
[4] Here *die Dorfbewohner*, 'the villagers'.   [5] In the sense of 'according to' *nach* usually follows the word it governs: *meiner Meinung nach*, 'in my opinion'; *der Zeitung nach*, 'according to the paper', etc.   [6] 'in the there (*dortig*) churchyard'; for *dortig* see p. 144.   [7] 'the people of Oberammergau', *die Oberammergauer*.   [8] 'to be allowed', use a Verb of Mood; see § 131 (i).   [9] Use *weiter halten* st. 'to go on holding'.
[10] Avoid a Relative Sentence (see § 185); 'to make a vow' = *eine Gelübde ab-legen* w.

62. THE ADVANCE[1] OF SCIENCE

Those who[2] formerly wished to find rest travelled into[3] the country for[4] recreation; to-day it is much more difficult, since the great progress which science has made in the realm of transport[5] has encroached on the country; soon there will be scarcely a single place to be found[6] where we can indulge in complete rest. Those who[2] a few years ago went for a walk only needed to evade horses or bicyclists; nowadays one ventures into the street at the peril of one's life[7]; private cars and lorries[8] of all sorts race past at full speed[9], motor-bicycles rattle by, and in order to make the noise complete[10], the whir of aeroplanes rushing[11] over the roofs is seldom absent[12].

¹ *die Fortschritte* (pl.); see § 215.   ² 'Those who', use one word.
³ *auf* (+Acc. since there is motion).   ⁴ Say 'to (*zu*) the recreation'.
⁵ 'in the realm of transport', *im Verkehrswesen*.   ⁶ Use the Active
Infinitive, § 192.   ⁷ 'at the peril of one's life', *mit Lebensgefahr*.
⁸ *Privat- und Kraftwagen*; for the use of the hyphen see p. 144.   ⁹ *mit
Blitzeseile*, 'with lightning speed'.   ¹⁰ 'to make complete', *vervoll-
ständigen* w.   ¹¹ Use *hinweg-sausen* w.   ¹² 'to be absent', here
fehlen w. 'to lack'.

63. THE BARON

It chanced, one November day, that the Baron had been
hunting[1] in the forest, and did not reach home till[2] nightfall.
There were[3] no guests with him for, as I hinted to you before,
the castle of[4] Arnheim seldom received[5] any[6] other than those
from whom its inhabitants hoped to gain augmentation of
knowledge. The Baron was seated alone in his hall, illuminated[7]
with torches. His one hand held a volume covered with characters
unintelligible to all save[8] himself. The other rested on the marble
table, on which was placed[9] a flask of Tokay wine. A page stood
in respectful attendance[10] near the bottom[11] of the large and
dim apartment, and no sound was heard[12] save that of the night
wind.

Scott, *Anne of Geierstein*

¹ 'to be hunting', *auf der Jagd sein*; 'to go hunting', *auf die Jagd gehen*;
jagen = 'to hunt' in the sense of 'to pursue', e.g. *der Hund jagt den Hasen*.
² 'not...till nightfall', *erst bei Einbruch der Nacht*; for *erst* see § 196.
³ Avoid *sein*; see § 207.   ⁴ Omit 'of'; cf. *die Stadt London*, 'the town
of London'; *die Insel Elba*, 'the Island of Elba', etc.   ⁵ *erhalten* or
empfangen? see p. 138 (2).   ⁶ Say 'any other except (*außer*) those from
whom'; for 'any' see § 66 (iii).   ⁷ Position of Past Participle? § 185.
⁸ Use *außer*; 'himself', *ihm* or *sich*? § 113.   ⁹ Use *sich befinden* st.;
the Reflexive Pronoun may precede the Subject; see § 77 (ii).   ¹⁰ 'to
stand in attendance', *zu Diensten stehen* st.   ¹¹ 'near the bottom',
am unteren Ende.   ¹² Avoid the Passive.

64. WHIPSNADE

A short time ago a zoological garden was laid out in England
after the pattern of the zoo at Stellingen in Germany, where all
the animals are kept in the open. At the moment this park
is still in its 'teens[1]' and it is hoped that the animals will
accustom themselves gradually to the variable English climate.

Most of the inmates[2] consist now of wolves, bears, buffaloes, foreign cattle and all sorts of stags and deer. In the summer three young lions are also to be seen[3]; these, however, are sent back to London in the winter, since at Whipsnade there is no warm accommodation[4] for tropical animals. The larger birds too, such as[5] storks, flamingos and so on[6], are obliged to change their quarters[7] in winter.

[1] 'in its teens', *in den Kinderschuhen*. [2] 'most of the inmates', say *der Hauptbestandteil*. [3] Passive or Active Infinitive? [4] Say 'there is a lack of hothouses'; for 'to lack' see § 152, *mangeln*. [5] 'such as', *wie*. [6] 'and so on', *und so weiter*. [7] 'to change quarters', use *über-siedeln* w. (literally 'to emigrate').

65. SHYLOCK

Shylock, the Jew, lived in Venice; he was a usurer, who had amassed an immense fortune by[1] lending money at high interest[2] to Christian merchants.

Shylock, being[3] a hard-hearted man, exacted the payment of the money he lent with such severity that he was much disliked by[4] all good men, and particularly by[4] Antonio, a young[5] merchant of Venice; and Shylock hated Antonio equally, because he used to lend money to people in distress, and would never take any interest for the money he lent. Therefore there was great enmity between this covetous Jew and the generous merchant, Antonio. Whenever Antonio met Shylock[6] on the Exchange he used to reproach[7] him with his usuries and hard dealings, which the Jew would bear with seeming[8] patience, while he secretly meditated revenge.

Lamb's *Tales from Shakespeare*

[1] Avoid the Present Participle; see § 186 (7). [2] 'at high interest', *zu hohen Zinsen*. [3] Say 'as Shylock had a heart of stone'. [4] Use *bei*. [5] This must stand in the Dative since it is in apposition to Antonio. [6] Say 'the Shylock'; the Definite Article is sometimes used to show that a person is well known. [7] See § 152, **vorwerfen**. [8] Say 'which he seemingly bore'.

66. A MAD SUMMER

After thirteen long weeks of work school was over at last, masters as well as pupils were looking forward to[1] the summer holidays and everyone scattered[2] hoping[3] for sunny days.

I had made arrangements[4] with two friends, to spend one half of the holidays with each. First I travelled to France in order to descend some rivers in a folding canoe[5], but incessant rain, sopping[6] ground and swollen rivers spoilt this[7] pleasure of which I am usually so fond.

So[8] I went to Germany in the hope of better weather and thought that I would be able to get plenty of bathing[9] and to make some fine expeditions in the mountains[10]. But it was a case of out of the frying pan into the fire[11]. Here it poured still harder, here the heavens were still greyer, the clouds still lower, and going out[12] was hardly to be thought of.

So[13] I passed this so-called summer in gazing[14] at the barometer and the other weather prophets. The weather reports were always announcing fine weather, the barometer was constantly rising, daily the swallows flew high over the roofs and the tree-frog sat eternally on the top rung of his ladder. I think they had[15] all gone mad.

[1] 'to look forward to', *sich freuen* w. (+ *auf* or *über*? § 163).   [2] Use *auseinander-stieben* st. 'to fly in different directions'.   [3] Say 'in expectation of sunny days'.   [4] Use *sich verabreden* w. *mit*, 'to make an appointment with'.   [5] 'folding canoe', *das Faltboot*.   [6] *durchgeweicht*, 'soaked through'.   [7] Say 'this otherwise (*sonst*) to me so dear pleasure'.   [8] Use *da* (§ 214), which is more graphic than *so*.   [9] Say 'to bathe much'.   [10] 'expeditions in the mountains', *Gebirgstouren*.   [11] Translate *doch ich kam vom Regen in die Traufe* ('the downpour'); for word-order after *doch* see § 70.   [12] Use the Infinitive as a Verbal Noun, *an ein Ausgehen war....*   [13] Say 'there passed this so-called summer in...', using *es* as the grammatical Subject; see § 205.   [14] 'in gazing at', *im Ausschauen nach*.   [15] Subjunctive or Indicative? § 182.

67. PHILIP II[1]

An honest tradesman entered a convent in which[2] Philip II of Spain was walking[3]. The tradesman admired many of the paintings hanging on the walls and asked the king, whom he

took[4] for one of the servants of the convent, to explain them
to him. Philip conducted him through the apartments and
acted the part that had been given to him to the best of his
ability[5]. At parting[6] the stranger shook him[7] by the hand, and
said, 'I am much obliged to you, my friend. I live at St Martin,
and my name is Michael Bombis; if you ever come my way[8],
and call upon me, a glass of good wine will be at your service[9]'.
'And my name', said the other, 'is Philip II; and if you will
call upon me at Madrid, I will give you a glass of as good[10]
wine.'

New London Jest Book

[1] For Titles see § 45.   [2] *worin*; see § 12.   [3] Use *spazieren gehen*;
see § 140 (i).   [4] 'to take for', *halten* st. *für*.   [5] 'to the best of his
ability', *aufs beste*; see p. 147.   [6] Use *bei*; see § 165 (ii).   [7] 'shook
to him the hand'.   [8] 'come my way', use *vorbei-kommen*, 'to pass'.
[9] 'to be at your service', *Ihnen zu Diensten stehen*.   [10] 'as good',
ebensogut; termination? § 22 III note.

68. NOTHING TO COMPLAIN ABOUT

A grim humour marks the story of the German spy, sentenced
to death, who had to walk some distance to the place where
the sentence was to be carried out. It was a cold, wet morning
and the German grumbled very much at having to walk so far.
His escort bore this patiently for some time, but at last the
soldiers got tired of the prisoner's continual and, as it seemed
to them, unreasonable complaints about the weather, and one
of them exclaimed: 'What have you to complain about? We've
got to walk back again!'

Quotable Anecdotes

69. THE MAN AND HIS FRIEND

A man quarrelled with his friend.
  'I have been much deceived[1] in you', said the man. And the
friend laughed at him and went away.
  A little later they both died, and came together before[2] the
Eternal Judge.
  'I find here some[3] record of a quarrel', said the Judge,
looking in his notes[4]. 'Which of you was in the wrong?'

'He was⁵', said the man. 'He spoke ill⁶ of me behind my back.'

'Did he so?' asked the Judge. 'And pray⁷ how did he speak about your neighbours?'

'Oh⁸, he had always a nasty tongue', said the man.

'And you chose him for⁹ your friend?' cried the Judge. 'My good fellow¹⁰, we have no use¹¹ here for fools.'

So the man was cast in the pit, while the friend laughed out aloud in the dark and remained there to be tried on¹² other charges.

Adapted from R. L. Stevenson

¹ 'to be deceived in', *sich täuschen* w. *in* (+ Dat.). ² Is this 'motion to' or 'motion at'? § 158. ³ Say 'a record of (*über*)'. ⁴ 'notes', *die Aufzeichnungen*. ⁵ Say 'he was it'; see § 61 (iii). ⁶ Use the Neuter of an Adjective; see § 28. ⁷ *bitte*. ⁸ Word-order after Exclamations? § 95. ⁹ *zu*. ¹⁰ *mein Lieber*. ¹¹ Say 'we cannot use (*brauchen* w.) fools here'. ¹² 'to be tried on', use *ab-urteilen* w. *wegen*.

70. AN UNEXPECTED ANSWER

During the war an English officer wished to ask¹ a favour of M. Briand and thought that it² would be well to flatter him first. 'These Bretons are a wonderful race!' he said, 'they make³ splendid soldiers—the best in the world; you yourself are a⁴ Breton, are you not?' The French minister nodded his assent⁵. 'Now how is⁶ it', continued the Englishman, 'that in a highly civilised⁷ country like France there are⁸ still such fanatical soldiers as these Bretons?' 'Quite simple', replied M. Briand, 'they are all peasants, ignorant creatures who know nothing of the world and believe everything they are told⁹. We just let them think¹⁰ that they are fighting against the English.'

¹ 'to ask a favour of someone', *jemand um eine Gunst ersuchen* w. ² Say 'he would do well to...'. ³ Translate 'out of them become splendid soldiers'. ⁴ With trades and nationalities the Article is omitted, e.g. *er ist Soldat, ich bin Engländer*, etc. ⁵ Say 'nodded assenting'. ⁶ Translate 'how comes it?' Insert a Particle; see § 193 (ii). ⁷ 'highly civilised', *hochkulturell*. ⁸ *geben* or *sein*? ⁹ Can the Passive be used here? § 108. ¹⁰ Translate 'We leave them in the belief that...'.

71. LUTHER AT WORMS. i

Having reached the town hall at last, Luther and those who accompanied him[1] were again prevented by the crowd from crossing the threshold. They cried, 'Make way[2]! Make way!' but no one moved. Upon this the Imperial soldiers by main force[3] cleared[4] a road, through which Luther passed[5]. As the people rushed forward to enter[6] with him, the soldiers kept them back with their halberds. Luther entered the interior of the hall: but even there every corner was crowded[7]. In the ante-chamber and embrasures of the windows[8] there were[9] more than five thousand spectators: Germans, Italians, Spaniards and others.

Merle D'Aubigné, *History of the Reformation*

[1] 'those who accompanied him', say 'his companions'.   [2] 'Make way!' *Platz da!*   [3] 'by main force', *mit Gewalt.*   [4] Use *öffnen* w.   [5] 'to pass', use *durch-schreiten* st. (+Acc.).   [6] Use *ein-dringen*, 'to press in'. [7] *dicht besetzt*, 'closely occupied'.   [8] 'embrasures of the windows', *die Fenstervertiefungen.*   [9] Use an alternative to *sein.*

72. LUTHER AT WORMS. ii

Luther advanced with difficulty[1]. At last, as he drew near the door which[2] was about to admit him into the presence of his judges, he met a valiant knight, the celebrated George of Frundsberg, who four years later, on the field[3] of Pavia, in[4] a great measure decided the captivity of the king of France. The old leader, seeing Luther pass, tapped him on the shoulder, and shaking his head, blanched[5] in many battles, said kindly: 'Poor monk[6]! Poor monk! Thou art now going to make a nobler stand[7] than I or any[8] other captains have made in the bloodiest of our battles! But if thy cause[9] is just, and thou art sure of it[10], go forward in God's name and fear nothing[11]! God will not forsake thee!'

Merle D'Aubigné, *History of the Reformation*

[1] 'with difficulty', *mit Mühe und Not.*   [2] Translate 'which ought to lead him before the face (*das Angesicht*) of his judges'.   [3] Here *das Schlachtfeld*, 'the battlefield'.   [4] Translate 'had the greatest share in the capture (*die Gefangennahme*) of the French king'.   [5] Translate 'the in many battles blanched head'.   [6] *Mönchlein! Mönchlein!* [7] *Ihr gehet einen edleren Gang,* 'you go a nobler way!' (use *Ihr* throughout). [8] *so mancher Führer,* 'so many a leader'.   [9] Here, *die Sache*, 'the affair'; *die Ursache* = 'the cause of material happenings'.   [10] 'of it', *derer*; see § 3 (iv).   [11] Say 'and do not be afraid (*sich fürchten* w.)!'

73. THE MODERN HOME

My brother, who has[1] previously been satisfied with his gramophone and who has spent an enormous amount of money in the purchase of gramophone records, has now had[2] a wireless installed in his room. By means of this[3] he is enabled[4] to hear without any special expense the finest concerts, the best singers, and every kind of news from the daily weather report to[5] the latest political items[6]. Fortunately he has procured a number of ear-phones, so that those who are not interested are not disturbed as is usually the case with[7] a loudspeaker.

[1] Omission of Auxiliary? § 209; 'to be satisfied with', *sich begnügen* w. *mit*.
[2] Use *lassen*; § 188. [3] 'by means of this', *hierdurch*. [4] Say 'the opportunity is given to him.' [5] *bis* + a Preposition; see § 166.
[6] 'the latest item', use *die Neuigkeit*. [7] *bei*.

74. A COMPROMISE

General Spears once told this story of the Peace Conference[1]. A meeting of the representatives of the five great powers[2] had lasted a whole morning. Punctually at 12 o'clock, M. Clemenceau, who always lunched[3] at that hour, rose and announced that the meeting was adjourned, adding, 'The question remains[4], at what time[5] we shall meet[6] this afternoon'. Signor Orlando, the Italian representative, requested that the meeting should[7] not be too soon after lunch as he liked[8] to take a little rest[9]; 'And[10] not too late', said Mr Lansing, the American, 'I must have some rest before dinner'. 'Well, gentlemen[11]', said Clemenceau, 'the meeting will take place at 3 o'clock. Signor Orlando will then be able to sleep before the conference, Mr Lansing after the conference and Mr Balfour and myself during it[12].'

[1] 'the Peace Conference', *die Friedenskonferenz*. [2] 'the great power', *die Großmacht*. [3] Use *essen* st. [4] Say 'it asks itself now'.
[5] *um wieviel Uhr*. [6] Reflexive? § 147 (ii). [7] Use *mögen*, which is politer than *sollen*; Mood? [8] Make use of *gern*; see § 144 (iii).
[9] 'to take a rest', *sich aus-ruhen* w. [10] Insert a Particle; see § 198 (i).
[11] 'gentlemen', *meine Herren*. [12] Use *derselbe*; see § 15.

75. ALICIA AUDLEY TO HER COUSIN
ROBERT AUDLEY

Audley Court.

My dear Robert, How cruel of you to run away[1] to that horrid St Petersburg before the hunting season[2]! I have heard that people lose their noses[3] in that disagreeable climate, and, as yours is rather a long one, I should[4] advise you to return before the severe weather sets in. What sort of a person is this young Mr Talbot? If he is very agreeable, you may[5] bring him home as soon as you return from your travels. Lady Audley tells[6] me to request you to secure her a set of sables. You are not to consider the price, but to be sure[7] that they are the handsomest that can be obtained[8]. Papa is perfectly absurd[9] about his new wife, and she and I cannot get[10] on together at all; not that[11] she is disagreeable to[12] me, for, as far as that goes[13], she makes herself agreeable[14] to everyone. Believe me to be[15], my dear Robert, your affectionate cousin[16].

Miss Braddon

[1] Use *fort-fahren* st. 'to travel away'.   [2] Say 'before the fox-hunting (*die Fuchsjagd*) begins'.   [3] 'the nose'.   [4] = 'should like to'. [5] Which Verb of Mood? § 131 (ii).   [6] Say 'asks me to commission (*auf-tragen* st. + Dat.) you to...'.   [7] Use *sich versichern* w.   [8] Insert a Particle; see § 201.   [9] 'is perfectly absurd about', translate *ist ganz vernarrt in* (+Acc.); cf. *verliebt in*, § 160.   [10] 'to get on together', *miteinander aus-kommen* st.   [11] *nicht als ob* followed by the Subjunctive.   [12] *gegen*.   [13] *was das betrifft*.   [14] Say 'she is the friendliness itself to...'.   [15] 'believe me to be', *mit herzlichem Gruß*. [16] *Deine Dich liebende Cousine.*

76. THE WEEKLY MARKET

This morning after breakfast we went to see the weekly market, which is held in the old square at the doors of the cathedral. The square is big, and yet not big enough for all the people who gather there. Even the pavements are covered with stalls, and peasant women sit on the steps of the old houses and close up against the cathedral walls. Mr Heriot and I stopped to buy some roses, and we got separated from the others, so we went on to the cathedral steps to look for them. The sight from there was a pretty one, for the women mostly wore bright dresses and red handkerchiefs on their heads; and the stalls and baskets were still filled with fruit and vegetables and flowers. There was a great deal of noise and movement, and it was very hot. 'Let us go into the cathedral', said Mr Heriot. We only stayed five minutes and enjoyed the twilight and the coolness. Then we came out, and stood on the steps again, and waited there a little.

77. THE WARTBURG

Deep in the Thuringian forest stands a famous castle whose[1] battlements tower far above the tops of the beech trees and whose[1] walls have witnessed a[2] large share of German history. Here in the Wartburg 'the minstrels' war[3]' took place which Wagner immortalised in his *Tannhäuser*. Here too lived Saint Elisabeth, and a few centuries later here[4] dwelt the famous reformer Martin Luther, who was offered[5] a place of refuge[6] by the Kurfürst of Saxony. In those small rooms, which are preserved in the same condition to this day[7], Luther completed his greatest work, the translation of the Bible. The visitor is still shown[5] there the inkstain, which, according to the legend, is said[8] to have been made when 'Junker Jörg' threw the inkpot at the Devil's head.

[1] For the Genitive of the Relative see § 9.   [2] Translate 'whose walls hide (*bergen* st.) a large part...'.   [3] 'the minstrels' war', *der Sänger-krieg*.   [4] Two Adverbial phrases cannot stand at the head of the Sentence; see § 75 (iii).   [5] Can the Passive be used with Verbs taking the Dative? § 108.   [6] 'place of refuge', *das Versteck*.   [7] 'to this day', *bis zum heutigen Tage*.   [8] Use a Verb of Mood; see § 128 (iv).

78. KING[1] HAROLD'S SAGAS

One summer a young man came to the court of King[1] Harold and was received there because he promised to tell sagas when-ever[2] he was requested to do so. When Christmas came near[3], the youth looked dejected, and the king thought that this was because he could find[4] nothing more to tell during the long winter evenings. When the king asked his guest why he seemed so little joyous, the young man answered, 'I have only one saga left, and I dare not tell that here, for it is[5] about your own adventures'. 'That is the saga I should most like to hear', said the king, and commanded him to make it so long[6] that it would last over[7] the Christmas festival. Never before had such stories been heard within those walls. The king, however, showed neither pleasure nor anger, and when on the sixteenth day the saga was finished, he had[8] the youth called before him[9] and inquired whether he was not curious to know[10] if[11] the king was content. 'I was afraid to ask about that', was the reply. 'I like it very well', said the king, 'but I want[12] to know how you succeeded in discovering my deeds.'

[1] For inflexion of Titles see § 44. *(auf-fordern* w.) him to it *(dazu)'.* [4] Say 'find no further *(weiter)* tales'. concern'; see § 163. [6] 'to make long', *aus-dehnen* w. see § 166. [8] *lassen*; see § 188. *erfahren* st. 'to find out'. [11] *wenn* or *ob?* § 130 (ii), N.B.
[2] Say 'whenever one requested [3] 'to come near', use *nahen* w. [5] Use *sich handeln* w. *um,* 'to [7] *bis über;* [9] *ihn* or *sich?* § 113. [10] Use [12] For 'want' see

79. THE FOREST GOES TO SLEEP

From now on winter[1] advanced with giant strides[2]. Autumn storms[2] came which whistled in so wild a way that the withered leaves fell down terrified from the branches, and[3] whirled[4] about in[5] the air, like an entire army of bright hunted butterflies.

So gradually the trees became bare. Only the fir trees were able to preserve their needles. For they have really quite small leaves which need very little[6] food, even in summer.

A great number of the oak leaves and the beech leaves[7] now said: 'We too have such beautiful brown weatherproof little[8] coats, that they will certainly protect us! We will remain all[9] the winter through, whatever happens[10]'.

And they really did remain there.

On the autumn storms followed, however, a whole series[11] of still days, days in which nothing was to be seen but mist. Then the wood went slowly to sleep.

¹ The Definite Article is required with days, months, seasons, etc., e.g. **am**
Samstag, **im** **Januar**, **im** **Sommer**, etc.   ² One word in German:
'giantstrides', 'autumnstorms'.   ³ *daß* is understood after *und*;
word-order?   ⁴ *drehen* w.; 'about', *umher* or *herum*? § 213.   ⁵ Is this
'motion at'? § 158.   ⁶ Is *wenig* declined in the singular? § 62.   ⁷ *der*
Eichen- und Buchenblätter.   ⁸ Translate by a Diminutive; see § 38 (i).
For 'coat' use *der Mantel*, 'the cloak'.   ⁹ Should *all* or *ganz* be used?
§ 58 (ii); 'through'=*hindurch*.   ¹⁰ Insert a Verb of Mood; § 130 (i).
¹¹ Say 'a whole row (*Reihe* f.)'.

80. THE RAIN. i

The rain began to come down in torrents¹ and a man, who had
been strolling down one of London's main² streets, reached the
shelter of a doorway just in time³. There he paused⁴ to watch
the passers-by hurrying in every direction until his attention
was caught⁵ by a young girl who, surprised⁶ like himself by the
rain, did not seem to know which way⁷ to turn. Her mind
once made up⁸ she ran as fast as she could to the doorway where
the man was standing and in her hurry nearly knocked⁹ him
over. He excused himself gallantly and the two soon fell¹⁰ into
a conversation.

¹ 'to come down in torrents', *in Strömen regnen* w.   ² 'main street',
use a compound word, see Prose 58, note 3.   ³ 'just in time', *gerade*
noch zur richtigen Zeit.   ⁴ Use *stehen bleiben*; see § 150 (ii).   ⁵ Use
ab-lenken w. *auf*, 'to turn to'.   ⁶ 'surprised' must stand at the end
of its clause: 'like himself (*er*) by the rain surprised'.   ⁷ Say 'whither
she **should** turn'; cf. *ich weiß nicht wie ich es tun sollte*, 'I do not know
how to do it'.   ⁸ 'her mind once made up', translate *plötzlich ent-*
schlossen.   ⁹ 'to knock over', *über den Haufen rennen* st.   ¹⁰ Say
'a conversation soon developed between the two'.

81. THE RAIN. ii

'The weather this summer has been awful', he remarked. 'Oh,
I don't complain of the weather, in fact I love the rain.' 'But
surely you can't mean that¹; one loves the sun, warmth, gaiety,
not rain, cold and melancholy—especially when one is young
and pretty.' The girl turned her head away. 'One can be at
the same time young and sad', she murmured. 'But if you are
unhappy there² must be³ some reason for it; won't you tell me

what it is?' 'Yes, there is a reason, I suppose[4], but what is the use[5] of talking about it?' 'Do[6], please, tell me; I am old enough[7] to be your father!' And at length after much persuasion[8] he learnt her story.

[1] *das ist doch nicht Ihr Ernst.*   [2] Insert *so*; see § 94.   [3] Insert a Particle; see § 198 (i).   [4] 'I suppose'; use a Particle; see § 202 (ii).   [5] 'what is the use of', *was nützt es* (+ Infin.).   [6] Translate 'but please tell it me'.   [7] Say 'according to the age I could be your father'; *nach* must follow the noun.   [8] *nach vielem Zureden.*

82. THE RAIN. iii

She was, it appeared[1], an orphan, who up till[2] a year ago had[3] lived happily with her only brother and had found in her love for him a consolation for the loss of her parents. He in his turn[4] had loved her dearly and had showered[5] on her all the gifts that her heart could desire. But a year ago he had died and even on his death-bed he had thought[6] of her and had given her a beautiful pearl necklace which she had worn night and day ever since. As she finished her story she raised her hand involuntarily to her neck. 'Oh[7]!' she cried in dismay, 'My necklace! it is gone[8], it is gone! I must have[9] dropped it somewhere in the street.' And she darted out[10] into the streaming rain with[11] the man at her heels.

[1] 'it appeared', *anscheinend*, 'apparently'.   [2] For 'up till' see § 199 (i).   [3] The Auxiliary may be omitted; see § 209.   [4] 'in his turn', *seinerseits*.   [5] Use *überhäufen* w. 'to heap on'; is this Prefix separable or inseparable? § 116.   [6] Use *gedenken* st. (+ Gen.); for 'of her' see § 4.   [7] Supply *um Gottes willen!*   [8] *weg.*   [9] Word-order? § 124 (ii).   [10] Use *hinaus-stürzen* w.   [11] Say 'whereupon the man followed her on the heels (*auf den Fersen*)'.

83. THE RAIN. iv

Ten minutes later the pair halted from[1] exhaustion; their search had been in vain. 'I know it would not be the same thing', he ventured, almost as near tears[2] as she was[3], 'but if you would allow me to replace the necklace....' 'Oh no! You are too kind!' 'But please, I insist[4]....'

After having given[5] a false address the girl returned home. A young fellow greeted her on the doorstep with the words 'Well, my dear[6]?' 'Wonderful[7]', she replied, 'that makes 32 necklaces and 4 bracelets, thanks to the rain and my story of the dead brother. In another[8] month we will be able to marry and fit out[9] a little jeweller's shop in some[10] provincial town free and for nothing[11].' 'Yes', grinned the young man, 'provided it rains!'

[1] Preposition? § 169 (ii).   [2] 'to be near tears', *dem Weinen nahe sein*.
[3] Say 'as the girl'.   [4] Supply 'on it'.   [5] 'to give', use *an-geben* st.
[6] 'my dear', *Schatz*.   [7] *großartig*.   [8] *ander* or *noch ein*? § 59.
[9] 'to fit out', *sich an-legen* w.   [10] = 'some or other'; see § 66 (iii).
'provincial town', *Provinzstadt*.   [11] 'free and for nothing', *umsonst*.

84. JANE EYRE AT SCHOOL

A quarter of an hour passed before lessons again began, during which the school-room was in a glorious tumult; for that space of time it seemed to be permitted to talk louder and more freely, and the girls used their privilege. The whole conversation ran on the breakfast, which one and all abused roundly. Poor things! it was the sole consolation they had. Miss Miller was now the only teacher in the room; a group of great girls standing about her spoke with serious and sullen gestures. I heard the name of Mr Brocklehurst pronounced by some lips; at which Miss Miller shook her head disapprovingly; but she made no great effort to check the general wrath; doubtless she shared in it. A clock in the school-room struck nine; Miss Miller left her circle, and standing in the middle of the room cried:

'Silence! go to your seats!'   Ch. Brontë, *Jane Eyre*

85. THE ISLAND OF[1] SARK

Every year thousands[2] of trippers visit this small island. The chief attraction lies[3] in the wild and rocky coast with its beautiful caves and pools. But there is also a charming valley which opens out[4] into a fine bay. Here the trees, sheltered from[5] the strong west winds, grow tall and straight and the bushes are so luxuriant that you could almost imagine yourself in the South. The three hundred inhabitants, who speak a curious language made up[6] of English and French, earn their bread by fishing[7] and farming. In[8] fine weather Sark is a Paradise, especially for those who like fresh air and bathing; but when the storms sweep[9] in from the Atlantic Ocean, it becomes[10] a prison and in winter the inhabitants are often cut off[11] from the mainland for many days on end.

[1] Since these words are in apposition *von* is not required.   [2] Noun or Numeral? § 52.   [3] Use *bestehen* st. *aus*, 'to consist in'.   [4] *aus-laufen* st. *in*, 'to run out into'.   [5] Preposition? § 169 (i).   [6] 'made up of', *gemischt aus*; position of Past Participle?   [7] 'by fishing and farming', *durch Fischerei und Landwirtschaft*.   [8] *bei*; cf. *bei einem schönen Frühlingstag*, 'on a fine spring day'.   [9] 'to sweep in', *herein-fegen* w.   [10] When *werden* is used in the sense of 'to turn into' it is often followed by *zu*, e.g. *es wird zu Staube, zu Wasser*, etc., 'it becomes dust, water, etc.'   [11] 'to cut off', *ab-trennen* w.

86. CHARLES XII'S TREASURE

In the middle of a large gloomy pine wood there[1] lay in dreamy silence[2] a small lake in which, according to the legend, Charles XII of Sweden was said[3] to have buried a part of his treasure. One day some peasants of the neighbouring estate found three Swedish coins. From that moment[4] on the treasure was the only subject of conversation[5], and finally the peasants asked the owner of the estate[6] to be allowed[7] to raise it. Thus it happened that the owner, with a dozen farm hands, went[8] to the lake armed with ropes and other implements. After three hours'[9] work they succeeded at length in finding something enormously heavy and everyone thought[10] they would soon see[10] a case of gold coins or valuables before their eyes. One more mighty heave and at the edge[11] of the pond appeared a huge, formless mass, which proved[12] to be the carcase of a bear. Master Bruin had probably had his winter sleep[13] on the ice, and surprised by a sudden thaw had[14] disappeared in[15] the depths and been drowned.

[1] Should *es* be omitted? § 205.   [2] 'in dreamy silence', *still und verträumt*.   [3] 'was said to', use a Verb of Mood; § 128 (iv). For 'to bury' use here *versenken* st. 'to submerge'.   [4] 'from that moment',

von nun an.   ⁵ Say 'one spoke only of',   ⁶ 'the owner of the estate', *der Gutsherr.*   ⁷ Use *dürfen*; Infinitive with or without *zu*? § 120.   ⁸ Use an alternative to *gehen*; see § 140 (iii).   ⁹ Translate 'three hours' by an Adjective; see § 55.   ¹⁰ The Subjects of the two Sentences are the same, so we can say, 'thought...to see'.   ¹¹ 'at the edge', *auf das Ufer.*   ¹² 'to prove to be', *sich erweisen* st. *als*, 'to show itself as'.   ¹³ 'to have his winter sleep', *seinen Winterschlaf halten* st. ¹⁴ May this Auxiliary be omitted? § 209.   ˙   ¹⁵ Motion is implied.

87. LORD BYRON TO GOETHE

You must therefore accept my most sincere acknowledgments¹ in prose—and in hasty prose too²; for I am³ at present on my voyage to Greece once more, and surrounded⁴ by hurry and bustle, which hardly allow a moment even to gratitude and admiration to express themselves. I sailed from Genoa some days ago, was driven back by a gale of wind, and have since sailed again and arrived here, Leghorn, this morning, to receive on board some Greek passengers for their struggling country. Here also I found your lines and Mr Sterling's⁵ letter; and I could not have had⁶ a more favourable omen, a more agreeable surprise, than a word of Goethe written by his own hand.

I am returning to Greece to see if I can be of any little use⁷ there: if⁸ ever I come back, I will pay⁹ a visit to Weimar to offer the sincere homage of one of the many¹⁰ millions of your admirers.

¹ Use the Singular; see § 215.   ² See § 203 (i).   ³ Alternative to *sein*? § 207.   ⁴ Say 'and am so harassed (*drängen* w.) and driven (*treiben* st.) that hardly a moment remains to me...'.   ⁵ See § 44, N.B. ⁶ Perfect Infinitive? § 135.   ⁷ Say 'if I can in any way (*irgendwie*) make myself somewhat (*etwas*) useful'.   ⁸ Alternative to *wenn*? § 89. ⁹ Use *ab-statten* w., which is more formal than *machen*.   ¹⁰ *viel* has the weak termination when preceded by the Article; so here, *der viele**n**.*

88. THE LAST STRAW¹

The barrister declared in addressing² the jury on behalf³ of the accused that the whole of the evidence⁴ in the case—with the exception of that⁵ of the ex-prisoner⁶ himself and of the watch which was found in the past month—had been in the hands of the police since March last year.

'Can you imagine', continued the barrister, 'such a man who knows that he is[7] under suspicion of murder, who knows that the police are only too ready to bring against him the witness[8] of his fellow[9] prisoners, can you imagine him picking up[10] a couple of complete strangers[11] and trusting[12] them in a conversation with an account of how he committed the terrible murder?'

'Gentlemen of the jury[13]', said the barrister heatedly, 'it is pure madness! It is unbelievable. That is the last straw[1]. It is the last weight that is thrown on the scales to turn[14] them against the accused.'

[1] *das fehlte gerade noch.*   [2] Say 'in his address to (*die Anrede an*)'.
[3] Say 'in his defence of'.   [4] 'evidence', here *das Beweismaterial*, 'the proofmaterial'.   [5] 'that of'; § 14 (ii).   [6] 'the ex-prisoner', *der ehemalige Gefangene*.   [7] Say 'stands'; see § 207. 'suspicion of murder', *Mordverdacht*.   [8] Here *die Zeugenaussage*.   [9] For 'fellow' see Prose 43, note 5.   [10] 'that he picks up (*auf-gabeln* w.)'.   [11] Termination? *der Unbekannte* is an Adjective used as a Noun; see § 27.   [12] 'trusts to them an account how.'   [13] *meine Herren Geschworenen.*   [14] 'to turn', *den Ausschlag geben.*

89. ZADIG'S JUDGMENT

After having given[1] away his daughter in marriage a famous merchant of[2] Babylon had[3] divided his property between his two sons and had left[4] in addition a gift of thirty thousand gold pieces to that son[5] who was considered[6] to have loved him best. After his death the elder built him[7] a tomb and the second increased the dowry of his sister with a part of his own inheritance; wherefore everyone said: 'The elder loves his father best, the younger prefers his sister; the thirty thousand crowns belong to the elder. Zadig had the two sons brought before him, one[8] after the other. He said to the elder: 'Your father is not dead at all, he has recovered from his illness and is returning to Babylon'. 'God be praised!' he replied; 'but all the same that tomb cost me a lot of money[9]!' Zadig then said the same to the younger. 'Thank God[10]!' replied the latter, 'I will restore everything to my father, but I should like him to let[11] my sister keep what I gave[12] her.' 'You will restore nothing at all', said Zadig, 'and you will have the thirty thousand crowns into the bargain; for it is[13] you who love your father best.'

Voltaire, *Zadig*

¹ 'to give away in marriage', *heiraten* or *verheiraten*? § 146.   ² *aus*; cf.
ich komme aus Paris, 'I come from Paris', etc.   ³ Use the Imperfect
to avoid the repetition of *hatte*.   ⁴ *hinterlassen* st.; Inseparable? § 116.
⁵ Say 'to him who...'.   ⁶ For 'consider' use *sollen*; 'was said to
have'.   ⁷ Case? § 175.   ⁸ In apposition to 'him'; case?   ⁹ 'a lot
of money', *viel Geld*.   ¹⁰ *Gott sei Dank*, 'to God be thanks'.   ¹¹ 'I should
like that he lets (use *lassen*) my sister keep that which...'.   ¹² Since
this is in conversation the Perfect should be used; see § 218.   ¹³ 'you
are it who...'.

90. THE SICK MAN AND THE FIREMAN

There was once a sick man in a burning house, to whom there
entered a fireman.

'Do not save me', said the sick man. 'Save those who are
strong.'

'Will you kindly tell me why?' inquired the fireman, for he
was a civil fellow.

'Nothing could be fairer', said the sick man. 'The strong
should be preferred in all cases, because they are of more service
in the world.'

The fireman pondered a while, for he was a man of some
philosophy. 'Granted', said he at last, as a part of the roof fell
in; 'but, for the sake of conversation, what would you lay down
as the proper service of the strong?'

'Nothing can possibly be easier', returned the sick man; 'the
proper service of the strong is to help the weak.'

Again the fireman reflected, for this excellent fellow never
hurried. 'I could forgive you being sick', he said at last, as a
portion of the wall fell in, 'but I cannot bear you being such
a fool.' And with that he heaved up his fireman's axe, for he
was eminently just, and split the sick man's skull.

Adapted from R. L. Stevenson

91. WELLINGTON AFTER THE BATTLE OF¹ WATERLOO

I met Lord Arthur Hill in the ante-room below, who, after
shaking hands, told me I could not go up to the Duke, as he
was then occupied in writing his despatch; but as I had been

invited, I of course proceeded. The first thing[2] I did, of course, was to put out my hand and congratulate the Duke upon his victory. He made a variety[3] of observations in his short, natural, blunt way, but with the greatest gravity all the time, and without the least approach to anything like[4] triumph, or joy. 'It has been a damned serious business[5]', he said, 'Blücher and I have lost 30,000 men. Blücher lost 14,000 on Friday night, and got so damnably licked[6] I could not find him on Saturday morning; so I was obliged[7] to fall back and to regain[8] my communications with him.'

Adapted from The Creevey Papers

[1] bei.   [2] For 'thing' use a Neuter termination; the Relative Pronoun cannot be omitted; should das or was be used here? § 19 (i).   [3] 'a variety of', eine Reihe von.   [4] Say 'which sounded like'.   [5] eine verdammt ernste Sache.   [6] verhauen st.   [7] Use an alternative to a Verb of Mood; see § 137.   [8] auf-nehmen st.

92. AN UNPLEASANT WELCOME

Paris, Aug. 20th.

A death sentence passed in 1919 on a certain Mr Mühler, a citizen of the United States, for[1] holding intelligence with the enemy during the war was revoked by the Paris military court to-day.

Mr Mühler had emigrated to America in 1872 to avoid conscription in Germany, and had never returned to Europe until[2] this year. He then visited his old home in[3] Alsace, and was surprised to find that he had been condemned to death as a[4] spy during his absence. He immediately went to the police to ask for an explanation, and was kept under arrest until information[5] confirming[6] the facts of his life during the last 58 years had been received from his present home in California. It appears that a Frenchman, accused of holding intelligence with the enemy from Switzerland[7], had[8] had identity papers forged in Mühler's name. The Frenchman was tried in October 1919 and was condemned to death.

The law did not permit the military court to give the real Mühler any damages[9] for the prejudice which the mistake had caused him, or for his imprisonment.

¹ Say 'because he had entered into communication with (*in Verbindung treten* st. *mit*) the enemy'. ² *bis zu*; for 'this' use the Adjective formed from *jetzt*; see p. 144. ³ *im Elsaß*. ⁴ Omit 'a'. ⁵ *Auskünfte* (Pl.). ⁶ This Relative Sentence is too long to be placed inside another Sentence (§ 96), so write 'until information from his home had been received which confirmed, etc.' ⁷ *von der Schweiz aus*. ⁸ Use *lassen*; Position of Auxiliary? § 124. ⁹ *Entschädigung* (Sing.); see § 215.

93. THE TWO MATCHES

A traveller riding through the woods of California dismounted to smoke a pipe. But when he felt¹ in his pocket he found he had only two matches. He struck² the first but it would not light².

'Here is a pretty state of things³!' said the traveller. 'Dying⁴ for a smoke, and only one match, and that will certainly not light. Was⁵ there ever a creature so unfortunate? And yet', thought the traveller, 'suppose⁶ I light⁷ this match and smoke my pipe and shake out the ash here on the grass—the grass might⁸ catch fire, and while I put out the flames in front, they would evade me and seize on⁹ that oak over there; how would the wind carry the flames through this inflammable forest! I hear in a moment the roar of the wind and fire¹⁰; I see myself gallop for my life; I see this pleasant forest burn for days; the cattle will be burnt¹¹, the springs dried up, the farmers ruined and their children turned¹² out on the world.

'How much hangs¹³ on this moment!'

With that he struck the match and it missed fire¹⁴.

'Thank God!' said the traveller and put¹⁵ his pipe in his pocket.

Adapted from R. L. Stevenson

¹ *greifen* st. ² *an-zünden* w. 'to strike'; *brennen* st.='to light' (i.e. to burn). ³ *eine schöne Bescherung*. ⁴ Say 'a violent longing for (*das Verlangen nach*) a pipe'. ⁵ Should *es* be dropped after *geben*? § 206, N.B. ⁶ *angenommen daß*. ⁷ = 'strike'. ⁸ Here *könnte*; § 133. ⁹ *erfassen* st. ¹⁰ *das Brausen des Windes und das Tosen des Feuers*. ¹¹ Use *verbrennen* st. 'to burn up'. ¹² 'to turn out on', *hinaus-werfen* st. *in*. ¹³ Use *abhängen* st.; see § 152. ¹⁴ 'to miss fire', *nicht brennen*. ¹⁵ See § 148 (iv).

SCENES FROM THE LIFE OF FREDERICK THE GREAT

I

94. FREDERICK'S FIRST TUTOR

At[1] the siege of Stralsund Frederick William I, King of Prussia, was much struck[2] by a young French nobleman named Duhan, who courageously exposed himself to every danger. The king had the officer presented to him[3] in the trenches and soon afterwards (in 1716) appointed[4] him tutor of the young crown prince, the[5] future Frederick the Great. Duhan, then[6] at the age of 31, was one of those distinguished officers such as[7] are frequently found in the eighteenth century: brave, learned and extremely well-bred[8]. For him as Calvinist and Refugee the world had no traditional limits; he was a broad-minded cosmopolitan. It was the task of this talented man to teach[9] the crown prince how to read maps[10], the history of the last hundred years, Biblical history and above all arithmetic.

[1] 'on the occasion of'; Preposition?   [2] Use *auffallen*; see § 152.
[3] This refers to the Subject of the Sentence. Should the Reflexive Pronoun be used?   [4] 'appointed him to (*zu*) the tutor.'   [5] Stands in apposition to 'prince'; case?   [6] *damals*, 'at that time'; for 'at the age of 31' use the Adjective formed from *das Jahr*; see § 55.   [7] 'such as', *wie*.   [8] *weltmännisch*.   [9] If we use *lehren*, what will be the case of the Indirect Object? § 173.   [10] Avoid a Dependent Clause by means of the Noun *das Kartenlesen*, 'map-reading'.

II

95. FREDERICK'S EDUCATION

Frederick William was accustomed to leave[1] nothing to chance, and he settled the course of his son's day[2] from one minute to another.

On week-days the prince had to[3] get up at 6 o'clock; as soon as he was out of bed he had to[3] fall on his knees and say[4] his morning prayer, then he dressed quickly and washed his[5] hands and face, but not with soap. While he was having his hair dressed⁶, he was⁷ to take tea and breakfast. At 6.30 the teacher and the domestics entered; a prayer and a chapter out of the Bible were read⁸ and a hymn was sung. From 7 to 10.45 were lessons⁹. After that the prince quickly washed his face and hands, the latter with soap this time, put on his coat and went to the king, with whom he stayed till 2 o'clock. Then the lessons were resumed¹⁰ till 5 o'clock. From 5 o'clock until he went to bed was play-time¹¹ for the prince, he could do what he liked¹² 'as long as¹³ it was not against God'. At 10.30 he had to be in bed.

¹ Here *überlassen* st.   ² 'the course of day', *der Tageslauf*.   ³ Verb of Mood? § 137.   ⁴ *sprechen* st.   ⁵ Do not use *sein*; see § 8.
⁶ Avoid a Dependent Clause; § 165 (ii).   ⁷ Use *sollen*; § 128.
⁸ Use *verlesen* st.   ⁹ Say 'lasted the instruction (*der Unterricht*)'.
¹⁰ Say 'took their course (*Fortgang nehmen* st.)'.   ¹¹ Use *frei haben*, 'to have a holiday'; cf. *freie Zeit*, 'spare time'; *freier Nachmittag*, 'half-holiday', etc.   ¹² = 'wished'.   ¹³ 'as long as', *wenn*.

III

96. FREDERICK'S FIRST LIBRARY

The young Frederick concealed his actions, good as well as bad. He began secretly to build up for himself a library of more than 3000 volumes. The first catalogue of this library, which the prince wrote with his own hand in 1727, contains the works of most of the great English, French, Spanish and Italian writers of the period, as well as a host of learned works on history, grammar, philosophy, etc.; above all Frederick valued his translations of the great French writers. These treasures were concealed in a house in the neighbourhood of the castle at Potsdam, and whenever the prince could snatch a moment from the duties and cares with which his days were filled he would hurry thither and consume a few pages with restless enjoyment. Had he been discovered by his father, what a scene there would have been! The king hated books to such an extent that he had employed the yearly allowance of 1000 Taler for the royal library as a pension for a retired general.

IV

97. FREDERICK'S ADDRESS TO HIS GENERALS ON THE[1] DEATH OF HIS FATHER

(June 1st, 1740)

I know what[2] a severe loss you have suffered: you know mine[3]. You have lost a king and a master whom I do not doubt[4] you loved even as well as he loved you. I lose in him as well a father. We must attempt to comfort ourselves for the common irreplaceable loss: I, in the hope that you will assist me to maintain the great army which you helped[5] my father to form; you, in the confidence—I promise you it—to find in me a master who does not love you less than he who is dead[6], who remembers with pleasure that[7] he has been your comrade, and who will not refuse due recognition for services which you perform for him. Take[8], therefore, unceasing care for the beauty and efficiency of my troops. Yet keep at the same time[9] two things in mind[10]: firstly, that I would[11] rather see them good than smart, and secondly, that they are[12] to protect my country and not to spoil it.

[1] *am.*   [2] When followed by an Adjective the termination is usually dropped from *welcher*; cf. *welch schöner Tag*, 'what a beautiful day', etc.
[3] See § 7.   [4] Say 'I do not doubt it *(daran)*'.   [5] Formation of the Past Participle? § 189.   [6] 'he who is dead', *der Verstorbene*.   [7] Since the Subjects are the same we may say 'to have been'.   [8] 'to take care for', *Sorge tragen* st. *um.*   [9] 'At the same time', *hierbei.*   [10] Say 'in the eye'.
[11] 'should like rather to'.   [12] This is a strong command; see § 103 (iii).

V

98. EXTRACT FROM THE DIARY OF HENRY DE GATT

(The King's reader, 1758–1780)

Ramenau, September 29th, 1758.

We spoke of Holland. 'The people are soft', said the king. 'And yet', I replied, 'the youth is engaged in the war.'

'Yes, youth[1] often does the opposite of what[2] it has been taught. If I had³ children, I should leave⁴ them to their nature and they could choose their calling themselves. If one wishes to be successful one needs strong ambition or strong self-love. That is a support, that is the mainspring of great deeds, for each man wishes to push himself forward⁵ in something. One cobbler maintains that he makes better boots than another, and so on⁶. Furthermore, this ambition must be great. It can show⁷ itself in many⁸ forms. I know mankind, I have seen them for⁹ twenty years as a private individual¹⁰. I can't be imposed¹¹ on. I get to the bottom¹² of reports which are made to me. Woe to him who deceives me!

'I remain true to my ideas, and you see that I do not fear death¹. When I do something wrong, I retire¹³ into myself, feel repentance and blush within myself for¹⁴ having failed in something or for having failed myself.'

¹ Abstract Nouns require the Definite Article; *die Liebe*, 'love', *der Tod*, 'death', etc.   ² 'of that which'; see § 18 (ii).   ³ Subjunctive? § 183 (ii).   ⁴ *überlassen* st.   ⁵ 'to push oneself forward', *sich hervor-tun* st.   ⁶ *und so weiter*.   ⁷ *sich äußern* w.   ⁸ Use *mancherlei*, 'many sorts of'.   ⁹ Not *für*; see § 56.   ¹⁰ *als Privatmann*.   ¹¹ Say 'one may (see § 131 (ii)) impose nothing on me'; 'to impose on' = *vor-machen* w. (+ Dat.).   ¹² 'to get to the bottom of', *auf den Grund gehen* st. (+ Dat.).   ¹³ 'to retire into oneself', *in sich gehen*.   ¹⁴ Say 'that I have failed something or have failed against myself'.

VI

99. FREDERICK'S DEATH

In the beginning of¹ April 1786, when the king had become very weak, he had himself carried on a fine day on to the so-called 'green stairs' of the castle at² Potsdam, where he refreshed himself in the warm spring sun. He had sat there a fairly long time before he noticed that the two grenadiers who were on guard were still standing to attention. He beckoned one of them to him and said: 'Walk up and down! You can't stand there as long as I can sit here'.

Six months afterwards in the early morning of the 17th of August 1786 the king passed away³ in his palace Sanssouci.

On the next day, laid out on his bier[4] in the concert hall of the castle, his officers and soldiers greeted him for the last time. He lay wrapped[5] in a light coat on his field-bed as if[6] he were resting after a day of battle.

His wish to find his grave in the garden of Sanssouci remained unfulfilled. He was buried in the garrison church at[2] Potsdam— near his father.

Anekdoten von Friedrich dem Großen

[1] Omit 'of'; cf. *Ende Juli*, 'at the end of July'.   [2] *zu?* § 170.   [3] *verscheiden* st.   [4] 'laid out on his bier', *aufgebahrt*.   [5] One would expect *in* to be followed here by the Dative, but in fact the Accusative is used; cf. *auf* **den** *Stock gestützt*, 'supported on the stick'.   [6] Omit *ob*; word-order? § 82.

100. THE MYSTERY OF THE UNIVERSE

The lecturer began with a characteristic figure to express the littleness of our world in space. A few stars were known, he said, which were hardly bigger than the earth, but the majority were so large that hundreds of thousands of earths could be packed inside each and leave room to spare; here and there we came upon a giant star large enough to contain millions of millions of earths. And the total number of stars in the universe was probably something like the total number of grains of sand on all the seashores of the world.

This vast multitude of stars travelled through a universe so spacious that it was an event of almost unimaginable rarity for a star to come anywhere near to another star. For the most part each voyaged in splendid isolation like a ship on an empty ocean. In a scale model in which the stars were ships the average ship would be well over a million miles from its nearest neighbour.   *The Times*

VOCABULARY

(§§ refer to sections in the Grammar)

Numerals, common pronouns and proper names which are the same in both languages have been omitted. For pronouns see §§ 4 *sq.*, for numerals § 50.
After verbs the following abbreviations have been used: st. (strong), w. (weak), tr. (transitive), intr. (intransitive). For the conjugation of strong verbs see p. 201. Verbs conjugated with *sein* are marked thus †. Verbs whose prefixes are separable have been printed so: *an-nehmen, aus-gehen, weiter-gehen*, etc.
Other abbreviations used are: acc. (accusative), adj. (adjective), adv. (adverb), conj. (conjunction), dat. (dative), gen. (genitive), inf. (infinitive), invar. (invariable), pl. (plural), prep. (preposition).
The plurals of nouns have been shown where necessary (i.e. where the plural cannot be found from the rules given in § 40) thus:

> der Fuß, ⸚e (i.e. die Füße),
> der Apfel, ⸚– (i.e. die Äpfel),
> der Schüler, – (i.e. die Schüler).

In nouns which decline weak and in a few other cases the genitive singular has been shown as well as the plural, e.g.

> der Soldat, –en, –en (i.e. des Soldaten, die Soldaten),
> der Gedanke, –ns, –n (i.e. des Gedankens, die Gedanken).

Most adjectives can in German be used also as adverbs; hence, if in the English an adverb is not given it may be looked for under its corresponding adjective, e.g. 'quickly' under 'quick', 'really' under 'real', etc.

a, ein § 1
able, to be, können *st.* § 126, vermögen *st.* (+ zu) § 137
about, über; **to be — to**, im Begriff sein...zu, wollen *st.* § 127 (iii)
above, über; **— all**, vor allem
absence, die Abwesenheit
absent, abwesend
abuse, to, schimpfen *w.* (auf)
accept, to, an-nehmen *st.*
acceptance, die Annahme
accompany, begleiten *w.*
according to, nach
account, der Bericht; **on — of**, wegen; **on that —**, deswegen
accuse (of), an-klagen *w.* (+ *gen.* or wegen), beschuldigen *w.* (+ *acc.*)

accused, der Angeklagte, –n, –n
accustom oneself (to), sich gewöhnen *w.* (an) § 161
accustomed, to be, pflegen *w.*
acknowledgment, die Anerkennung
acorn, die Eichel
acquaintance, die Bekanntschaft
act, to, spielen *w.*
action, die Handlung
active, energisch
actor, der Schauspieler
add, to, hinzu-fügen *w.*
addition, in, noch dazu, außerdem (*besides*)
address, die Adresse (*postal*); **— (to)**, die Ansprache (an)

12-2

adjourn, to, vertagen w.

admiration, die Bewunderung

admire, to, bewundern w.

admirer, der Verehrer, –

advance, die Fortschritte (pl.); to
—, weiter-schreiten† st., heran-
rücken w. (draw near)

adventure, das Abenteuer, –

advise, to, raten st. (dat.)

aeroplane, der Flugzeug, –e

affectionate, liebevoll, treuherzig

afraid, to be, Angst haben

after, nach, nachdem, nachher § 87;
— which, worauf

afternoon, der Nachmittag; this
—, heute nachmittag

again, wieder, noch einmal (once
more)

against, gegen, wider

age, das Alter; at the — of, im
Alter von

ago, vor § 162

agreeable, angenehm

aim, to, zielen w.

air, die Luft

alarmed (at), bestürzt (über)

alive, lebendig

all, all, ganz § 58; — sorts of,
allerlei (invar.)

allow, to, erlauben w. (dat.); to be
allowed, dürfen st. § 131

allowance, der Zuschuß

alms, das Almosen

alone, allein

aloud, laut

already, schon

also, auch, ebenfalls

although, obgleich

always, immer, stets

amass, to, zusammen-scharren w.

amazement, das Erstaunen

ambassador, der Botschafter

ambition, der Ehrgeiz

America, Amerika

American, der Amerikaner

among, unter

and, und

anger, der Zorn

angry, zornig

animal, das Tier, –e

announce, melden w. (people), an-
kunden w. (facts), erklären w.
(declare)

annoy, verdrießen st., ärgern w.

another, ander, noch ein § 59

answer (to), die Antwort (auf);
to —, erwidern w. (dat.), antworten w. (dat.), beantworten w.
(letters)

ante-room, das Vorzimmer

anxious, besorgt

any, irgend § 66 (iii), etwas § 66 (i)

anyone, irgend jemand, man

anything, irgend etwas § 66 (iii),
alles

apartment, das Gemach, ⸚er

appear, to, erscheinen st.

apple, der Apfel, ⸚–

appoint (to), to, ernennen st. (zu)

approach, to, sich nähern w. (dat.),
nahe-kommen† st. (dat.)

archbishop, der Erzbischof

argue, to, besprechen st. (tr.)

arithmetic, das Rechnen

arm, der Arm

armchair, der Lehnstuhl

armed (with), bewaffnet (mit)

army, das Heer, die Armee

arrest, die Haft; under —, in Haft

arrive (at), to, an-kommen† st.
(in + dat.)

artist, der Künstler

as, wie § 33, als, da § 83; as...as,
so...wie § 34; — soon as,
sobald; — well, noch dazu; —
well as, sowie

ash, die Asche

ashamed, verschämt; to be —
(of), sich schämen w. (vor)

aside, zur Seite

ask (for), to, fragen w. (nach),
bitten st. (um) § 138; — a question, eine Frage stellen w.

asleep, to be, schlafen st.

ass, der Esel

assenting, zustimmend

assertion, die Behauptung

assist, to, bei-stehen st. (dat.)

astonished, erstaunt
astonishment, das Erstaunen; in
—, in Erstaunen
at, an, in, zu §§ 164, 170; — last,
   endlich; — once, sofort
Atlantic, der atlantische Ozean
attempt, to, versuchen w.
attendants, das Gefolge
attention, die Aufmerksamkeit
attraction, der Reiz
augmentation, die Erweiterung
aunt, die Tante
Austrian, der Österreicher
autumn, der Herbst
average, durchschnittlich (adv.)
avoid, to, entgehen† st. (dat.)
awake, to, erwachen w.
away, weg, fort, davon
awe, die Ehrfurcht
awful, entsetzlich
awhile, eine Zeitlang
axe, die Axt

back, der Rücken, zurück (adv.)
bag, der Beutel
ban, to, verbieten st.
bandage, die Binde
bank, das Ufer
barber, der Barbier
bare, kahl (of trees, etc.)
bargain, der Kauf
bargain, into the, noch obendrein
bark, to, bellen w.
barometer, das Barometer
barrister, der Rechtsanwalt
basket, der Korb, ⁼e
bathing, das Baden
battle, die Schlacht, –en
battlement, die Zinne
bay, die Bucht
be, to, sein
bear, der Bär, –en, –en
bear, to, leiden st., aus-halten st.
   (put up with)
beard, der Bart
beautiful, schön
beauty, die Schönheit
because, weil
beckon, to, winken w.

become, to, werden
bed, das Bett
bee, die Biene
beech, die Buche
beer, das Bier
before, (prep.) vor, (conj.) ehe,
   bevor; (adv.) vorher, zuvor § 87
beg, to, bitten st. (request)
beggar, der Bettler; — woman,
   die Bettlerin
begin, to, beginnen st., an-fangen st.
beginning, der Anfang; at the —,
   am Anfang
behave, to, sich betragen st.
behaviour, das Benehmen, das
   Betragen
behind, hinter
belief, der Glaube, –ns, –n
believe (in), to, glauben w. (an)
   § 161
belong, to, gehören w. (dat.)
below, unten (adv.)
bend, to, sich beugen w.
best, best, am besten § 31
better, besser
between, zwischen
Bible, die Bibel
Biblical, biblisch
bicycle, das Rad
bicyclist, der Radler
bid, das Angebot (offer)
bid, to, heißen st. § 187
big, groß
bird, der Vogel, ··–
birthday party, die Geburtsfeier
bishop, der Bischof
bitter, bitter
bitterly, bitterlich
black, schwarz
blackboard, die Tafel
blanched, ergraut
bless, to, segnen w.
blind, blind
bloody, blutig
blow, der Schlag, der Hieb
blunt, derb
blush, to, erröten w.
board, on, an Bord
book, das Buch, ⁼er

boot, der Stiefel, –

both, beide § 60; — ... and, sowohl...wie

bottle, die Flasche

bottom, der Grund; at the —, auf dem Grunde

bow, die Verbeugung

box, die Loge (*theatre*)

boy, der Junge, –n, –n, der Bube, –n, –n

bracelet, das Armband, ⁻er

branch, der Ast, ⁻e

brandy, der Kognak

brave, tapfer, mutig

bread, das Brot

break, to, brechen *st.*, zerbrechen *st.* (*to pieces*); — out, ausbrechen *st.*

breakfast, das Frühstück; to have —, frühstücken *w.*

Breton, der Bretone, –n, –n

bride, die Braut

bridge, die Brücke

bright, hell

bring, to, bringen *st.*

broad, breit; — minded, großzügig

brook, der Bach

brother, der Bruder, ··–

brown, braun

Bruin, Petz

buffalo, der Büffel

build, to, bauen *w.*, errichten *w.*

bundle, das Bündel

burn, to, brennen *st.*, verbrennen *st.*

burning, brennend

bury, to, vergraben *st.*, bestatten *w.*

bushes, das Gebüsch

business, das Geschäft

but, aber, sondern, allein § 71, doch § 194

butterfly, der Schmetterling, –e

buy, to, kaufen *w.*

by, von, durch

California, Kalifornien

call, der Besuch (*visit*); to —, rufen *st.*; to — on, besuchen *w.*

called, to be, heißen *st.* § 139; so —, sogenannt

calling, der Beruf (*profession*)

Calvinist, der Kalvinist, –en, –en

can, können *st.* § 126

candidly, offen

canny, schlau

cap, die Mütze

captain, der Hauptmann

car, das Auto

carcase, die Leiche

care, die Sorge

carriage, der Wagen

carry, to, tragen *st.*; — off, forttragen, entführen *w.* (*abduct*); — out, voll-strecken *w.* (*a sentence*)

case, der Fall, ⁻e, die Kiste (*box*); in any —, jedenfalls

cast, to, werfen *st.*

castle, das Schloß, die Burg (*citadel*)

cat, die Katze

catalogue, der Katalog

catch, to, fangen *st.*; — fire, sich entzünden *w.*

cathedral, der Dom

cattle, das Rind, –er

cause, die Ursache; to —, verursachen *w.*

cave, die Höhle

celebrated, berühmt

century, das Jahrhundert, –e

certain, gewiß, sicher (*safe*)

chair, der Stuhl, ⁻e

chance, der Zufall; to —, sich ereignen *w.*

change, to, verändern *w.*

chapter, das Kapitel

character, der Buchstabe, –n, –n (*letter*)

characteristic, charakteristisch

charge, die Anklage (*accusation*)

chariot, der Wagen

charity, die Wohltat

Charles, Karl

charming, reizend

chase, to, jagen *w.* (*hunt*)

cheap, billig

check, to, dämpfen (*quell*)

chemist's shop, die Apotheke
child, das Kind, –er
childishly, kindlich
choose, to, wählen *w.*
Christ, Christus (*gen.* Christi)
Christian, christlich
Christmas, Weihnachten
church, die Kirche; — yard, der
  Kirchhof
circle, der Kreis
citizen, der Bürger
city, die Stadt
civil, höflich
class, die Klasse
class-room, das Klassenzimmer
clever, geschickt
cliff, der Fels, –ens, –en
climate, das Klima
climb, to, steigen† *st.*, klettern† *w.*
clock, die Uhr
close (to), nahe (an)
clothe, to, kleiden *w.*
clothing, die Kleider (*pl.*), die
  Kleidung
cloud, die Wolke, –n
club, die Verbindung
coast, die Küste; — resort, das
  Seebad
coat, der Rock
cobbler, der Flickschuster
coin, die Münze
cold, kalt, die Kälte
collect, to, sammeln *w.* (*things*);
  sich versammeln *w.* (*assemble*)
Cologne, Köln
combine, to, verbinden *st.*
come, to, kommen† *st.*; — back,
  zurück-kommen† *st.*;—in, herein-
  kommen† *st.*; — up to, zu-kom-
  men† *st.* (auf) § 152
comfort (for), to, trösten *w.*
  (über)
comfortable, bequem
commit, to, begehen *st.*
common, gemein
communications, die Verbindung
companion, der Begleiter
company, die Gesellschaft
compare, to, vergleichen *st.*

compartment, der Abteil
complain (of), to, sich beklagen *w.*
  (über), klagen *w.*
complaint, die Klage
complete, völlig, vollkommen; to
  —, vollenden *w.*
composed (of), to be, bestehen *st.*
  (aus)
compromise, der Kompromiß
comrade, der Kamerad, –en, –en
conceal, to, verstecken *w.*
concert, das Konzert; — hall, die
  Konzerthalle
condemn (to), verurteilen *w.* (zu)
condition, der Zustand
conduct, das Benehmen; to —,
  führen *w.* (*lead*)
confidence, die Zuversicht
confirm, to, bestätigen *w.*
congratulate (on), to, gratulieren
  w. (zu)
conjurer, der Zauberkünstler
conjuring trick, das Kunststück
conscription, der Militärdienst
consist (of), to, bestehen *st.* (aus)
consolation, der Trost
constantly, beständig, immer
consume, to, verschlingen *st.*
contain, to, enthalten *st.*, umfassen
  st. (*include*)
content, zufrieden, das Behagen
continual, beständig
continually, fortwährend
continue, to, fort-fahren† *st.*
contrary (to), das Gegenteil (von);
  on the —, im Gegenteil
convent, das Kloster
conversation, die Unterhaltung
coolness, die Kühle
cord, der Strick, –e
corner, die Ecke, der Winkel
correct, richtig
cosmopolitan, der Kosmopolit
cost, to, kosten *w.*
count, der Graf, –en, –en; to —,
  zählen *w.*
countess, die Gräfin
country, das Land; in the —,
  auf dem Lande

couple, das Paar
courageous, kühn
course, of, selbstverständlich
court, der Hof, das Gericht (*of justice*); in —, vor Gericht
cousin, der Vetter
cover, to, bedecken *w.*
covetous, habgierig
creep, to, schleichen† *st.*, kriechen† *st.*
criticise, kritisieren *w.*
cross, to, überschreiten *st.*
crowd, die Menge
crown prince, der Kronprinz, –en, –en
cruel, grausam
cry (exclaim), to, rufen *st.*, ausrufen *st.*
cupboard, der Schrank
curiosity, die Neugierde (*inquisitiveness*), die Kuriosität, –en
curious, neugierig (*inquisitive*), sonderbar (*strange*)
curtain, der Vorhang
customer, der Kunde, –n, –n
cut, to, schneiden *st.*; — off, abhauen *st.*

daddy, Vati
daily, täglich
damages, die Entschädigung § 215
dance, to, tanzen *w.*
danger, die Gefahr
dangerous, gefährlich
dare, to, wagen *w.*
dark, in the, im Dunkeln
daughter, die Tochter
dawn, der Tagesanbruch; at —, mit Tagesanbruch
day, der Tag, –e
dead, tot, verstorben
deal, to, versetzen *w.*, geben *st.*
dealing, die Handlung
dean, der Dechant, –en, –en
dear, teuer (*price*), lieb
dearly, zärtlich
death, der Tod; — bed, das Totenbett; on the —, am Tode
deceive, to, betrügen *st.*

decide, to, sich entscheiden *st.*, entschließen *st.*
decidedly, entschieden
decision, der Entschluß
declare, to, erklären *w.*
deed, die Tat, –en
deep, tief
deer, das Reh, –e
defence, die Verteidigung
degree, der Stand
dejected, traurig
deliver, to, überbringen *st.*
depart, to, fort-gehen† *st.*
descend, to, absteigen *st.* (*horse, etc.*), hinunter-fahren† *st.*
deserted, verlassen
desire, to, wünschen *w.*, begehren *w.*
desk, der Schreibtisch
despatch, die Depesche
destination, der Bestimmungort
determine, to, sich entschließen *st.*
determined, entschlossen
develop, to, entwickeln *w.*
devil, der Teufel
devote, to, widmen *w.* (*dat.*)
diary, das Tagebuch
die, to, sterben† *st.*
different (from), verschieden (von), anders
difficult, schwer, schwierig
difficulty, die Schwierigkeit, die Mühe (*trouble*)
dig, to, graben *st.*
digest, to, verdauen *w.*
dim, matt erleuchtet (*dimly lit*)
dine, to, speisen *w.*
dining room, das Speisezimmer
dinner, das Abendessen; — party, die Tischgesellschaft
diplomatic, diplomatisch
direct (to), to, weisen *st.* (nach)
direction, die Richtung
disagreeable, unangenehm
disappear, to, verschwinden† *st.*
disapprovingly, mißbilligend
discover, to, entdecken *w.*
dish, die Schüssel
disliked, unbeliebt

dismay, in, bestürzt
dismount, to, ab-steigen† *st.*
dispute, die Widerrede
distinguish, to, unterscheiden *st.*
distinguished, ausgezeichnet
distress, in, in Not
disturb, to, stören *w.*
divide, to, teilen *w.*
do, to, tun *st.*
doctor, der Arzt (*medical*), Doktor (*title*)
dog, der Hund, –e
domestics, die Dienerschaft
donkey, der Esel
door, die Tür, –en; — step, die Schwelle; — way, der Torweg
dormouse, die Haselmaus
doubt, der Zweifel; to —, zweifeln *w.* (an)
doubtless, zweifellos
down, hinunter, herunter § 210
dowry, die Mitgift
dozen, das Dutzend
drain, to, aus-trinken *st.*
draw, to, ziehen *st.* (*pull*), zeichnen *w.* (*sketch*); — water, Wasser schöpfen *w.*
drawbridge, die Zugbrücke
dress, das Kleid, –er; to —, sich an-ziehen *st.*, sich kleiden *w.*, frisieren *w.* (*the hair*)
dried up, ausgetrocknet
drink, to, trinken *st.*
drive, to, treiben *st.* (*of cattle*), fahren† *st.* (*vehicles*); — on, weiter-fahren† *st.*
drop, to, fallen lassen *st.* § 188
drown, to, ertrinken† *st.*
drowned, ertrunken
dry, trocken; to —, trocknen *w.*
due, gebührend
duke, der Herzog
during, während
duty, die Pflicht, –en
dwell, to, wohnen *w.*

each, jeder
early, früh
earn, to, verdienen *w.*

earphone, die Ohrenklappe
earth, die Erde
east, der Orient
easy, leicht
eat, to, essen *st.*
edge, der Rand
education, die Erziehung
efficiency, die Tüchtigkeit
effort, die Bemühung; to make an —, sich Mühe geben *st.*, sich bemühen *w.*
elm, die Ulme
emigrate, to, aus-wandern *w.*
eminently, äußerst, vor allem
employ, to, verwenden *w.*
empty, leer; to —, leeren *w.*
enchanting, bezaubernd
encourage, ermutigen *w.*
encroach (on), to, über-greifen *st.* (auf)
end, der Schluß, das Ende; in the —, am Ende, endlich, schließlich; on —, hintereinander
endure, to, dulden *w.*
enemy, der Feind, –e
engage, to, an-stellen *w.*
engaged in, to be, sich betätigen *w.* (in)
English, englisch
Englishman, der Engländer
enjoy, to, sich unterhalten *st.*, genießen *st.* (*tr.*)
enjoyment, der Genuß
enmity, die Feindschaft
enormous, riesig, ungeheuer
enough, genug
enter, to, ein-treten† *st.* (in), betreten *st.* (+ *acc.*) § 152
entire, ganz
equally, ebensosehr
escort, die Begleitung
estate, das Gut
etc., u.s.w.
eternally, ewig
Euphrates, Euphrat, –en
Europe, Europa
evade, aus-weichen† *w.* (*dat.*)
even, selbst, sogar, gar
evening, der Abend, –e

ever, jemals, je; — since, seitdem
every, jeder (each), alle (all)
everyone, jedermann, alle
everything, alles
everywhere, überall
exact, to, verlangen w.
examine, to, untersuchen w.
Excellency, His, Seine Exzellenz
excellent, vortrefflich
exception, die Ausnahme
exceptional, außerordentlich
Exchange, die Börse; on the —,
    an der Börse
exclaim, to, aus-rufen st.
excuse, die Ausflucht; to —, ent-
    schuldigen w.
exhausted, erschöpft
exhaustion, die Erschöpfung
exit, der Ausgang
expect, to, erwarten w.
expense, die Kosten (pl.)
experience, die Erfahrung
explain, to, erklären w.
explanation, die Aufklärung
expose (oneself), to, sich aus-
    setzen w. (dat.)
express, aus-drücken w.
expression, der Ausdruck
extent, der Grad
extract (from), der Auszug (aus)
extraordinary, sonderbar
extremely, äußerst
eye, das Auge, -s, -n
eyesight, das Augenlicht

face, das Gesicht
fact, die Tatsache; in —, tatsächlich
fail, verfehlen w.
faint, to, in Ohnmacht fallen† st.
fair, gerecht
fairly, ziemlich
fall (off), to, fallen† st. (von);
    — back, sich zurück-ziehen st.;
    — in, ein-fallen† st.
false, falsch
famous, berühmt
fanatical, fanatisch
fancy (oneself), to, sich vor-
    stellen w.

far, weit; — and wide, weit und
    breit
farm hand, der Knecht, -e
farmer, der Landmann, der Bauer,
    -n, -n
fast, schnell
fat, dick
father, der Vater
fault, die Schuld
favour, die Bitte (request)
favourable, günstig
favourite, der Liebling, -e
fear, to, fürchten w., sich fürchten
    w.
feast, das Fest
feat, das Kunststück
feeble, schwach
feel, to, fühlen w., empfinden st.
fellow, der Geselle, -n, -n, der Kerl
    (colloquial)
festival, das Fest
fetch, to, holen w.
few, a, einige, ein paar
field, das Feld; — bed, das Feldbett
fight, to, kämpfen w., fechten st.
figure, die Gestalt, das Bild (picture)
fill, to, füllen w.
finally, endlich
find, to, finden st.; — oneself, sich
    befinden st.
fine, schön, fein
finish, to, beenden w.
fire, das Feuer, der Kamin (fire-
    place)
fireman, der Feuerwehrmann
first, erst; at —, zuerst
fish, der Fisch, -e; to —, fischen
    w.
fix, to, heften w.
flame, die Flamme
flamingo, der Flamingo, -s
flask, die Flasche
flatter, to, schmeicheln w. (dat.)
fling, to, werfen st.; to — oneself,
    stürzen w.
floor, der Boden (ground), der Stock
    (storey); on the first —, im
    ersten Stock
flower, die Blume

fly, die Fliege; to —, fliegen† *st.*, fliehen† *st.* (*flee*)
following, folgend
food, das Essen, die Nahrung
fool, der Narr, –en, –en
foolish, töricht
foot, der Fuß; on —, zu Fuß
for, (*prep.*) für, (*in expressions of time*) auf, seit § 56; (*conj.*) denn § 70
forbid, to, verbieten *st.* (*dat.*)
foreign, ausländisch
forest, der Wald, ⁼er
forge, to, fälschen *w.*
forget, to, vergessen *st.*
forgive, to, vergeben *st.* (*dat.*)
fork, die Gabel
form, die Form, –en; to —, bilden *w.*
former, jener
formerly, früher
formless, formlos
forsake, to, verlassen *st.*
fortunately, glücklicherweise
fortune, das Vermögen
forward, vorwärts
found, to, begründen *w.*
Fred, Fritz
Frederick, Friedrich
free, frei; to —, befreien *w.*
French, französisch
Frenchman, der Franzose, –n, –n
frequently, häufig
fresh, frisch
friend, der Freund, –e
from, von, aus
front, in, vorne
fruit, das Obst
full, voll
funny, komisch, drollig
further, weiter
furthermore, übrigens
future, zukünftig

gaiety, die Freude
gain, to, gewinnen *st.*
gale, der Sturm
gallant, galant
garden, der Garten, ⁼–
garrison, die Garnison

gather, to, sammeln *w.* (*things*), sich versammeln *w.* (*people*)
general, der General, –e; in —, im allgemeinen
generous, großzügig
Genoa, Genua
gentleman, der Herr, –n, –en
gently, sanft
George, Georg
German, deutsch (*adj.*), der Deutsche, –n, –n
Germany, Deutschland
gesture, die Gebärde
get, to, bekommen *st.*; — up, sich erheben† *st.*, auf-stehen *st.* (*from bed*); — tired of, satt werden (+ *gen.*)
giant, der Riese, –n, –n
gift, das Geschenk, die Gabe
girl, das Mädchen
give, geben *st.* (*dat.*), schenken *w.* (*dat.*)
gladly, gerne
glass, das Glas
gloomy, düster
glorious, herrlich
glow, glühen *w.*
go, to, gehen† *st.* § 140; — on, fortfahren† *st.* (*of speech*); — out, aus-gehen† *st.*
God, Gott
gold, das Gold
good, gut; — natured, gutmütig
gradually, allmählich, nach und nach
grain (of sand), das Sandkorn, ⁼er
grammar, die Grammatik
gramophone, das Grammophon; — record, die Schallplatte
grant, to, erfüllen *w.*
granted, zugegeben
grass, das Gras
gratitude, die Dankbarkeit
grave, das Grab
gravity, der Ernst
great, groß
Greece, Griechenland
Greek, griechisch (*adj.*)
green, grün

greet, to, begrüßen *w.*, grüßen *w.*
grenadier, der Grenadier, –e
grey, grau
grim, grimmig
grin, to, schmunzeln *w.*
ground, der Boden
group, die Gruppe
grow, to, wachsen† *st.* (*grow*), werden *st.* (*become*)
grumble, brummen *w.*
guard, die Wache; to be on —, Wache halten *st.*
guest, der Gast, ⸚e
gun, die Kanone

hair, das Haar, –e
halberd, die Hellebarde
half, halb, die Hälfte § 53
hall, die Halle, der Saal
halt, to, stehen bleiben† *st.* § 150 (ii)
hand, die Hand, ⸚e
handkerchief, das Taschentuch, ⸚er
handsome, schön
hang, to, hangen *st.* (*intr.*), hängen *w.* (*tr.*) § 141
happen, to, geschehen† *st.*
happy, glücklich
hard, hart, heftig (*violent*)
hardly, kaum
harm, to, schaden *w.* (*dat.*), verletzen *w.* (*injure*)
hasten, to, eilen *w.*
hat, der Hut
hate, to, hassen *w.*, verabscheuen *w.* (*things*)
hatter, der Hutmacher
have, to, haben
head, der Kopf, ⸚e
health, die Gesundheit
hear, to, hören *w.*
heart, das Herz
heartily, herzlich
heatedly, hitzig
heave, der Ruck
heaven, der Himmel
heavy, schwer
hedge, die Hecke
heed, to, beachten *w.*

Henry, Heinrich
here, hier; — and there, hie und da
hide, to, verstecken *w.*, verbergen *st.*
high, hoch
hint, to, an-deuten *w.*
history, die Geschichte
hit, to, schlagen *st.*
hive, der Bienenstock, ⸚e
hoarse, heiser
hold, to, halten *st.*
hole, das Loch
holidays, die Ferien (*pl.*)
homage, die Huldigung
home, die Heimat (*home country*), das Haus, nach Hause (*motion*) § 168; at —, zu Hause
honest, ehrlich
honey, der Honig
honey-comb, die Wabe
hope, die Hoffnung; to —, hoffen *w.*
horn, das Horn, ⸚er
horrible, schrecklich
horrid, gräßlich
horse, das Pferd, –e
host, der Gastgeber, die Menge (*crowd*)
hot, heiß
hotel, das Hotel
hothouse, das Warmhaus, ⸚er
hour, die Stunde; quarter of an —, die Viertelstunde; for hours, stundenlang
house, das Haus
how, wie; — many, wie viele
however, jedoch § 91, N.B.
humbly, demütig
humour, der Humor
hundred, hundert, das Hundert § 52
hungry, hungrig
hunt, die Jagd; to —, jagen *w.*
hunting dress, der Jagdanzug
hurry, die Eile; to —, eilen† *w.*, sich beeilen *w.* (*hurry up*)
husband, der Gatte, der Mann
hymn, das Kirchenlied

ice, das Eis

idea, die Idee, –n
identity papers, die Ausweis-
papiere (*pl.*)
if, wenn, ob § 88
ignorant, unwissend
ill, krank
illness, die Krankheit
illuminate, to, erleuchten *w.*
imagine, to, sich vor-stellen *w.*
(*dat.*); — oneself, sich wähnen *w.*
immediately, sofort
immense, riesig
immortalise, to, verherrlichen *w.*
impatient (at), ungeduldig (über)
imperial, kaiserlich
implements, das Gerät
important, wichtig
imprisonment, die Haft
in, into, in; — order to, um...zu
§ 190; — spite of, trotz
incessant, unaufhörlich
inconvenient, unangenehm
increase, to, vermehren *w.*
indeed, wirklich
indefinite, unbestimmt
indignantly, entrüstet
indulge (in), to, sich hin-geben *st.*
(*dat.*)
industrious, emsig, fleißig
industry, der Fleiß
inflammable, entzündbar
inform, to, mit-teilen *w.* (*dat.*)
information, die Auskunft
inhabitant, der Einwohner, —
inheritance, die Erbschaft
injure, to, verletzen *w.*
inkpot, das Tintenfaß
inkstain, der Tintenfleck
inn, das Wirtshaus
innocent, unschuldig
inquire, to, sich erkundigen *w.*
(nach), fragen *w.*
inquisitive, neugierig, naseweise
insist (on), to, bestehen *st.* (auf)
install, to, ein-richten *w.*
intend, to, beabsichtigen *w.*
intention, die Absicht
interest, die Zinsen (*pl.*); to —,
interessieren *w.*

interior, das Innere
interrupt, to, unterbrechen *st.*
introduce, to, vor-stellen *w.* (*dat.*)
invalid, der Kranke, –n, –n
invite, to, ein-laden *st.*
involuntarily, unwillkürlich
irreplaceable, unersetzlich
island, die Insel
isolation, die Abgesondertheit
Italian, der Italiener, –, italienisch
(*adj.*)

Jack, Hans
jacket, die Jacke
Japanese, japanisch (*adj.*)
jester, der Hofnarr, –en, –en
Jew, der Jude, –n, –n
jeweller's shop, der Juwelier-
laden
John, Johann
joke, der Spaß, der Witz
journey, die Reise, die Fahrt
joy, die Freude
joyous, vergnügt, fröhlich
judge, der Richter
judgment, das Urteil
jump, to, springen† *st.*; — about,
umher-springen† *st.*
June, Juni
jury, die Geschworenen (*pl.*)
just, gerade (*adv.*), gerecht (*adj.*);
— now, eben
justice, die Gerechtigkeit

keep, to, halten *st.*, behalten *st.*
key, der Schlüssel
kick, der Fußtritt
kill, to, töten *w.*
kind, gut, gütig, freundlich
king, der König
kitchen, die Küche
knee, das Knie, –
knife, das Messer
knight, der Ritter
knock, to, klopfen *w.*
know, to, wissen *st.*, kennen *w.*
§ 142
knowledge, Kenntnisse (*pl.*) § 215
known, bekannt

lack, to, mangeln *w.* (an), § 152
lad, der Bursche, –n, –n
ladder, die Leiter
lady, die Dame; **the young —,** das Fräulein
lake, der See
lament, to, jammern *w.*
landgrave, der Landgraf
landgravine, die Landgräfin
language, die Sprache
large, groß
last, letzt; **to —,** dauern *w.*
late, spät
later on, später
latter, dieser
laugh (at), to, lachen *w.* (über)
laundress, die Waschfrau
law, das Gesetz
lay, to, legen *w.*; **— down,** hin-legen *w.,* auf-stellen *w.* (*rules*); **— out,** an-legen *w.* (*gardens, etc.*)
lead, to, führen *w.*
leader, der Führer, der Anführer
lean (out of), to, sich lehnen *w.* (aus)
learn, to, lernen *w.,* erfahren *st.* (*find out*)
learned, gelehrt
leave, die Erlaubnis; **to —,** lassen *st.,* verlassen, ab-reisen *w.* § 143; **— out,** aus-lassen *st.*
lecturer, der Vortragende, –n, –n
left, link, übrig (*remaining*)
leg, das Bein, –e, der Fuß, ⸚e
legend, die Legende, die Sage
Leghorn, Livorno
lend, to, leihen, verleihen *st.* (*dat.*)
less, weniger
lesson, die Stunde (*hour*), die Lehre
let, to, lassen *st.* § 188
letter, der Brief
library, die Bibliothek
lid, der Deckel
lie, to, liegen *st.*
life, das Leben
light, leicht; **to —,** an-zünden *w.,* brennen *st.* (*burn*)
like, wie, als § 33
like, to, mögen, gern haben, gefallen *st.* § 144

limit, die Schranke
line, die Linie, die Zeile (*of letters*)
lion, der Löwe, –n, –n
lip, die Lippe
listen, to, zu-hören (*dat.*)
little, klein (*small*), wenig; **a —,** ein wenig, etwas
littleness, die Winzigkeit
live, to, leben *w.,* wohnen *w.* (*dwell*)
living, lebendig
long, lang, lange (*adv.*)
look, der Blick; **to —,** aus-sehen *st.* § 145; **— at,** an-sehen *st.* (+ *acc.*); **— for,** suchen *w.* (+ *acc.*)
lordship, die Lordschaft
lose, to, verlieren *st.*; **— the temper,** in Wut geraten† *st.*; **— the way,** sich verirren *w.*
loss, der Verlust
loudspeaker, der Lautsprecher
Louis, Ludwig
love, die Liebe; **to —,** lieben *w.,* gern haben § 144
lover, der Liebende, –n, –n
low, tief, niedrig
lunch, das Mittagessen
luxuriant, üppig

mad, verrückt, wahnsinnig; **to go —,** wahnsinnig werden
madness, der Wahnsinn
magician, der Zauberer
magnificent, herrlich
mainland, das Festland
mainspring, die Triebfeder
maintain, behaupten *w.* (*assert*), erhalten *st.* (*preserve*)
majesty, die Majestät
majority, die Hauptanzahl
make, to, machen *w.*
man, der Mann, der Mensch, –en, –en
mankind, die Menschen
map, die Karte
marble, der Marmor
March, März
mark, to, kennzeichnen *w.*
market, der Markt
marriage, die Hochzeit

married, verheiratet

marry, to, heiraten w., sich verheiraten w., sich verheiraten w. § 146

mass, die Fülle, die Masse

master, der Lehrer (*teacher*), der Herr, der Meister

match, das Streichholz, ⸚er

matter, die Sache, die Angelegenheit

may, mögen, können, dürfen, § 132

meal, die Mahlzeit

mean, to, bedeuten w., wollen (*wish*) § 127

meaning, die Bedeutung

meanwhile, unterdessen

meditate, to, brüten w.

meet, to, begegnen† w. (*dat.*), treffen *st.* § 147

meeting, die Sitzung

melancholy, die Traurigkeit

memory, das Gedächtnis

mend, to, aus-bessern w.

merchant, der Kaufmann (*pl.* Kaufleute)

message, die Botschaft

messenger, der Bote, –n, –n

middle, die Mitte; in the — of, mitten in

mighty, mächtig

mile, die Meile

military, militärisch

milk, die Milch

milkman, der Milchmann

miller, der Müller

million, die Million

minister, der Minister

minute, die Minute

mirror, to, spiegeln w.

mist, der Nebel

mistake, der Irrtum, der Fehler

misunderstanding, das Mißverständnis

model, die Modelle

modern, modern

moment, der Augenblick

money, das Geld

monkey, der Affe, –n, –n

month, der Monat

more, mehr § 63

morning, der Morgen; this —, heute morgen

most, meist, am meisten; for the — part, meistenteils

mother, die Mutter

motor-bicycle, das Motorrad, ⸚er

mount, to, steigen† *st.* (auf), besteigen *st.* (*acc.*)

mountain, der Berg

mourn (for), to, trauern w. (um)

mouse, die Maus, ⸚e

mouth, der Mund, das Maul (*of animals*)

move, to, bewegen w. (*tr.*), sich rühren w. (*stir*)

movement, die Bewegung

much, viel, sehr § 64 (ii)

multitude, die Menge

murder, der Mord

murmur, to, flüstern w.

must, müssen *st.* § 129

mystery, das Geheimnis

nail (on), to, nageln w. (an)

name, der Name, –ns, –n

named, namens

Narcissus, Narziß

natural, natürlich, selbstverständlich

nature, die Natur

near, neben, bei, an § 164; — by, nahe

nearest, nächst

neck, der Hals

necklace, die Halskette; pearl —, die Perlenkette

need, to, brauchen w.

needle, die Nadel

neighbour, der Nachbar, –n, –n

neither...nor, weder...noch § 93

never, niemals, nie; — before, noch nie

new, neu

news (of), die Nachricht (über)

next, nächst

nice, nett

night, die Nacht; by —, bei Nacht

no, nein, kein (*adj.*)

no one, niemand

nobleman, der Edelmann
nod, to, nicken w.
noise, der Lärm
noiseless, geräuschlos
none, kein § 30
nose, die Nase
not, nicht § 76; — at all, gar nicht
note, der Zettel
note-book, das Heft, –e
nothing, nichts; — at all, gar
    nichts; — but, nichts als
notice, to, bemerken w.
now, jetzt, nun; from — on, von
    nun an
nowadays, heutzutage
nudge, to, an-stoßen st.
number, die Nummer, die Zahl, die
    Anzahl; total —, die Gesamt-
    anzahl

obey, to, gehorchen w. (dat.)
object, der Zweck
obliged, verbunden
observation, die Bemerkung
obtain, to, sich verschaffen w.,
    erstehen st.
occupied (in), beschäftigt (mit)
occur, to, vor-kommen† st.
of, von § 174
offer, to, bieten st. (dat.), an-bieten
    st. (dat.)
officer, der Offizier, –e
often, oft
oh! ach!
old, alt
omen, das Vorzeichen
on, auf, oben (adv.)
once, einst, einmal; — more, noch
    einmal
one, ein §§ 1, 30, man § 65
only, nur, einzig (adj.)
open, offen, auf; to —, öffnen w.,
    auf-machen w.; in the —, im
    Freien
opera, die Oper
opinion, die Meinung
opportunity, die Möglichkeit
opposite (to), das Gegenteil (von)
or, oder

order, der Befehl; to —, befehlen
    st. (dat.), verordnen w. (medical)
orphan, die Waise
other, ander § 25
otherwise, anders, sonst
out of, aus
outbreak, der Ausbruch
outside, draußen
over, über (prep.), vorbei (adv.);
    — there, da drüben
own, eigen (adj.)
owner, der Besitzer
ox, der Ochs, –en, –en

pack up, to, ein-packen w.
paddock, die Weide
page, die Seite (of a book, etc.);
    der Edelknabe (servant)
painting, das Gemälde
pair, das Paar
palace, der Palast, das Schloß
paradise, das Paradies
pardon, to, entschuldigen w. (ex-
    cuse), verzeihen st. (dat.)
parents, die Eltern
parliament, das Parlament
parson, der Pfarrer
part, die Rolle (in a play), der Teil
    (share); to — (with), sich trennen
    st. (von)
particular, besonder
particularly, besonders
partridge, das Rebhuhn, ⸚er
party, die Gesellschaft
pass, to, reichen w. (dat.) (reach),
    vorbei-schreiten† st. (go past)
    § 152, vergehen† st. (of time),
    fällen w. (über) (sentence on)
passenger, der Passagier, –e
Passion Play, das Passionspiel
past, vergangen
patience, die Geduld
patiently, geduldig, mit Geduld
pattern, das Muster
pavements, das Pflaster
paw, das Pfötchen, –
pay, der Sold; to —, bezahlen w.
payment, die Bezahlung
peace, die Ruhe (quiet)

peaceful, friedlich
peasant, der Bauer, –n, –n
peasant-woman, die Bäuerin, –nen
pencil, der Bleistift
pension, die Pension
people, die Leute (pl.), das Volk (nation)
perform, to, aus-führen w. (plays), leisten w. (a service)
performance, die Ausführung
perhaps, wohl § 202, vielleicht
period, die Periode
permission, die Erlaubnis
permit, to, erlauben w. (dat.), gestatten w. (dat.)
Persian, persisch
person, der Mensch, –en, –en
persuade, to, überreden w.
pestilence, die Seuche
philosopher, der Philosoph, –en, –en
philosophy, die Philosophie
pick up, to, auf-heben st.
picture, das Bild, –er
piece, das Stück
piety, die Frömmigkeit
pinch, to, kneifen st.
pine, die Tanne
pine-wood, der Tannenwald
pious, fromm
pipe, die Pfeife
pit, die Grube
pity on, to have, sich erbarmen w. (+ gen.)
plague, die Pest
plain, die Ebene
plead, to, flehen w.
please, bitte; to —, gefallen st. (dat.), befriedigen w. (acc.)
pleasure, das Vergnügen, die Freude; with —, mit Vergnügen
plenty, genügend
plough, to, pflügen w.
pocket, die Tasche
point (to), to, zeigen w. (auf)
pole, die Stange
police, die Polizei
policeman, der Polizist, –en, –en
police-station, das Polizeiamt; at the —, auf dem Polizeiamt

politeness, die Höflichkeit
political, politisch
pond, der Teich
ponder, to, sich besinnen st.
pool, der Tümpel
poor, arm
Pope, der Papst
porter, der Hausdiener
portrait, das Bild
possess, to, besitzen st.
possible, möglich
post, der Posten
potato, die Kartoffel
pour, to, gießen st.; — out, aus-gießen st.
power, die Macht
praise, to, loben w.
prayer, das Gebet
preach, to, predigen w.
prefer, to, vor-ziehen st. § 144 (iii)
prejudice, das Unrecht
premonition, die Vorahnung
prescription, die Verordnung
present, anwesend, jetzig, gegenwärtig, das Geschenk (gift); at —, augenblicklich; to —, vor-stellen w. (dat.) (introduce)
preserve, to, erhalten st., behalten st. (keep)
pretty, hübsch
prevent, to, verhindern w.
previously, bisher
price, der Preis, –e
priest, der Geistliche, –n, –n
prince, der Prinz, –en, –en
princess, die Prinzessin, –nen
prison, das Gefängnis
privilege, das Vorrecht
probably, wahrscheinlich, wohl
proceed, to, weiter-gehen† st.
procure, to, sich an-schaffen w.
professor, der Professor, –en
progress, die Fortschritte (pl.)
promise, to, versprechen st. (dat.)
proper, besonder (special)
property, das Besitztum
prophecy, die Voraussagung; to prophesy, prophezeien w.
proposal, der Vorschlag

prose, die Prosa
protect, to, beschützen *w.*
proud, stolz
prove, to, beweisen *w.*
provided (that), vorausgesetzt daß
provisions, das Lebensmittel
Prussia, Preußen
pull, to, ziehen *st.*
punctually, pünktlich
pupil, der Schüler, –
purchase, der Ankauf; to make
—s, Einkäufe machen *w.*
pure, rein
purr, to, schnurren *w.*
pussy, Mieze
put, to, legen *w.*, setzen *w.*, stellen
w. § 148; stellen *w.* (*a question*);
— on, an-ziehen *st.*; — out, aus-
löschen *w.*

quarrel, der Streit; to —, streiten
st.
queen, die Königin
question, die Frage
quick, rasch, schnell, geschwind
quiet, ruhig
quite, ganz

rabbit, das Kaninchen
race, das Geschlecht; to —, rasen *w.*
rail, by, auf der Eisenbahn
railway carriage, der Eisenbahn-
wagen
rain, der Regen; to —, regnen *w.*
raise, to, auf-heben *st.*, heben *st.*
rascal, der Schelm
rather, ziemlich, lieber (*preferably*)
rattle, to, knattern *w.*
raven, der Rabe, –n, –n
reach, to, erreichen *w.*, gelangen *w.*
(zu)
read, to, lesen *st.*; to — aloud, vor-
lesen *st.*
reader, der Verleser
readily, bereitwillig
ready, bereit
real, wirklich
reason, der Grund, die Ursache
(*cause*)

receive, to, erhalten *st.*, empfangen
st.
recently, kürzlich
recognition, die Anerkennung
recover, to, genesen† *st.*, sich
erholen *w.*
recreation, die Erholung
red, rot
reflect, to, sich besinnen *st.*
reformer, der Reformator
refresh oneself, to, sich erquicken
w.
refugee, der Flüchtling
refuse, to, sich weigern *w.*, ver-
sagen *w.* (*tr.*)
regiment, das Regiment, –er
regret, to, bedauern *w.*
relate, to, erzählen *w.* (*dat.*)
remain, to, bleiben† *st.*
remark, die Bemerkung; to —,
bemerken *w.*
remarkable, merkwürdig
remember, to, sich erinnern *w.*
(an) § 161
repentance, die Reue
replace, to, ersetzen *w.*
reply, die Antwort; to —, antworten *w.* (*dat.*)
report, der Bericht, –e
represent, to, vertreten *st.*, aus-
führen *w.* (*portray*)
representative, der Vertreter, –
reprimand, der Verweis
reproach, vor-werfen *st.* (*dat.*) § 152
request, das Gesuch, die Bitte; to
—, bitten *st.*
respectful, respektvoll, ehrerbietig
rest, die übrigen (*pl.*), die Ruhe
(*quiet*); to —, ruhen *w.*, sich
aus-ruhen *w.* (*repose*)
restaurant, das Restaurant
restless, ruhelos
restore, to, zurück-geben *st.*
retired, außer Dienst
return, die Rückkehr; to —,
zurück-kehren *w.*; to — home,
heim-kehren *w.*
reveal, to, offenbaren *w.*
revenge, die Rache

review, to, mustern *w.*
revoke, to, widerrufen *st.*
rich, reich
ride, to, reiten† *st.*; — by, vorbei-
reiten† *st.*
ring, to, klingeln *w.*
rise, to, steigen† *st.*, auf-stehen *st.*
(*get up*)
river, der Fluß, (*pl.* Flüsse)
road, der Weg, die Straße; by
the —, am Wege
roar, das Brausen
rob (of), to, berauben *w.* (+ *gen.*)
§ 152
rocky, felsig
roof, das Dach, ¨er
room, das Zimmer, der Platz (*space*)
rope, der Strick
rose, die Rose
round, um
royal, königlich
rucksack, der Rücksack
ruin, to, ruinieren *w.*
rule, die Regierung (*government*),
die Regel; to —, regieren *w.*
run, to, laufen† *st.*, rennen† *st.*
(*a race*), lauten *w.* (*purport*)
rung, die Sprosse
rush, to, sich stürzen *w.*
rusty, rostig

sables, set of, die Zobelgarnitur
sad, traurig
saddle, to, satteln *w.*
saga, die Sage
sail, to, segeln† *w.*
Saint Elisabeth, die heilige Elisabeth
salmon, der Lachs
same, derselbe § 15; all the —,
immerhin
satisfaction, die Befriedigung, die
Zufriedenheit
satisfied, zufrieden, begnügt
save (from), to, retten *w.* (von)
Saxony, Sachsen
say, to, sagen *w.* (*dat.*)
scales, die Wagschale
scarcely, kaum

scene, die Szene
school, die Schule; at —, auf der
Schule
school-room, das Schulzimmer
science, die Wissenschaft
Scot, der Schotte
Scotland, Schottland
scoundrel, der Schelm, der
Halunke, –n, –n
scourge, die Geißel
sea, das Meer, die See
search, das Suchen; to —, suchen
w.
seashore, der Strand, das Meeres-
ufer, –
seat, der Platz
secret, das Geheimnis
secretly, heimlich, insgeheim
secure, to, besorgen *w.*
see, to, sehen *st.*
seek, to, suchen *w.*
seem, to, scheinen *st.*
seize, to, ergreifen *st.*, erfassen *w.*
self, selbst, selber § 111
self-confidence, das Selbstver-
trauen
self-love, die Eigenliebe
sell, to, verkaufen *w.*
send, to, senden *st.*, schicken *w.*
sentence, das Urteil
sentry, die Schildwache
separate, to, trennen *st.*
serious, ernst
sermon, die Predigt
servant, der Diener
serve, to, dienen *w.* (*dat.*)
service, der Dienst, –e; to be of
—, dienen *w.*
set in, to, ein-treten† *st.*
set off, to, sich auf den Weg
machen *w.*
settle, to, fest-setzen *w.*
several, mehrere § 24
severe, streng, schwer (*heavy*)
severity, die Strenge
shadow, der Schatten, –
shake, to, schütteln *w.*
share (in), der Anteil (an + *acc.*);
to —, teilen *w.*

sharp, scharf, spitz (*pointed*)
shave, to, rasieren *w.*
shed, to, vergießen *st.*
shell, die Muschel
shelter, der Schutz; to —, schützen *w.*
shepherd, der Schäfer
shilling, der Schilling
ship, das Schiff
shirt, das Hemd, –en
shop, der Laden
short, kurz, lakonisch
shoulder, die Schulter
shout, to, schreien *st.*
show, to, zeigen *w.* (*dat.*)
shut, geschlossen (*adj.*), zu; to —, zu-machen *w.*, schließen *st.*
sick, krank
side, die Seite
siege, die Belagerung
sight, die Sehenswürdigkeit, der Anblick (*view*)
significantly, bedeutsam
silence, die Ruhe
silver, das Silber, silbern
similar, ähnlich
simple, einfach
simple–minded, einfältig
since, da (*cause*), seitdem (*time*) § 83; (*adv.*) seitdem
sincere, aufrichtig
sing, to, singen *st.*
singer, der Sänger
single, einzig
sink, to, sinken *st.*
sir, Herr, mein Herr, geehrter Herr (*in letters*)
sister, die Schwester
sit, to, sitzen *st.*; — down, sich nieder-setzen *w.*
size, die Größe
skull, der Schädel
sleep, der Schlaf; to —, schlafen *st.*; to go to —, ein-schlafen† *st.*
sly, schlau
small, klein
smell, der Geruch
smile, to, lächeln *w.*
smoke, to, rauchen *w.*

smoking, das Rauchen
snail, die Schnecke
snatch, to, ergreifen *st*
sneeze, to, niesen *w.*
snow, der Schnee
so, so
soap, die Seife
sob, to, schluchzen *w.*
soft, sanft, weichlich
soldier, der Soldat, –en, –en
sole, einzig
some, etwas, einige § 66
somebody, jemand; — else, jemand anders
something, etwas
somewhere, irgendwo
son, der Sohn, ⸚e
soon, bald
sorry, to be, bedauern *w.*
sort, die Art, –en
sound, to, klingen *st.*
south, der Süden; — side, die Südseite
space, der Weltraum
spade, der Spaten
Spain, Spanien
Spaniard, der Spanier, –
Spanish, spanisch
spare, to, verschonen *w.*
spare–time, die Mußezeit
speak (of), to, sprechen *st.* (über *or* von)
special, besonder
spectator, der Zuschauer, –
speech, die Rede
spend, to, verbringen *st.* (*time*), aus-geben *st.* (*money*)
spite of, in, trotz
splendid, prachtvoll, prächtig
split, to, spalten *w.*; — in pieces, zersplittern *w.*
spoil, to, verleiden *w.*, verderben *st.*
spoon, der Löffel
spring, der Frühling
spy, der Spion
square, der Platz
squint, to, schielen *w.*
stable, der Stall
stag, der Hirsch, –e

staircase, die Treppe
stall, die Bude
stand, to, stehen *st.*; — to attention, stramm stehen *st.*
star, der Stern, –e
state, der Staat, der Zustand (*condition*)
station, der Bahnhof
station-master, der Bahnhofsvorsteher
statue, die Bildsäule
stay, to, bleiben† *st.*, sich auf-halten *st.*
steal, to, stehlen *st.*
step, die Stufe
stern, streng
still, noch, (*adj.*) still
sting, der Stachel
stone, der Stein, steinern
stop, to, bleiben† *st.*, auf-hören *w.*, an-halten *st.*, übernachten *w.* § 150
store up, to, auf-speichern *w.*
stork, der Storch, ⸚e
storm, der Sturm, ⸚e
story, die Geschichte
straight, gerade
stranger, der Fremde, –n, –n, der Unbekannte, –n, –n
streaming, strömend
street, die Straße
stretch, to, strecken *w.*, dehnen *w.*
strict, streng, strengstens (*adv.*)
stride, der Schritt
strike, to, an-zünden *w.* (*matches*), schlagen *st.* (*hit*)
stroll, to, schlendern† *w.*
strong, stark
struggle, to, ringen *st.*
student, der Student, –en, –en
study, das Studierzimmer
succeed, to, gelingen† *st.* (*dat.*) § 152
successful, erfolgreich
such, solch § 67; — as, wie
suddenly, plötzlich
suffer, to, leiden *st.*, erleiden *st.* (*a loss*)
suffering, das Leiden

suit, der Anzug, ⸚e
suitcase, der Handkoffer
suitor, der Bewerber
sulkily, mürrisch
sullen, mürrisch
summer, der Sommer; in —, im Sommer
sun, die Sonne
sunny, sonnig
sunrise, der Sonnenaufgang
sunset, der Sonnenuntergang
support, die Stütze
sure, sicher
surprise, die Überraschung; to —, überraschen *w.*
surprised (by), überrascht (von)
swallow, die Schwalbe
Sweden, Schweden
Swedish, schwedisch
swim, to, schwimmen† *st.*
Switzerland, die Schweiz
swollen, geschwollen
sword, das Schwert

table, der Tisch; at —, bei Tisch
take, to, nehmen *st.*; — from, ab-nehmen *st.* (*dat.*) § 152; — off, ab-nehmen; — leave, Abschied nehmen *st.*; — place, statt-finden *st.*
talented, begabt
talk, to, reden *w.*, plaudern *w.* (*chatter*)
tall, hoch, groß
tap, to, klopfen *w.*
task, die Aufgabe
tea, der Tee; — party, die Tischgesellschaft
teach, to, lehren *w.*, bei-bringen *st.* (*dat.*)
tear, die Träne
tell, to, sagen *w.* (*dat.*), erzählen *w.* (*a story*) § 151
terminus, die Endstation
terrible, entsetzlich, schrecklich
terrified, erschrocken
than, als
thank, to, danken *w.* (*dat.*)
thanks to, dank (+ *dat.*)

that, jener, dieser § 3, daß (*conj.*);
in order —, damit
thaw, das Tauwetter
the, der § 1
theft, der Diebstahl
then, dann, da § 214, damals (*at that time*)
there, da, dort; — **is**, es gibt, es ist § 206
therefore, daher
thick, dicht
thief, der Dieb, -e
thin, dünn
thing, das Ding, -e
think (of), to, denken *st.* (an), meinen *w.* (*to be of the opinion*)
thirsty, durstig
this, dieser § 2
thither, dahin
though, obgleich
thought, der Gedanke, -ns, -n
thousand, tausend, das Tausend § 52
threshold, die Schwelle
through, durch
throw (at), to, werfen *st.* (nach)
thunderbolt, der Donnerkeil
Thuringia, Thüringen
Thuringian, thüringer (*adj.*)
thus, so
ticket, die Fahrkarte
ticket-collector, der Schaffner
tidy, ordentlich
tie, to, binden *st.*
tight, eng
till, (*conj.*) bis (daß), (*prep.*) bis § 166
time, die Zeit, das Mal § 57; **at the same** —, zu gleicher Zeit; **for some** —, eine Zeitlang
tired, müde; — **out**, ermüdet
to, zu, nach, in § 167; **in order** —, um...zu § 190
tobacco, der Tabak
to-day, heute
together, zusammen, miteinander
Tokay, Tokaier
tomb, die Grabstätte
tone, der Ton

tongue, die Zunge
too, auch (*also*), zu
top, oberst, der Wipfel
torch, die Fackel
touch, to, berühren *w.*
tour, die Tour, -en
tower, der Turm; **to** —, ragen *w.*
town, die Stadt, ⁻e; — **hall**, das Rathaus
townsman, der Städter
tradesman, der Kaufmann
traditional, traditionell
train, der Zug
translate, to, übersetzen *w.*
translation, die Übersetzung
travel, to, reisen† *w.*, fahren† *st.* (*in a vehicle*) § 140 (ii), die Reise
traveller, der Reisende, -n, -n
treacle, der Sirup
treasure, der Schatz, ⁻e
treat, to, behandeln *w.*
tree, der Baum, ⁻e; **fir** —, der Fichtenbaum
tree-frog, der Laubfrosch
trench, der Laufgraben
trick, to, betrügen *st.*
tripper, der Ausflügler
triumph, der Triumph
troops, die Truppen (*pl.*)
tropical, tropisch
trouble, die Mühe
troupe, die Schar
trousers, die Hosen (*pl.*)
true, wahr, treu (*faithful*)
truly, wahrlich
trust, to, trauen (*dat.*), vertrauen *st.* (*dat.*), an-vertrauen (*dat.*)
try, to, versuchen *w.*, suchen *w.*, an-klagen *w.* (*in court*)
tumult, der Aufruhr
turn, to, drehen *w.* (*of a wheel, etc.*), sich wenden *st.* (*of people*); — (**into**), ein-biegen *st.* (in + *acc.*), verwandeln *w.* (*transform*); — **out**, ein-treten† *st.* (*of weather*); — **round**, sich um-drehen *w.*
tutor, der Erzieher
twilight, das Zwielicht

unable, nicht imstande (+ *inf.*)
§ 187
unbelievable, unglaublich
unceasing, unablässig
under, unter
underneath, unten, darunter
understand, to, verstehen *st.*
undisturbed, ungestört
unexpected, unerwartet
unfortunate, unglücklich, arm; to
be —, Pech haben
unfulfilled, unerfüllt
ungainly, vierschrötig
uniform, die Uniform
unintelligible, unverständlich
United States, die Vereinigten
Staaten
universe, das Weltall
university, die Universität
unlock, to, auf-schließen *st.*
unlucky, unglücklich
unpleasant, unangenehm
unreasonable, unvernünftig
until, bis (daß), bis (*prep.*) § 166
up, hinauf, herauf § 210; — and
down, auf und nieder
upon, auf; — this, darauf, hier-
auf
use, to, gebrauchen *w.*
used to, to be, pflegen *w.*
useful, nützlich
usual, gewöhnlich
usurer, der Wucherer
usury, die Wucherzinsen (*pl.*)

vain, vergeblich; in —, vergebens
valiant, tapfer
valley, das Tal
valuable (*noun*), die Kostbarkeit
value, to, schätzen *w.*
variable, unbeständig
various, verschieden
vase, die Vase
vast, ungeheuer
vegetables, die Gemüse (*pl.*)
Venice, Venedig
venture (into), to, sich begeben
st. (auf)
very, sehr, recht

vexed, verdrossen
victim, das Opfer
victory, der Sieg
Vienna, Wien
village, das Dorf
violent, heftig
visit, der Besuch, –e; to —,
besuchen *w.*
voice, die Stimme
volume, der Band, ⸚e
vow, to, geloben *w.*
voyage, die Reise

wade, to, waten *w.*
wag (the tail), to, wedeln *w.* (mit
dem Schwanz)
wait (for), to, warten *w.* (auf)
wake up, to, auf-wachen *w.*
walk, der Spaziergang; to —,
gehen† *st.*; go for a —, spazieren
gehen† *st.* § 140
wall, die Mauer (*outside*), die Wand,
⸚e (*inside*)
wander, to, wandern† *w.*
want, to, wünschen *w.*, wollen *st.*
(*wish*), mögen § 130
war, der Krieg, –e
warm, warm
warn, to, warnen *w.*
warning, die Warnung
wash, to, sich waschen *st.*
watch, die Uhr (*clock*); to —,
beobachten *w.*
water, das Wasser
wax, das Wachs
way, der Weg, die Weise (*manner*);
by the —, am Wege; — out, der
Ausweg
weak, schwach
wear, to, tragen *st.*
weather, das Wetter; — report,
der Wetterbericht
weatherproof, wetterfest
week, die Woche; — day, der
Wochentag
weekly, wöchentlich
weep, to, weinen *w.*
weight, das Gewicht
welcome, das Willkommen

well, wohl, gut, nun, also; **the —**, der Brunnen

west, der Westen

wet, regnerisch (*of weather*)

what, was § 16; **— a**, welcher § 21

when, wenn, wann, als § 81

whenever, wenn § 81, wenn auch

where, wo

wherefore, weshalb

whereupon, worauf

whether, ob

which, der, welcher § 9; **— of**, welcher von

while, während (*conj. and prep.*), indem (*conj.*) § 86; die Weile

whir, to, schwirren *w.*

whistle, to, pfeifen *st.*

who, der, welcher § 9

whole, ganz § 58 (ii)

why, warum

wife, die Frau

wild, wild

will, der Wille, –ns, –n

William, Wilhelm

wind, der Wind, –e

window, das Fenster

wine, der Wein

winter, der Winter

wireless, der Radioapparat

wise, klug, weis

wish, der Wunsch; **to —**, wollen *st.*, wünschen *w.*

wit, der Witz

with, mit, vor § 169 (ii)

withdraw, to, zurück-ziehen *st.* (*tr.*), sich zurück-ziehen *st.* (*intr.*)

wither, to, verwelken *w.*

within, innerhalb (+ *gen.*)

without, ohne; **— further ado**, ohne weiteres

woe (to), wehe (+ *dat.*)

wolf, der Wolf, ⸚e

woman, die Frau, –en, das Weib, –er

wonderful, wunderbar

word, das Wort, –e or ⸚er § 216

work, die Arbeit (*labour*), das Werk; **to —**, arbeiten *w.*

workman, der Arbeiter

world, die Welt

wrap, to, hüllen *w.*

wrath, der Zorn

write (to), to, schreiben *st.* (an)

writer, der Schriftsteller, –

wrong, alsch; **in the —**, im Unrecht

yard, der Hof

yawn, to, gähnen *w.*

year, das Jahr, –e

yearly, jährlich

yellow, gelb

yes, ja, jawohl

yesterday, gestern

yet, noch (*still*), doch (*however*) § 194

young, jung

youth, der Jüngling (*young man*), die Jugend

Zoo, der Tiergarten

zoological, zoologisch

TABLE OF STRONG VERBS

STRONG VERBS

Infinitive	Imperfect Indicative	Past Participle	Present Indicative 3rd Sing.	English
befehlen	befahl	befohlen	befiehlt	*command*
beginnen	begann	begonnen	beginnt	*begin*
betrügen	betrog	betrogen	betrügt	*deceive*
biegen	bog	gebogen	biegt	*bend*
bieten	bot	geboten	bietet	*offer*
binden	band	gebunden	bindet	*bind*
bitten	bat	gebeten	bittet	*beg*
bleiben	blieb	geblieben	bleibt	*remain*
brechen	brach	gebrochen	bricht	*break*
empfehlen	empfahl	empfohlen	empfiehlt	*recommend*
essen	aß	gegessen	ißt	*eat*
fahren	fuhr	gefahren	fährt	*ride, drive*
fallen	fiel	gefallen	fällt	*fall*
fangen	fing	gefangen	fängt	*catch*
finden	fand	gefunden	findet	*find*
fliegen	flog	geflogen	fliegt	*fly*
fliehen	floh	geflohen	flieht	*flee*
fließen	floß	geflossen	fließt	*flow*
geben	gab	gegeben	gibt	*give*
gehen	ging	gegangen	geht	*go*
gelingen	gelang	gelungen	gelingt	*succeed*
gelten	galt	gegolten	gilt	*be worth*
genesen	genas	genesen	genest	*recover*
genießen	genoß	genossen	genießt	*enjoy*
geschehen	geschah	geschehen	geschieht	*happen*
gewinnen	gewann	gewonnen	gewinnt	*win, gain*
gießen	goß	gegossen	gießt	*pour*
gleichen	glich	geglichen	gleicht	*resemble*
graben	grub	gegraben	gräbt	*dig*
greifen	griff	gegriffen	greift	*seize*
halten	hielt	gehalten	hält	*hold*
hangen	hing	gehangen	hängt	*hang* (intr.)
hauen	hieb	gehauen	haut	*hew*
heben	hob	gehoben	hebt	*heave, lift*
heißen	hieß	geheißen	heißt	*bid, be called*
helfen	half	geholfen	hilft	*help*

Infinitive	Imperfect Indicative	Past Participle	Present Indicative 3rd Sing.	English
klingen	klang	geklungen	klingt	*sound*
kneifen	kniff	gekniffen	kneift	*pinch*
kommen	kam	gekommen	kommt	*come*
kriechen	kroch	gekrochen	kriecht	*creep*
laden	lud	geladen	lädt	*load, invite*
lassen	ließ	gelassen	läßt	*let*
laufen	lief	gelaufen	läuft	*run*
leiden	litt	gelitten	leidet	*suffer*
leihen	lieh	geliehen	leiht	*lend*
lesen	las	gelesen	liest	*read*
liegen	lag	gelegen	liegt	*lie*
meiden	mied	gemieden	meidet	*avoid*
nehmen	nahm	genommen	nimmt	*take*
pfeifen	pfiff	gepfiffen	pfeift	*pipe, whistle*
raten	riet	geraten	rät	*advise*
reißen	riß	gerissen	reißt	*tear*
reiten	ritt	geritten	reitet	*ride*
ringen	rang	gerungen	ringt	*wrestle*
rufen	rief	gerufen	ruft	*call*
scheiden	schied	geschieden	scheidet	*separate*
scheinen	schien	geschienen	scheint	*appear*
schießen	schoß	geschossen	schießt	*shoot*
schlafen	schlief	geschlafen	schläft	*sleep*
schlagen	schlug	geschlagen	schlägt	*strike*
schleichen	schlich	geschlichen	schleicht	*sneak, slink*
schließen	schloß	geschlossen	schließt	*shut*
schneiden	schnitt	geschnitten	schneidet	*cut*
schreiben	schrieb	geschrieben	schreibt	*write*
schreien	schrie	geschrieen	schreit	*cry, shriek*
schreiten	schritt	geschritten	schreitet	*step, stride*
schwimmen	schwamm	geschwommen	schwimmt	*swim*
sehen	sah	gesehen	sieht	*see*
singen	sang	gesungen	singt	*sing*
sinken	sank	gesunken	sinkt	*sink*
sinnen	sann	gesonnen	sinnt	*think, muse*
sitzen	saß	gesessen	sitzt	*sit*
sprechen	sprach	gesprochen	spricht	*speak*
springen	sprang	gesprungen	springt	*spring*
stechen	stach	gestochen	sticht	*sting*
stehen	stand	gestanden	steht	*stand*
stehlen	stahl	gestohlen	stiehlt	*steal*
steigen	stieg	gestiegen	steigt	*mount*
sterben	starb	gestorben	stirbt	*die*
stoßen	stieß	gestoßen	stößt	*push*
streiten	stritt	gestritten	streitet	*quarrel*

Infinitive	Imperfect Indicative	Past Participle	Present Indicative 3rd Sing.	English
tragen	trug	getragen	trägt	carry, wear
treffen	traf	getroffen	trifft	hit
treiben	trieb	getrieben	treibt	drive
treten	trat	getreten	tritt	tread
trinken	trank	getrunken	trinkt	drink
tun	tat	getan	tut	do
verbergen	verbarg	verborgen	verbirgt	hide
verderben	verdarb	verdorben	verdirbt	spoil
verdrießen	verdroß	verdrossen	verdrießt	vex
vergessen	vergaß	vergessen	vergißt	forget
verlieren	verlor	verloren	verliert	lose
verschlingen	verschlang	verschlungen	verschlingt	devour
verschwinden	verschwand	verschwunden	verschwindet	disappear
verzeihen	verzieh	verziehen	verzeiht	pardon
wachsen	wuchs	gewachsen	wächst	grow, wax
waschen	wusch	gewaschen	wäscht	wash
weichen	wich	gewichen	weicht	yield
weisen	wies	gewiesen	weist	show
werfen	warf	geworfen	wirft	throw
ziehen	zog	gezogen	zieht	draw
zwingen	zwang	gezwungen	zwingt	compel

Verbs which modify their vowels in the 3rd Person Sing. of the Present Indicative also modify in the 2nd Pers. Sing. e.g.

ich befehle, du befiehlst, er befiehlt.

ich fahre, du fährst, er fährt.

Some verbs for the sake of euphony may drop -es in the 2nd Pers. Sing. of the Present Indicative, e.g. du fließ(es)t, du wäsch(es)t, etc.

Similarly the final -t is dropped from the 3rd Pers. Sing. of the Present Indicative of **gelten**, **halten** and **raten**: **er gilt**, **er hält**, **er rät**.

The Imperative Singular of all verbs whose vowels modify from e to ie or i in the Present Indicative is formed by dropping -st from the 2nd Pers. Sing. of the Present Indicative, e.g. du befiehlst, Imperative befiehl; du brichst, Imperative brich, etc.

Other strong verbs form their Imperative like weak verbs except that the final -e is omitted in a few common verbs (e.g. geh, halt, komm, lauf, steh, etc.).

The terminations of the Present and Imperfect Subjunctive are the same in strong as in weak verbs; in the Imperfect Subjunctive the stem vowel generally modifies, e.g. gab—gäbe; zog, zöge; schlug, schlüge. Some irregular subjunctives are given in § 102.

MIXED VERBS

Infinitive	Imperfect	Imperfect Subjunctive	Past Participle	English
brennen	brannte	brennte	gebrannt	*burn*
bringen	brachte	brächte	gebracht	*bring*
denken	dachte	dächte	gedacht	*think*
kennen	kannte	kennte	gekannt	*know*
nennen	nannte	nennte	genannt	*name*
rennen	rannte	rennte	gerannt	*run (a race)*
senden	sandte	sendete	gesandt	*send*
wenden	wandte	wendete	gewandt	*turn*
wissen	wußte	wüßte	gewußt	*know*

The **Present Indicative** of these verbs is regular except for *wissen* which conjugates:

ich weiß, du weißt, er weiß, wir wissen, ihr wisset, sie wissen.